Trees for the New Zealand Countryside
A Planter's Guide

Trees
for the
New Zealand Countryside
A Planter's Guide

John and Bunny Mortimer

BUTTERWORTHS BOOKS

National Library of New Zealand
Cataloguing-in-Publication data

MORTIMER, John (John Bracken), 1923-
  Trees for the New Zealand countryside :
a planter's guide / John and Bunny Mortimer. —
Wellington, N.Z. : Butterworths of N.Z. ;
Auckland : Silverfish, 1987. — 1 v.
  Reprint. Originally published: Auckland, N.Z. :
Silverfish, 1984.
    ISBN 0-409-60478-X
          634.99909931
    1. Wood-lots — New Zealand. 2. Trees — New
Zealand. I. Mortimer, Bunny, 1924-.
II. Title.

Published by Butterworths 1987

Butterworths of New Zealand Limited
205-207 Victoria Street
C.P.O. Box 472
Wellington, New Zealand

ISBN 0-409-60478-X

Design and Production by Silverfish, Auckland
First published by Silverfish 1984
Copyright © John and Bunny Mortimer 1984
          Butterworths of N.Z. Ltd 1987

Contents

Foreword

For over a hundred years we felled and burnt our native forests with gay abandon and everywhere we cut down any trees great or small which stood in the way of the works of man. We wanted the land and we took it relentlessly. Farming became a favoured way of life and the main source of our national wealth. But now there is little unprotected land and the plundering of the forests is almost over. Feeling a little guilty about the past desecration, we seek to preserve the stands of native bush still surviving and to undertake the selective planting of trees across our farming landscape.

This timely and unique book is in the spirit of this growing enthusiasm for the growing of trees. It is the outcome of long practical experience, a continuing accumulation of ideas and opinions and the patient observation of the way trees behave in many and varied conditions.

It is a comprehensive guide to rural tree planting. The authors modestly disclaim that it is a complete guide and refer the reader to other sources of supplementary information but in its text and illustrations it covers most of what the tree planting farmer would need to know to make the best and the most of his trees. The authors give practical guidance on the selection of trees for the most suitable sites and the best trees where the only available sites are not ideal. The advice on the handling and planting of trees and their protection and sheltering from the wind and the frost and the weeds and the insects and animals will save many a young tree from an early death and many a tree planter from despair.

The authors discuss the value of shelter and shade, not only for the protection of stock but for greater productivity and soil improvement, raising new dimensions for farm forestry not yet fully evaluated but pointing to positive gains. The intriguing prospects for two tier farming with trees and pasture together and with tree crops of nuts or fruit as well as timber is another areas of possible future development upon which the authors have made interesting observations. There are two charming chapters on the need for bees and birds in the rural environment and the kinds of trees which will provide the pollen and nectar and berries and seeds to attract those small partners in the farming world.

There is a fascinating chapter on planting design by Diane Lucas with illuminating drawings by Ines Stäger showing how the recognition of the natural landforms can be the basic framework for effective farm forestry.

On my own land at Reikorangi I have about ten acres of native bush well preserved and adequately fenced, a woodlot of *Pinus radiata* reaching for the sky and hundreds of native and exotic trees which I have planted year by year. My one regret about this book is that I did not have it years ago when I first started to plant trees. It would have saved some sad mistakes and guided me in better ways.

New Zealand is a land of great natural scenic beauty but we have much to do to make our landscape as beautiful as the British countryside dressed as it is with magnificent trees, copses and hedgerows. There are encouraging signs that as a nation we are beginning to see this vision of a land enriched with trees. This book contributes to making that vision come true and for its authors John Mortimer (now President of the New Zealand Farm Forestry Association) and his wife Bunny, that will be their best reward.

John Marshall

Rt. Hon. Sir John Marshall, G.B.E., C.H.
Patron of The New Zealand Farm Forestry Association.

Preface

"The planter of trees is a man of vision. He has the wisdom to realise that trees are needed for his physical comfort and his spiritual welfare. He knows that they are necessary for the well-being of his land and for the protection of his stock. Above all, he knows that trees are the vital heritage of the future."

These are the opening words of the preface to F.B. McWhannell's book *Eucalypts for New Zealand Farms, Parks and Gardens* published in 1958. They are entirely appropriate to any book which sets out to encourage tree planting, but especially so to this book since some of Mr McWhannell's earlier writings have been used by us.

We do not set out to provide sufficient information to enable identification of tree species, rather we hope to identify the many purposes for which trees can be used. We want trees to be seen as part of the total landscape: they can not only improve production but can have a considerable impact on the quality of life for both people and the animals which provide them with a living.

So many farmers provide shelter around the homestead as a first priority but leave their livestock exposed to cold winds and hot suns. There are landowners who persist in trying to farm a piece of low-producing land when a well designed and managed woodlot would be better landuse and a good form of diversification. Water is a crucial ingredient in production and storage dams provide summer supplies for irrigation and drinking. At the time when the need is greatest hot summer winds cause unnecessary evaporation losses which could be reduced by planting trees on the windward side. We take for granted the vital role which bees play in pollinating our plants. We think hardly at all about the steady destruction of the very environment necessary for them to live and do their job. We should be planting trees to ensure that there is a constant food supply throughout the seasons. We can also make provision for bird food and habitats by planting suitable trees, for a world without birdsong would indeed be a sad place, probably filled with many more undesirable insects.

Because of our tendency to try and extract the last dollar, small wet spots are frequently drained to pro-

duce another few miserable blades of grass. So often greater benefit would be gained by planting moisture-loving trees which can help dry out the area and provide wonderful autumn colours. All over New Zealand the effects of erosion can be seen as our precious topsoil slips away to the sea, never to be replaced unless we provide a new forest cover to supply more humus and to hold the land together. Flat areas too are losing topsoil and tree barriers can prevent a loss of tilled topsoil in times of high winds. The staple diet of our grazing animals is grass and clover — almost as much a monoculture as some of our pine forests. Seasonal changes bring feeding shortages which could be alleviated by planting suitable forage trees. These not only provide food but bring benefits through the additional nutrients contained in the foliage, fruit and nuts.

If your home is near a factory or motorway planting of trees is a most effective acoustic barrier as well as a visual one. So many farms have iron sheds and white-painted water tanks which would be the better for having a few trees to hide them from neighbours and passing motorists. Often such unsightly structures are hidden from the farm house, but the effect of them on the landscape generally (and therefore on other people) is overlooked.

Farmers and the many other people who make decisions affecting our countryside need to accept that they have a responsibility to the whole of the community, for the view from the road belongs to us all. History clearly tells the story of how our native forests have been destroyed (a process which unfortunately still continues in some areas). Original forest cover is replaced by a farming landscape which now has to be moulded into not only a productive asset but also one which should make a positive contribution to our environment. Unless we preserve the small pockets of native trees which remain on our farms, and keep on planting trees (both indigenous and exotic) in accordance with good design principles our descendants will give us scant thanks for what we have bequeathed them.

There is nothing difficult about planting trees — the rewards far outweigh the effort required to establish them, and once that is accomplished they continue to grow and contribute their many values with hardly any additional input by the landowner. There should be no conflict between production and tree growing; it should be the converse for there is an interaction between trees and most living things on the farm and these can be complementary. Landowners, those working on the land, city dwellers and the domesticated animals on whom we depend, all benefit both directly and indirectly from trees. The multiple landuse concept, now so much more acceptable, has trees as essential ingredients. Let us acknowledge the diverse values and functions of trees and how greatly they contribute to our landscape values and to the environment of those who live and work in our rural areas.

"We should do our utmost to encourage
the beautiful for the useful encourages itself."
(Goethe)

Introduction

This book has been compiled to help those responsible for land management to make greater use of trees. It may sometimes assist with the identification of trees but is not intended to be used for this purpose, nor is it a do-it-yourself propagation manual. The book has been written to help in the choice of species for specific sites, whatever the object in planting might be. The planter should think in terms of the effect that is required and then select the tree best suited to the site. There is nothing more liable to failure in every way than a plant that is in an environment to which it has not adapted. Everyone likes to see a strong-growing healthy tree and this means avoiding planting in unfavourable sites or planting trees with susceptibility to insect damage and diseases. Unsuitable sites result in slow growth, defoliation and vulnerability to secondary infections — and the trees look awful.

As practising Farm Foresters we have found that there is no New Zealand publication which can serve as a handbook for larger landscape planting. There is plenty of information available in the many gardening and horticultural books, but only one has so far been published with the farmer in mind. This is George

Stockley's *Trees Farms and the New Zealand Landscape* published by the Northern Southland Farm Forestry Association. It contains much information that is not in this book and has detailed instructions on propagation, as well as covering many smaller species which are not included here. We have confined our subject to trees, a term which generally does not cover anything likely to be less than seven metres high when mature. For the enthusiast Stockley's book should certainly be on the shelf, and we would like to think the two books are complementary. In our experience no single book supplies all the answers and it is frequently necessary to refer to several to get the information one seeks.

We have been very involved in tree planting ourselves and this has led to our acting in an advisory capacity to other farmers. Visiting their farms and discussing their objectives, we have so often been at a loss to leave them something which would continue to act as a guide after the specific recommendations which we have made are carried out. We have also made the assumption that what is a common tree to us means nothing to someone just starting to plant. It has been impracticable to carry a library of books with

This dam on the authors' farm was made, fenced and planted 12 years ago.

us and yet it seemed desirable to be able to show by illustration which tree we were talking about. While pondering this deficiency in available literature we were approached by Mrs Rhoda McWhannell to see whether we could make use of some material written by her late husband, Mr Fred McWhannell.

Mr McWhannell's specialty and great love was the eucalypts in which he first became involved in 1927 when he was farming near Hamilton. He saw possibilities of growing them for the production of strong, useful and very durable timber as well as for their beauty. He imported seed of many species and distributed the resulting seedlings for planting out on trial areas: he gave away over 10 000 in 1938. He later established a commercial nursery, developed a reputation as a most knowledgeable authority on eucalypts and published the book referred to on page 269. He wrote articles on other trees as well, many of which were published in the *New Zealand Farmer*. Thus we were provided with the genesis of this book.

As it developed we were constantly aware of the range of questions which were being asked about trees on farms. For many years we have staffed a Farm Forestry stand at the agricultural field days run by the New Zealand National Fieldays Society and handled hundreds of inquiries from a never-ending stream of interested people. This resulted in an ever-widening content, which was originally intended to consist of just notes and photographs of the more common species which could be used on farms. Many people with whom we spoke indicated they wanted more information, hence the addition of the other sections.

We did not intend to enter controversial areas, but felt obliged to cover topics which were not clear-cut. Not everyone will agree with what has been written.

Shelter

Interest in shelter is now so great that a chapter finally had to be included and we are most grateful to Murray Faulkner of Centrepoint Nurseries for supplying a first draft and to Ian Nicholas of the NZ Forest Service for helping to edit it. On its own it is a subject to fill a book. Much has been written on shelter so our contribution can hardly be termed comprehensive although we feel it sets out some useful guidelines.

Shade

Shade and its effect on animals and pasture seems to be a somewhat neglected subject. There is practically no scientific literature based on New Zealand research, and little that we could find based even on observation or interest. When we see how animals use shade and how we ourselves appreciate its availabil-

Eucalyptus maculosa growing on Mrs Rhoda McWhannell's farm.

ity, its seems worthwhile including some aspects of its effect on livestock even if only to stimulate further interest.

Indigenous Forest Remnants

New Zealand's long-term future is affected as much by the actions of today as the pioneers influenced the environment we inherited. We believe that the country will be the better for the preservation of what little indigenous forest remains. Many private land owners control pockets of bush but do not realise how easy it is to provide for their protection; this section of the book sets out the present position. Most steps which can be taken are affected by some sort of legislation so the situation is bound to change from time to time. It is not always necessary to make legal preservation though this is best, and it is the only way to protect anything in perpetuity. A farmer who fences off native bush takes a positive and worthwhile step. It is within the means of many land owners to do this without the aid of the bureaucratic machine. They just need to get up a little earlier.

Special Purposes

Allied to preservation of native species is substitution

Fine remnant native bush now fenced off from stock.

with exotic hardwoods. The reasoning behind the advocacy of a limited number of species being planted for this purpose is set out in the NZFS Policy on Exotic Special Purpose Species (Appendix 1).

On these species and on other exotic trees being grown in New Zealand, a good deal of research is being carried out, so the planter should always get the latest information from the appropriate source. Genetic quality is being systematically improved, provenance selection made more specific, and site preparation, planting and sylvicultural techniques are constantly being bettered as information comes to light. When planting and managing a woodlot the best results will be achieved only if the latest research results are implemented.

Planting Design
We start the book off with the design section by Diane Lucas because we would rather nothing was planted until this has been read, if not completely digested. The community has the right to ask of the land owner that he or she take into account the effects his or her actions will have on the surrounding countryside. More intensive land use and a steadily growing population occupying small holdings is rapidly

changing the view from the road, mostly for the worse. Our vistas are framed by power and telephone poles and lines: a plethora of galvanised unpainted iron sheds despoil the country, situated as they often are close to the road on the 4 ha farmlet or on the skyline of the larger farm.

On a visit to England during the course of preparing this book, we were, as are most travellers, overwhelmed by the beauty of that country. On analysis it appeared that most of the pleasing aspect was manmade — if one can include under that heading the planting of trees. Only very rarely were power or telephone lines seen. New Zealand's reputation for beauty depends almost entirely on its natural physical characteristics — the mountains, the rivers, the forests and the coastlines. The cultivated parts of the country are becoming less beautiful as civilisation imposes its ugly additions. In England there are stringent regulations on what can and cannot be done to the environment and while it is a landscape planner's paradise it is a nightmare to anyone wanting to put a building up in a rural area. The result however is a satisfying and comfortable blend of agriculture and buildings, with neither shouting at the other. It is a unified, harmonic scene, and with the work

Most farm sheds do not improve the view from the road.

A well-loved dairy shed.

being carried out by the Countryside Commission, England has a charm all of its own and remains one of the world's most beautiful countries.

New Zealand has so much to start with that it is shameful that we take our city habits out into the country. Stand on a hill overlooking a peri-urban area and note the 'spotty' effect of white houses and silver sheds. Do the same in England and you will see the mellowness of buildings of brick and stone, the natural materials of the area and in harmony with the landscape. Can we not learn from this and have a care for our rural scene? We hope that the design chapter will assist you in planning your farm so that it becomes more attractive from every point of view, making it a more pleasant environment to work in, more satisfying to those who just look at it and maybe adding capital value to it as well.

We do however recognise that putting into practice a planting scheme in accordance with the best design principles as set out in Chapter 1 is not easy. There are many areas of conflict and planters will have to work out their own priorities. We anticipate farmers and foresters disagreeing with what has been written, but no apology is required. It is important that the approach to planning be made with the ideal in mind, although almost inevitably compromises will be necessary. If only a proportion of the objectives are achieved, then the landscape will still look the better for them.

Climate

The narrow width of New Zealand and the distance between Cape Reinga and the Bluff give it a most variable climate. Exposure is generally the main difficulty in establishing trees in coastal areas, but there is plenty of wind inland too. Altitude differences add to problems, so in this book we have tried not to be too specific as to where a tree will or will not grow. Microclimates will produce variations in survival and growth.

Remember that whatever the statistics might say there is always the likelihood of unseasonable weather conditions, the late frost being the one most likely to do damage.

The change to metrics has meant that we can no longer use degrees of frost as an indication of severity of cold. The book mentions frost, but generally describes tolerance to cold in terms of degrees Celsius. For those who still think in terms of Fahrenheit these Celsius equivalents may be of some assistance:

1° frost = -0.6 °C
5° frost = -2.8 °C
10° frost = -5.6 °C

15° frost = -8.3°C
20° frost = -11.1°C

Frost effects can be minimised by ensuring that there is adequate air drainage. Cold air gets as close to the ground as possible and then rolls downhill if there is no physical barrier. If frost is an inhibiting factor in tree establishment make sure you leave an escape hole for it to go through. If you have protectors such as old drums leave a gap at the bottom for air drainage (both cold and hot). Young trees which are slightly frost tender should be hardened off before planting out. Don't take them straight from a protected nursery area, exposing them to a temperature which they have not experienced. Gradually move them out into the colder areas so that if they should be subjected to late frosts after planting they are less likely to suffer. Autumn frosts can damage soft tissues, so if they are expected a scrim cover can help. Late spring frosts are unpredictable and you have to take your chance. Careful site choice and pre-planting treatment will help to minimise damage. Eventually trees will grow above frost damage so protection may be required for only a year or two.

Choice of Species

This is a book about trees, so you will not find any detailed description of species which do not normally grow to at least 7m at maturity. Smaller trees are mentioned in the specialised areas such as shelter, bee fodder, fruit etc, where they may have a specific role to play.

In assembling the list of species we had in mind general farm planting rather than the farm homestead garden. We hope however that this book will be used by others who plan the planting of large open spaces such as around schools, country halls, cemeteries and golf courses. These are sometimes bleak, unattractive and utilitarian. Some of the flowering species are included as they are well suited to planting near many rural buildings.

It should not be inferred that because we have included a tree it is necessarily obtainable from your local nursery. Sometimes we have felt that a tree is worth growing although not commonly seen and therefore warrants inclusion. You may well have to hunt around for a *Lagunaria patersonii* but you will be well rewarded if you find one.

Fruit Trees

Most farmers agree that livestock thrive on grass and clover. They resent the presence of weeds, and some regard trees as unnecessary, whether for shade, shelter or supplementary fodder. Others believe trees

encourage diseases through stock "camping" under them. But many think that feeding animals on deep-rooting plants such as certain "weeds" and trees provides stock with minerals which are not found in the top few centimetres of soil occupied by surface-rooting plants. Trees recycle these minerals by the dropping of their leaves which, if not eaten by animals (or even if they are) return their elements to the topsoil as they decompose.

For those who are interested in supplementary food sources, some information on fruit trees is included in the chapter on exotics. Most of the trees named are decorative, hardy and easily grown, and provide useful but not top quality fruit for man and beast, with practically no attention.

Timber Uses

To produce quality timber nearly all trees require some training and form pruning. Ideally the bole should be free of side branches for 6m — this distance being related to the size of plywood which is normally in sheets 2.4m x 1.2m. A log pruned to 6m allows a little wastage at top and bottom and can then be veneered into suitable sizes. This length is also acceptable from a miller's point of view, should the log be destined to produce clearwood.

The expression "of no commercial value" is sometimes used. This means that the timber is not normally in demand by the marketplace and would be difficult to sell. It does not mean that it is worthless —we have found that almost all the trees mentioned in this book are widely used in their country of origin and have many intrinsic qualities. It is usually the size of the resource that puts a value on timber. The marketplace has to be able to rely on continuity of supply if millers, manufacturers and retailers are to be equipped to handle the wood and the finished products. It is for this reason that the Forest Service has formulated a policy advocating plantings of a limited number of species other than *Pinus radiata* to supply future requirements of special purpose timbers.

"No commercial value" may mean you cannot sell your tree to the local miller, but you may well be able to have it milled on your own account and use it at home. This may be for the farm, for firewood or to meet the needs of a woodwork hobby. You could even sell off the surplus to neighbours or the local woodcarver. The section on wood properties may help in deciding whether it is worthwhile making the effort to convert an unwanted tree into something useful.

Descriptions

An attempt has been made to cover various aspects of

Pruned branches should be cut off flush with the trunk. The one on the right is occluding well, whereas those on left will never heal, possibly resulting in disease.

each species and though not separately itemised each tree has been classified as to:

Country of origin
Deciduous or Evergreen
General description of form
Estimated height and/or width
Site conditions most to its liking
Wood properties and uses
Method of propagation

During editing there has been some criticism that the information used has not been sourced. We must state that this is not a scientific work and does not purport to be anything other than a guide to rural planting. In the first place information from local sources has always been used when available and appropriate. However many of the New Zealand publications contain information which is drawn from overseas. Quite frequently one can come across identical wording in local and overseas literature — we can assume that the movement has been southwards rather than the reverse (except perhaps in the case of New Zealand's indigenous plants)! When no local data on exotic trees has been located we have had to rely on overseas sources.

The general description and size of the trees tends sometimes to be a bit too broad. Site conditions are such an important factor that a tree develops its full potential only when it is in a perfect environment. So while many trees will survive in conditions less than ideal they are likely to be disappointing. It would be reasonable to assume that trees will assume their optimum proportions only when they are on sites to which they are best suited.

All too frequently the literature advises that "a moist, well drained loamy soil" is what the tree likes and in which it grows best: given these conditions there is a good chance most species will finish up as fine healthy well-grown trees. However these conditions are frequently not available, and part of the purpose of this book is to assist in the selection of suitable species for less than desirable sites.

The method of propagation is mentioned as a "one liner" as a matter of interest. For those who are really wishing to do their own propagation we advise you to obtain copies of George Stockley's book and *Cultivation of New Zealand Trees and Shrubs* by L.J. Metcalf. Some people with sticky fingers like to pick up a seed or sneak a cutting as they roam around and the information given may help them improve their chances of success.

It should be noted that in some species seeds take more than one season to germinate: eg Black Walnuts can pop out of the ground several years after planting.

Wood Properties
Wood qualities are mentioned for the benefit of those

who like to consider a tree as something still useful even when horizontal. For exotics there is some information available in New Zealand, but for obvious reasons most is of overseas origin. Uses of timber are therefore mostly based on the experience and history of the wood in its country of origin. In the case of indigenous timbers much use has been made of earlier literature. At present very little native timber is put into the commercial market, but the earlier settlers were dependent on a great variety of native trees for everyday requirements. The uses to which these timbers were put is included as a matter of interest rather than of practical importance.

Illustrations
Neither of us could be classified as anything but a rank amateur photographer. The wonders of modern technology have enabled us by clicking the camera often enough to acquire a collection of usable photographs. Our initial approach to the book was to have a photograph for every species described, but this has proved impossible in the time available, unless we were to use what we considered unsuitable photos.

Until we set about finding trees to photograph we had not realised how many telephone and power lines there are in New Zealand. The difficulty of being in the right place, at the right time of the year, the right time of the day and in the right weather has not aided the early publication of this book. More than one visit to a particular area has been necessary sometimes with less than satisfactory results — especially when a camera fault develops.

The photos are not an end in themselves, but an adjunct to the text. We hope that readers will study the description of a tree, which in itself is never entirely adequate, and then the photo will fill out the mental picture and so help in decision-making. It may be that a photo tempts the reader to inquire further into the conditions required for such a tree, with a view to planting that species.

We have resisted the temptation to use photos of trees which are not in rural situations. It would have been easy to fill in the gaps by visiting the parks and botanical gardens where fine specimens are known to exist, but we do not wish it to be said that it is all very well growing a tree in such a sheltered site, but how will it do out in the countryside? Similarly we have not for the most part used trees in nicely manicured garden situations — we have preferred to take photos which depict typical farm sites using fencing and animals as scale indicators. If these have not be present we have not been averse to including long grass and thistles. Thus we hope the photos will be in sympathy with the practical nature of the book.

Although dogs are unable to read, we would like to record our thanks for their co-operation. Punch 'n' Nello learnt to pose by a tree for the camera when it was necessary to give scale. They would sit anxiously waiting for the camera to click, when they would bound off as if their day's work were done. In February 1983 Nello vanished and has not been seen since. We still have Punch who at the age of 10 has to pose alone when required.

We have been through some other collections of slides and photographs, but it surprised us how few were suitable for our purposes. Most people who have large numbers of photos tend to be specialists and it would seem that our area of interest is another form of specialisation. We have been unsuccessful in locating in quantity exactly what we want, although we have used some other people's photos and these have been acknowledged.

Most photos have been taken on farms, with a few in other rural situations such as schools. Some of the trees with neatly mown surrounds are growing on the Westlands Golf Course near Hamilton. This course was previously part of our farm and was converted by us into a golf course in 1968. We carried out an extensive planting programme and have continued to watch the growth of the trees with interest. While there are now no stock, and only boundary fences, we consider it still to be a truly rural situation.

This is not a "coffee table" book which has as its prime purpose the satisfaction of the reader's eye. Our photos are to help you in your choice of species and to encourage you to plant more trees. We hope they serve this purpose.

Except for those used in Chapter 1, all the black-and-white line drawings and diagrams have been done by our daughter Jane.

Farm Foresters
One of the most effective ways of tapping the resources of other people's experiences is to join the New Zealand Farm Forestry Association, whose members have done so much of it all before. It is disheartening to start off with failures, so many of which are avoidable if you talk to experienced growers.

We emphasise here, as elsewhere in the book, that planters must look around their own neighbourhood to see how species perform. Inquire from those who have achieved success with their trees. Don't be diffident about knocking on the door of a farmhouse where there is evidence of successful establishment. Keen tree-growers are almost invariably delighted to help others interested in doing some planting by passing on the stories of their successes and failures. (See Appendix 6.)

Acknowledgements

Mrs Rhoda McWhannell of Ohaupo really planted the seed of this book. It germinated and has been cultivated by us. With advice and help from those mentioned it has grown into the specimen it now is and we are sure that if only a few more trees are planted as a result of its publication, Mrs McWhannell will be very happy. We thank her for inspiring it and for her never-failing interest in its progress.

The book has been written by laypeople for laypeople. Nevertheless a number of professional foresters and scientists have given us a great deal of help by checking drafts. In acknowledging and thanking members of the N.Z. Forest Service staff at the Forest Research Institute in Rotorua we must make it quite clear that they have had no formal input and can in no way be held responsible for any of its contents, nor do they necessarily agree with what has been written. In particular we acknowledge the help of Ian Nicholas who gave considerable assistance with the chapter on shelter and generally made some most helpful comments in other areas. The late Doug Revell advised on the eucalypt section, Tony Beveridge went through the native tree section and Dr John Butcher checked that on timber properties. Chris Ecroyd has carefully verified and updated the botanical nomenclature and if there are any mistakes that have slipped through they are certainly not his fault. We also thank Clive Anstey and Karen Nichols from the landscape section of the N.Z. Forest Service in Christchurch.

Chris van Kraayenoord of the Ministry of Works and Development Soil Conservation Centre at Aokautere has been a good friend to farm foresters for many years and did not fail us when we asked for information on poplars, willows and soil conservation. Murray Faulkner, an experienced forester, was running the Centrepoint nursery in Albany when we discussed the book with him and he felt that a chapter on shelter was essential, then backed up his assertion by drafting it for us. The chapter on shade could only be written because animal behavioural scientist Dr Ron Kilgour of Ruakura Agricultural Research Centre gave us access to his library.

So many farm foresters have been called on for information and comment that we cannot mention them all. In particular we thank Bob Berry of Tiniroto for going through the section on oaks and John Mackay from Heriot gave us information on snow shelter. Ian McKean has one of the finest collections of conifers in the country and twice gave us hospitality at Rangiwahia, as well as checking the text. David McNeil of Te Poi spent many hours on field trips helping to identify specimens and patiently waiting while the photos were taken. To him, to Richard Davies-Colley (Past President of the N.Z. Farm Forestry Association) and to Bruce Treeby we extend thanks for encouragement and comment.

We also wish to thank all those who have unwittingly contributed to the book's contents through ownership of photogenic trees, and have provided interesting views from the road. Sandra Stephens coped with reams of almost illegible writing and typed late into the night to meet deadlines so that we could finally submit a tidy completed script.

We were babes in the woodlot when it came to publishing a book so we are grateful for the assistance given by Michael Gifkins, who did some heavy pruning and thinning in a most professional manner and right on time, too. Our designer Colin Maclaren (Silverfish) took control of all the technical processes and led us over entirely new ground, safely escorting us out of the woodlot. We thank them for their skill, efficiency and enthusiasm and for the pleasant working relationship so quickly established among those involved in the final stages of the book's preparation.

1
Planting Design

Diane Lucas

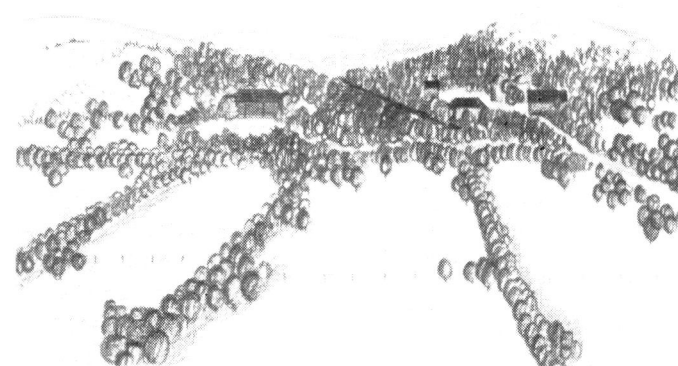

Productive open spaces within a productive wooded countryside.

Much of the New Zealand countryside is dominated by arbitrary, formal patterns defined by property boundaries, roads, fences, and plantings. These straight lines and grid patterns would mostly disappear if the rural land were left unworked and ungrazed, for trees and shrubs are the natural cover for most of the country. Natural patterns would reappear, patterns which relate to the underlying landform, with its variety of soil, moisture availability, aspect and microclimate. The landform or topography pattern is the basic component of any landscape, and is emphasised by vegetation. Even in a functional farming landscape the topographic pattern can still be emphasised by vegetation. By planting to show the variations in topography, soils and climate, local character for every different area of the country can be developed. Emphasis on *natural* variety should

be a priority, otherwise the whole of New Zealand would look the same.

Although variety is important it is not desirable to have random mixtures of exotic trees spread haphazardly about the country with no relationship to the locality. Exotic, ornamental mixtures can be very destructive of local character. Care is needed in species choice and siting to ensure that all plantings will look as though they belong and are not imposed "unsympathetically". Plan all plantings as components of a pattern of open and wooded landscape. The shapes of the plantings, and the openings, need to be closely related to the shapes of the underlying landform. The size of the spaces will depend primarily on the intensity of the landuse, particularly in relation to the amount of shelter required: systems of productive open spaces within a productive wooded countryside.

Countryside dominated by formal, arbitrary patterns . . .

and the patterns which would develop naturally.

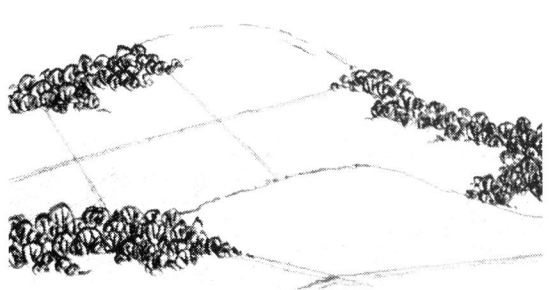

Planting which relates to topography.

A landscape that displays a sense of naturalism is universally preferred to that which is obviously man-dominated. The principal aim in planting layout should therefore be to do away with, or soften, any straight lines. Remember too that the landscape does not stop at property boundaries. Design your plantings to emphasise the landform features that continue from one property to another (eg ridges, valleys, waterways). Discuss plans with your neighbours to ensure that you work to complement one another and enhance the local character in this way.

In designing farm planting, care is needed to avoid destroying the beauty that already exists. Before planting any tree or tree mass, consider the relationship with the surroundings. Generally a tree should not be a prominent feature in complete contrast to the surroundings. Instead, the scale, colour, shape, and texture should be in sympathy with the landforms and with other vegetation. Formal plantings and arrangements are often unsatisfactory because of individual failures and growth rate variations. Also, formality usually conflicts with landform patterns. It is very difficult to develop a formal planting that really looks right, as the scale of the planting is critical in relation to the spaces. If formality is wanted, it is best achieved within an informal framework, but of course the transition from formal to informal needs to be carefully designed.

Because of their small size, shrubs and small ornamental trees look too fussy for the rural landscape. They belong in town gardens, or within larger tree frameworks of rural gardens. To use shrubs and small trees successfully in the rural landscape they must be massed together so that none appears as an individual specimen.

In the choice of species make maximum use of local vegetation, using local native species which are particularly adapted to the conditions, and exotics that grow well in your area. Even 'weed' species of trees and shrubs can be useful. Take note of what is growing well already. A design with many healthy trees,

even if a limited number of species, will be more successful than a design that uses a wide variety of trees, some of which struggle under the conditions.

Trees should be part of the working landscape, not mere decoration. Tree planting on farms should aim at fulfilling as many functions as possible: to modify the climate, provide timber, fuel, fodder, fruits and nuts, and protect soil and water resources.

Trees should also meet visual requirements for framing views and screening, enclosing spaces, integrating structures with their surroundings and enhancing local character. Each planting should fulfil as many functions as possible whilst aiming at maximum beauty in the landscape. Multi-purpose plantings can be achieved by using a mixture of species, with each species having one or more function. A single species can be used to meet a number of needs, but for ecological and visual reasons it is not desirable to have very extensive single species plantings.

Mass trees together so that none appears as an individual specimen.

Local Character

The visual character of a landscape is influenced by the topography, the existing scale, type and pattern of vegetation and landuse, and the prevailing colour of rock, soil, and structures. This character determines not only the extent, types, and patterns of planting that will look right, but also the appropriate siting, forms, materials and colours for any structures.

The extremely varied topography throughout New Zealand and the resultant variety of climate, soils and plants is of international significance. A unique flora developed in isolation over some 80 million years: various types of forest, shrublands, wetlands, grasslands, etc, displayed the natural variety of the land.

Until recently a framework at least of the various types of native vegetation remained to emphasise landform patterns and express the character of local soils and climate. Together with buildings largely constructed of local materials, some significant local character was assured even in developed rural areas. But with techniques and pressures to intensify agri-

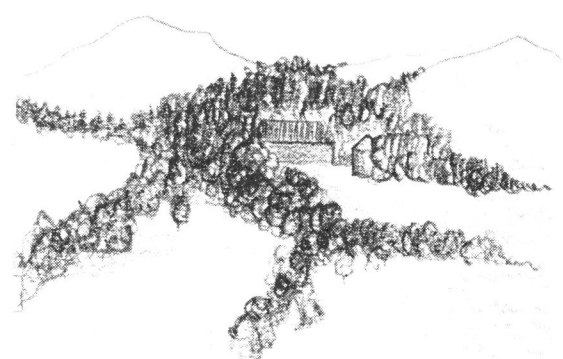

Buildings can nestle into a planting network.

Special tree groups fitted into the network.

culture and expand exotic forestry, and with the use of a large variety of non-local building styles and components, much of the character of rural landscapes has been lost. Pine forestry has been extended over, and now dominates, much of the country. A passion for tidiness often destroys the last remnants of natural diversity which is inadequately replaced by superficial 'tarting up' such as white-painted fences and garish, coloured-foliage planting.

Local character can only be enhanced by recognising the natural diversity of the landscape through maximum use of local native plants, mixed with useful exotics or alone. If these plantings are designed in relation to the landform, a suitable and logical landscape character can be developed.

Framework Planting

Each farm planting, whether for shelter, timber, shade, screening or beauty, needs to be designed as part of a framework which reflects the patterns of the natural landscape and visually absorbs the various rural developments. Buildings and silos can be nestled into a planting network so that these structures become an acceptable part of the landscape. Existing vegetation including native bush and shrubland remnants, riverside willows and woodlots can be used as a basis. Extend these with plantings for shelter, etc, but always in a pattern which follows the topography.

If particular ornamental trees are wanted they must be fitted into this framework and not be set apart as isolated elements or decoration. Groups and groves of special tree species should serve some functional purpose: screening, shade, fruit or nut crops, valuable timber, or to highlight particular soils or microclimate. There should not be an obvious contrast between trees for use and trees for decoration. All planting should do both — be beautiful and useful.

Trees and Climate

Trees change the microclimate for people, animals and other plants.

Temperature

Trees make the climate milder. Within trees temperatures are modified, so it is cooler on a hot day, and frosts are rare.

Dense planting across a slope can dam cold air, increasing frosts. Cold air is heavier than warm air, so

it slowly flows off hills into valleys, collecting in frost hollows. Even flatter ridge tops and plateaus can have pools of cold air, so that these sites can experience frosts almost as severe as valley sites. The upper slopes of the valleys have least frost — the thermal belt. Maximise such sites for planting and living, as in all districts upper north-facing slopes will have the highest minimum temperatures.

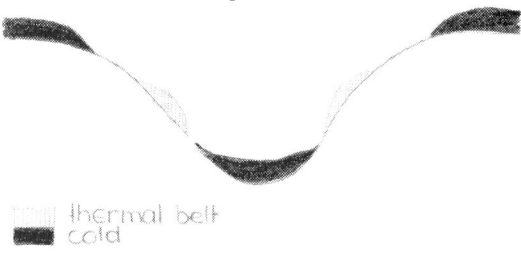

thermal belt
cold

Maximise the warmer sites.

rain shadow

Most rain comes from the south or west.

The main damage from frost occurs when the sun reaches frozen plants. By planting in shaded areas (shaded at least from morning sun) the plants will thaw slowly so that damage is less likely. Plants in bare ground are less likely to frost than those in mulch.

Dense plantings such as shelterbelts reduce winds and may dam cold air so that temperatures are colder at night. But during the day soil and air temperatures in the sheltered areas are significantly higher. Dense shelter plantings can be sited above and shaped to deflect the cold air away from critical sites.

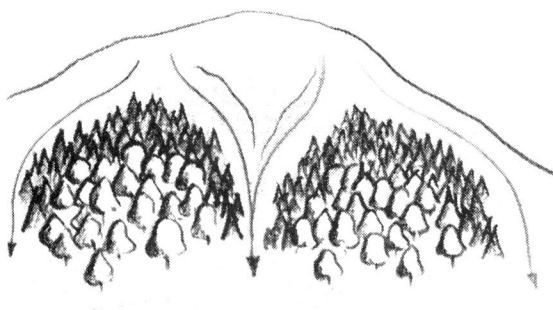

Moisture

Trees also modify moisture levels. Because of shade and shelter the soil under trees usually dries out less, depending on whether trees are shallow rooting or not. As much of New Zealand's rain comes from the south and west, the northern sunny sides of plantings will be drier than the rain-catching sides. The dry northern side that is sheltered from rain is the 'rain shadow' area.

Moisture limitations may decide the minimum spacing of trees: trees need to be wider spaced in drier

areas, and closer in moister sites. Weed control and mulching significantly reduce watering needs.

Too much moisture is a major limiting factor for tree growth. Tree species which tolerate "wet feet" can be used to reduce excess soil moisture and less tolerant tree species (or crops) can then be interplanted. For this technique to be effective, winter-growing evergreen species are necessary. Trees can also be used instead of a drainage system to lower the water table through high rates of evapo-transpiration, but this should be done sparingly. It is not necessarily desirable to drain or dry out wetland areas whether by tree planting or earthworks and thus cause a loss of landscape and ecological diversity.

Deep-rooting trees tap moisture and nutrients and supply these as stock fodder in times of drought when shallow-rooting species (eg grass) are under stress.

Tree species which naturally grow alongside streams can often be used to enhance valley and waterside character (eg willow, poplar, alder, fuchsia). They are associated with lush sites, so their appearance gives a visual key to the site even when the water is not visible. But care is needed to avoid destroying natural plant and animal habitats alongside water and to avoid the trees spreading where not wanted. Dull, fine, dry-looking plants (eg pines,

Lush growth gives a visual key, even when surface water is not visible.

many eucalypts, acacias) convey a dryland character, signalling higher or drier sites. The change in plant character from watercourse to upland slope is a visible reinforcement to the landform pattern.

In tree crops too the soil moisture can be displayed in crop choice, with juicy crops generally on the lusher lowlands, and dry crops (almond, olive, carob) on dry hillsides. The presence of irrigation can be boldly displayed by integrating the lusher trees in shelter and crop plantings, and along border dykes.

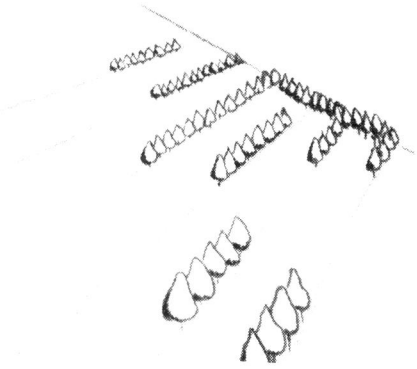

Sunlight

It is critical to supply enough shade to avoid concentration of stock under just a few trees (see Chapter 5). Scatter trees and tree groups around paddocks to ensure adequate summer shade. The trees can extend from shelterbelts or woodlots to soften the layout; they can be grouped strategically to frame good views, screen bad views, produce a nut or fruit crop (walnut, chestnut, macadamia), produce special timber (oak, ash, beech, poplar), and create interest in the landscape.

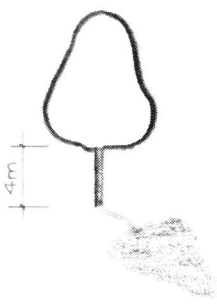

Deciduous trees with clear trunks at least 4m high provide good stock shade. The shade is projected away from the base of the tree and moves around during the day. The stock move with the shadow so that their camping is not concentrated in one place. Winter shade is minimal.

Late-leafing deciduous trees can be used where maximum winter and spring sunshine is needed on crops, etc. Align shelter plantings north-south wherever possible to obtain maximum sunshine on the area between the groves or rows of shelter plantings.

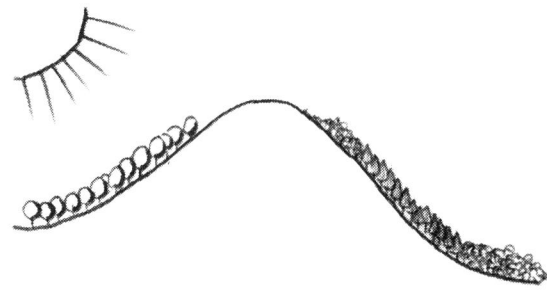

Edges of plantings and slopes which face north receive maximum solar radiation. They can be used for trees and tree crops which require greatest heat and light (most fruits, honey locusts). Likewise sites shaded by topography or trees can be used for trees which prefer or tolerate such sites (hazel, most conifers, native bush).

Wind

Wind is a major limitation to tree growth in New Zealand (see Chapter 4). Without wind, moisture stress is markedly reduced. Shelter planting on New Zealand farms is a major use of trees, but care in design and management of these plantings is essential to avoid the trees causing other problems.

The subtleties of rural landscapes must be especially respected in shelter design. As shelter planting often forms the basic framework of a farm landscape, it must be carefully planned with more than just shelter in mind. Too often the shelterbelts carve up a landscape with formal plantings that destroy the local character. Shelter design should not automatically involve the laying of a grid over the farm. Study the natural shelter created by the topography and vegetation and develop a shelter planting design around the landform patterns as an extension of this natural shelter.

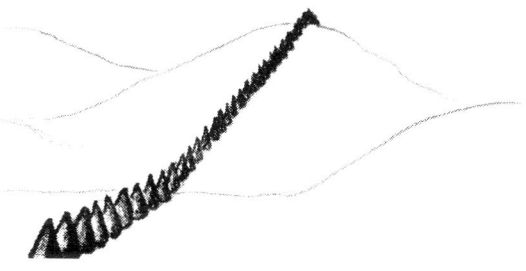

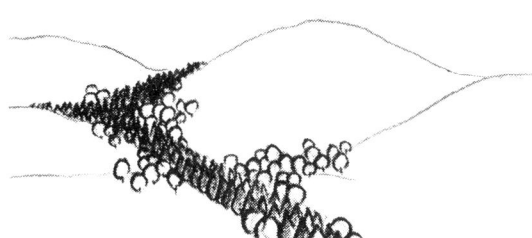

Shelter planting related to the topography.

An existing fencing layout should not automatically be used as the shelter layout pattern. Fences and gateways not sympathetic to the landform need to be left unplanted, or be resited. Nor does shelter necessarily need to be in the form of straight rows of trees.

In pastoral situations it may be preferable to use irregular groves and clumps of trees scattered about to diffuse and lift the winds. (Landuses such as cropping may limit the suitability of scattered tree clumps.)

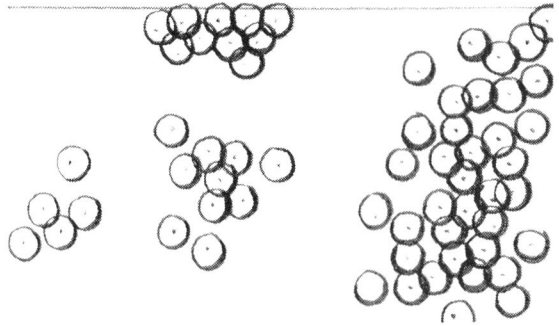

Tree clumps to diffuse the winds.

Not only are there visual problems with long rows of trees, but if the shelter belt does not lie at right angles to the path of the wind, then the wind can be accelerated along the belt. If the long row is broken by a gap for a gateway or power lines, this gap will become a wind funnel.

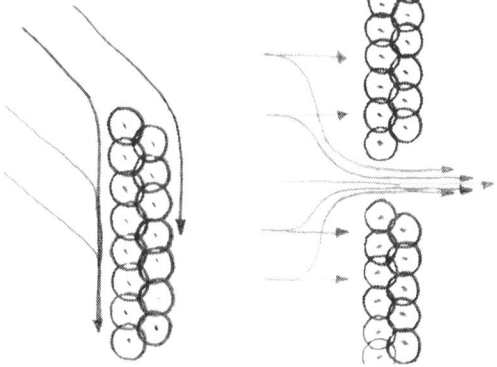

Where rows of windbreak planting are required, always try to run them *with* the lines of the land — the valleys, terraces, swales, waterways, soil boundaries, etc. A layout that does not relate to the landform will soon dominate the landscape. Permeable windbreaks of rounded form and soft colour will disrupt the landscape less than windbreaks of dark, dense, formal trees. Generally, broadleaved trees are less disruptive than conifers.

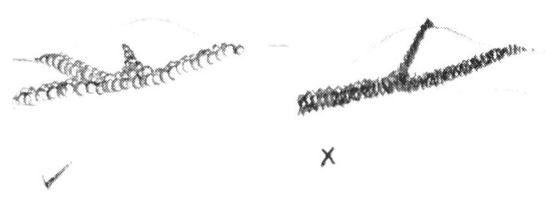

A straight-row shelterbelt should not suddenly start or stop. Each belt needs to be linked with other plantings, having a wider end group, and continue some way in another direction. If only lineal plantings are used, considerable care is needed with their siting as any straight line or geometric shape will become a dominant element. In rolling or hilly country if the siting, form, or colour of a shelterbelt is not sympathetic to the landform, or is isolated and not tied into a general landscape framework, it can visually destroy a far greater area than the actual farm.

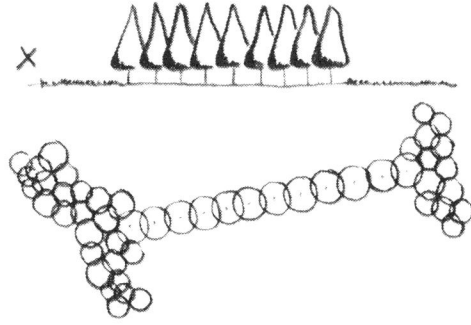

Avoid abrupt, straight shelterbelts.

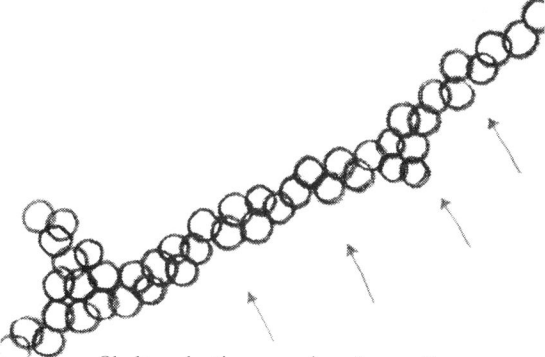

Shelter plantings running along valley.

Developing shelter plantings from local native vegetation would help a lot to produce distinctive local character. These plantings could also be valuable for creating a network of wildlife habitat, and for providing bee fodder. Fussy, garden-style, ornamental trees and shrubs should not be added to shelter belts as they do not suit the farm-scale landscape. Mix species informally in all plantings: never alternate different kinds.

Native waterside tree and shrub species added to exotic trees, or used alone, will give considerable character and interest. Take care not to encroach on the riparian zone with inappropriate plantings. Protect buffer zones between productive land and waterways; protect any remnant or regenerating native vegetation, especially that surrounding a spring.

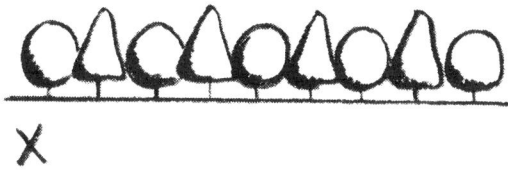

Use shelter planting to emphasise the landform pattern:
a. Where shallow valleys lie across the path of the wind, the valley system can be emphasised and good shelter provided by planting along the line of the drainage pattern. Not the exposed ridges, but the valley floors or lower slopes are better sites for tree growth. Tall trees grown in the valley bottom will give shelter to adjoining ridges. Even if a single or double row is planted along the watercourse, make it less formal by widening out into groups particularly at change points — on the outside of a curve; up into a tributary; extending to form shelter plantings running at right angles to the valley.

b. Valleys which are wind funnels will require planting across them. To retain the continuity of the valley landform, use shelter trees of open form and soft green colour. Use lush-looking species, possibly deciduous.

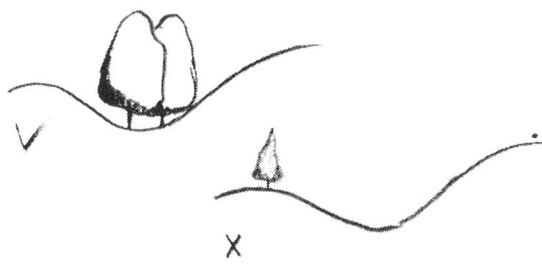

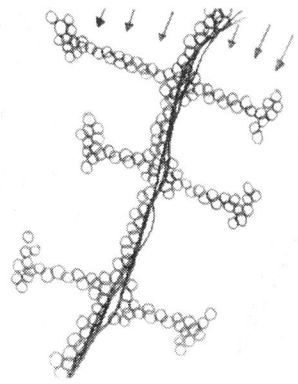

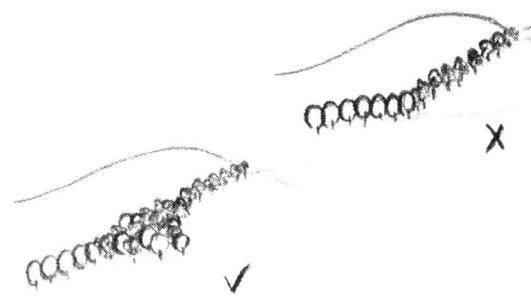

If the belts are required to extend up the sides of the valley, there should be a gradual change in tree species to relate to the change in landform. But employ a similar soft shape, eg poplars on valley floor, eucalypts and acacias on drier valley sides. Soften the change from one to the other with group plantings of a mixture of each as a small woodlot, two-tier, or corner copse. Sudden changes and sharp contrasts should be avoided.

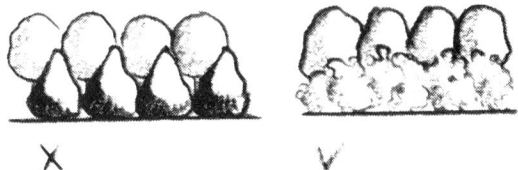

Add lower, denser shelter to the high, permeable trees only if absolutely necessary, such as for critical stock or crop shelter. Any density immediately cuts the visual landscape flow (and could pond cold air). Soft form and colour in the lower storey is essential —never use conifers.

If an understorey is needed, use a mixture of local native trees and shrubs, possibly adding some multi-use exotic plants such as fruiting, bee and stock fodder trees and shrubs.

Ensure any shelterbelts that cross a valley are strongly linked into more dominant plantings along the waterway. The cross shelterbelts should appear as extensions from this central spine.

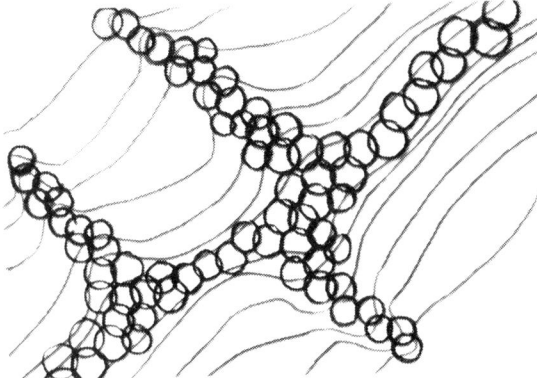

c. Hills and ridges suffer considerably from wind exposure, so they are most difficult places on which to grow shelter trees. The higher and steeper they are in comparison with surrounding landforms, the more important they will be in the landscape. Skylines will be the most prominent sites. Because of this visual prominence, as well as the adverse conditions (wind exposure, moisture extremes) any hill planting needs to be carefully designed if it is not to become a "blot" on the landscape. Generally, rounded tree forms which are not very much darker than the surrounding landscape are preferable.

No shelterbelt should go straight up and over a hill or ridge. If it is necessary to run a belt over a ridge, then ensure the species vary with the different sites. Try to avoid planting the ridge-top areas. Often trees do not do well in such a situation, yet will be visible for many kilometres around. Subtly link the shelterbelts into woodlots, gully plantings, and those extending up from the valley, so that no shelter is a lone strip across a slope.

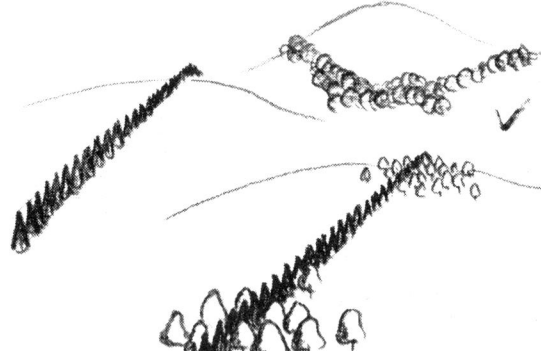

Soften the appearance of all straight-line plantings by extending them to fit the contour of the land. Wherever there is room, an awkward corner, or a change in slope or moisture, widen the planting to form substantial groups, possibly extending some trees out into the paddock to give a more gradual transition to pasture.

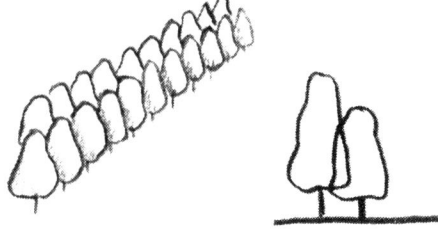

Visual contrasts between rows should be minimal. For example, if there is a contrast in colour, say slightly lighter and darker greens, then they should be of similar form and texture. Generally it is preferable to contrast just one aspect — either form, or texture, or colour. With formal shelter-planting layouts, contrasts in two or more aspects look unhappily contrived.

If exotic conifers must be used for one or more rows of a shelterbelt, an informal mixture of different conifer species will lessen the starkness of the belt.

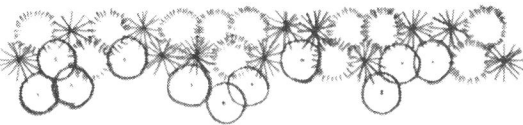

Formality will be reduced by adding groups of broadleaved trees but avoid any stark contrasts between the different species. Only slight variety within the rows is desirable. If conifers are used, then an informal mixture of two or more different species which have similar growth rates will be preferable to a row of one species. The same applies to broadleaved trees.

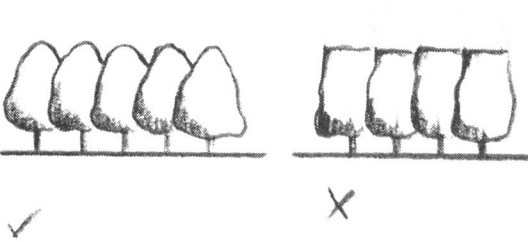

Relatively even tree height is desirable for effective shelter. But avoid topping or hedging trees. Instead, plant trees that will grow to the desired height.

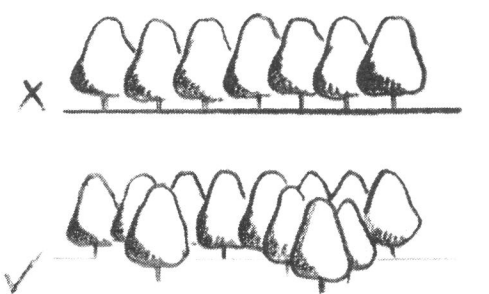

Sometimes only a single row of shelter trees is required, such as for an intermediate planting to subdivide between major windbreaks. To improve the visual depth and balance, add further trees to widen the row at some points. As with widening out any shelterbelt, these extra groups should show some relation to the landform and help create more interesting spaces within the farmland.

In planning the layout and design of shelter be sure to work with the existing landscape, complementing the landform patterns and the natural shelter. Take care to protect and encourage any remnants of native forest and shrubland that do remain.

Woodlot Design

Developing a woodlot which is a beautiful feature of the landscape does not mean adding a few ornamental trees around the edges of a standard block of pines! There are wonderful opportunities on so many New Zealand farms to develop small, interesting woodlots of special-purpose timber trees. Hill and downland farms are often particularly suited to varied woodlot development.

The actual productive forestry planting must be carefully sited and designed to complement the local landscape. If it is not, instead of an asset the woodlot can become an ugly blot on the landscape.

The location, shape and extent of forestry plantings are critical. Forestry can add to the beauty of a landscape through adding interest and variety that looks logical and sensitive. Or, as too often happens, forestry can totally ruin it with insensitive plantings which obliterate or dominate natural beauty and character.

Forestry planting should not be considered in isolation, but must be developed as part of a total plan. Aim for best landuse, multiple use, and coordination of all plantings into an overall framework that complements the natural landscape.

Carefully protect any remnant native forest or shrubland that you have by fencing out completely with no gates. Retain the bush for local identity, interest, wildlife values, and to protect soil and water resources. It is distressing to see a distinctive vegetation being cleared to be replaced with a monoculture of exotic timber plantings which do nothing for development of local identity and which could be anywhere. The need is to build local character, not to destroy it.

Instead of trying to clear, spray or burn areas of shrubland to develop pasture in areas which will require high maintenance input or place soil stability at risk, use the shrubland as the first stage in the development of forest. Either allow or encourage native regeneration, or interplant with native and/or compatible exotic timber trees. It is a waste of resources to continually clear shrubland — manuka, gorse, broom, etc — on land that is obviously better suited for tree growth.

There is a need for high-quality timber trees to be grown, and these require soils of reasonable quality. The planting of small, special-purpose woodlots on good soils scattered throughout New Zealand could be very beneficial: such landuse diversity gives variety in work opportunity and products and at the same time adds to the beauty of each property.

In the siting and design of a woodlot, take care with:

1. Relating the woodlot to the landform pattern.
   a. Fit the overall shape of the woodlot to the topography. The steeper or more visible the land the more care is needed with designing the shape.
   b. Relate the outline to natural boundaries. Never follow geometric boundaries, nor have the edge of a woodlot running straight across or up a slope. Avoid sharp-angled edges on a hillside. Do not automatically follow fencelines or property boundaries.
2. Avoiding skyline planting.
   The boundary between land and sky is a very important landscape feature. Take care not to disrupt this boundary. Never suddenly start or stop a plantation on a skyline — a careful transition is essential.

Preferred forestry on any ridge or hill top is hardwoods for long-term selective logging. These are usually of softer form and colour than conifers. The selective logging does not have the devastating visual effects of clear-felling. Avoid short-rotation, clear-fell forestry systems on ridges and hilltops.

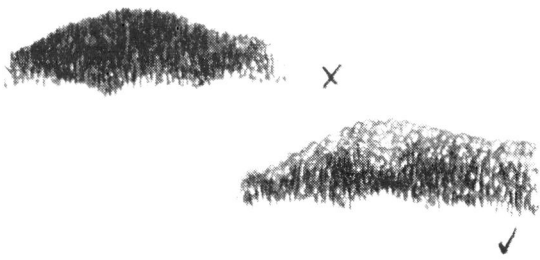

3. If trees must be in rows, have the rows running around the hillside with the contour. Do not have rows running up and down a hillside.

4. Mixing species.

a. All woodlots should have a mixture of tree species. The only exceptions are small woodlots of broadleaved trees (eucalypts, blackwoods, walnuts, oaks, etc) which can be beautiful as pure stands.

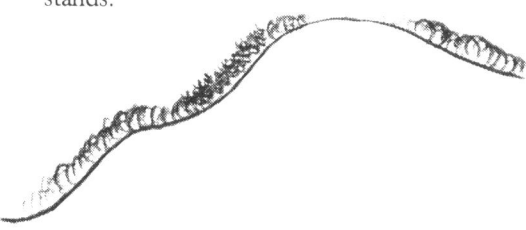

b. A continuous plantation disguises the underlying details of the landscape. Therefore it is important to mix species in such a way as to display the details rather than disguise them. Change species where there is a change in soil, aspect, moisture or slope.

c. Plant long-rotation hardwoods to give a framework when the other species are felled. This framework should follow the main pattern of the landform — the waterways particularly, suitable spurs and ridge lines, and parts of the outer margins of the plantation.

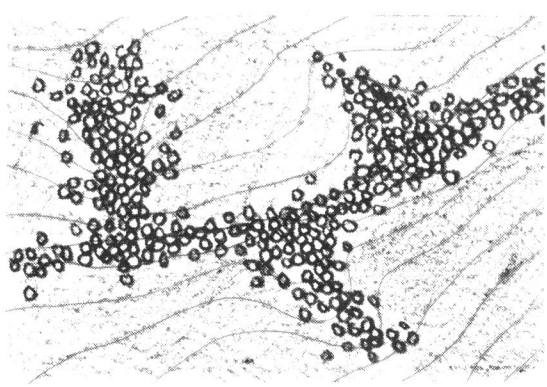

It does not need to be continuous, and should not be of constant width, but vary informally, widening out into groves at strategic points and narrowing to nothing at others.

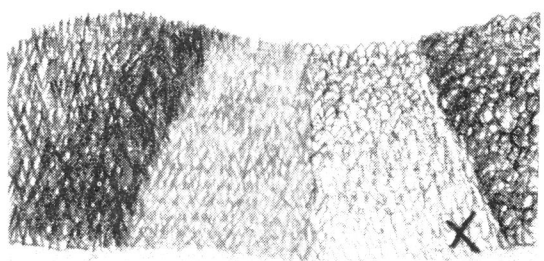

d. Do not have sudden changes from a block of one species to a block of another. Mix the species where they meet, merging one type into the other. A guideline for the amount of mixing required for a plantation containing two species is to have a third to a quarter of the area in a mixture of the two species, the remaining two-thirds to three-quarters being pure stands of each species.

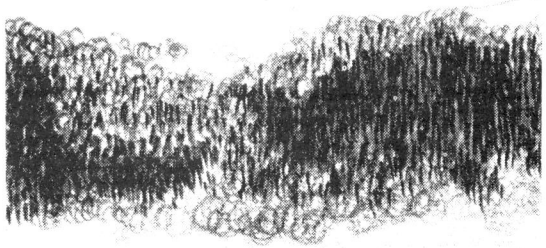

e. Temporary plantation mixtures such as a nurse crop and the species it protects can be quite ugly. Alternate rows of contrasting trees should not be visible, and never run up a hillside.

If two different types must be closely mixed to produce both a nurse crop and a long-term crop, plant them in mixed groups, not in long rows.

X

Even though the main plantation may be high-pruned for timber production, reduce the amount of pruning toward the edges, so that the transition trees have a balanced shape. These transition trees will also be more windfirm, and may be capable of remaining when the main crop is felled.

X

5. Treatment of edges.
    Avoid straight, sharp edges. Those of a woodlot need to be softened to create a pleasant transition from forest to pasture. Do not plant a narrow fringe of ornamental trees around the edge. Instead:
    a. Plant large groups and groves of other productive trees, and have them drift back into the main crop. The drifts should relate to the landform pattern — run up gullies, ridges, or terraces.

X

6. Forest-farming combined.
    Although there are many benefits from closely combining timber trees and pasture, the visual results of this combination can be ugly.
    Never plant wide-spread rows of trees across rolling or hilly land. The effect is very dominating.
    Wide-spaced trees are beautiful when combined with pasture if they are grouped. The forest-farming concept is very successful where the trees are carefully sited in an informal arrangement which meets the needs of both industries.

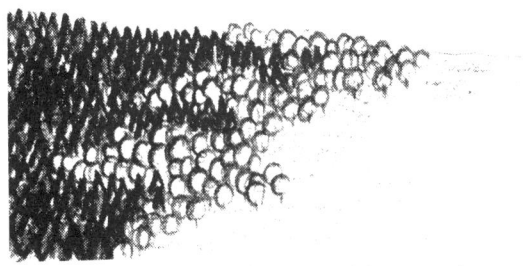

b. Have the plantation trees wider spaced toward the edges. Create a gradual transition from dense plantation to grassland. Distribute the trees irregularly — not in rows.

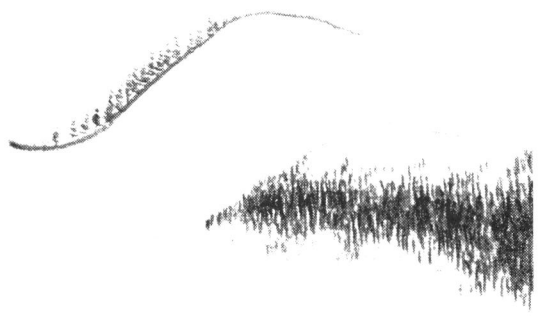

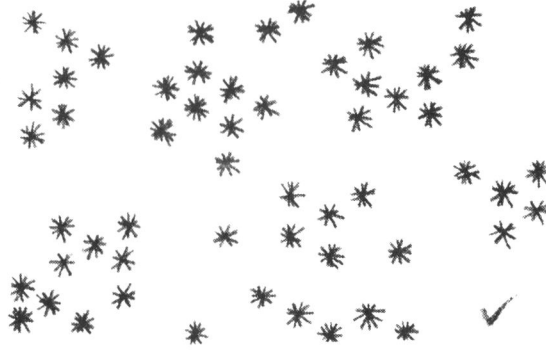

✓

Quincunx pattern used as a basis for planting layout.

Trees and Buildings

Most structures in the New Zealand countryside appear as an intrusion: they often look as though they have just been dropped there. There is no sense of belonging, either in their siting or their design.

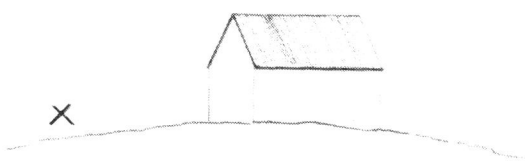

Although it is desirable that all structures be of dull, earthy colours — with walls at least as dark as the surrounding landscape, and roofs much darker — it is not always practical to paint existing large sheds. Nonetheless no building should sit stark and shiny in the landscape. If a building cannot be suitably coloured, then use trees to screen and soften the structure. Even two or three trees can be a great help.

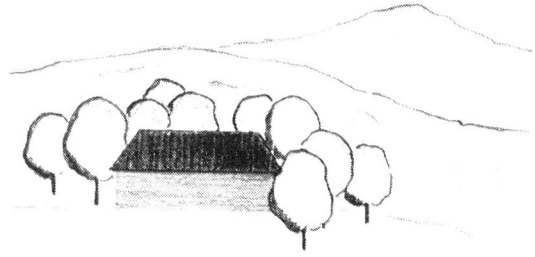

All buildings should be sited so that they have a backdrop, preferably of land as well as of trees. Nestle structures against existing vegetation wherever possible, and supplement with additional planting where necessary. The backdrop planting should be tall enough to appear well above the roof, but need not be planted close to the building.

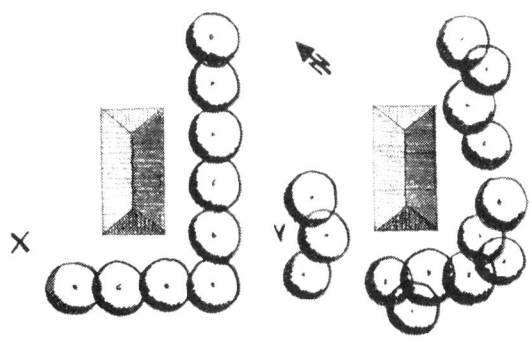

Trees forming a backdrop or screen should not be planted as a row around a structure. It is not usually necessary to block out a building completely, but merely to reduce its impact. Group trees so as to integrate the structure subtly into the surrounds. Tall trees should be sited around the south side of buildings. These trees can be a deciduous and evergreen mixture, with the latter being an understorey to give good low shelter. They can be as much as 15 to 25 metres back from the building, although they can often be much closer. It is visually important that the planting is extended around the ends of buildings, softening their outline and thus relating them better to the surrounding land.

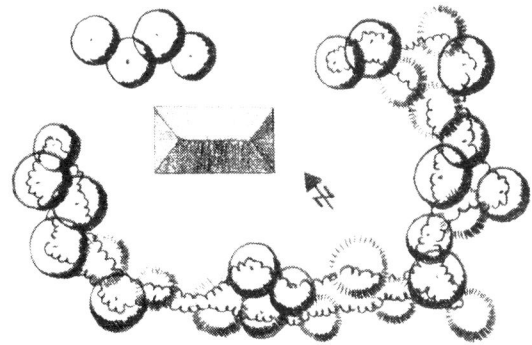

Plant tall, deciduous trees out from the north side of buildings. These will make a building look more interesting, as glimpses are always more exciting than total exposure. At the building these north-side trees will give some shelter, summer shade, privacy and beauty. Views out may be possible under the tree canopy.

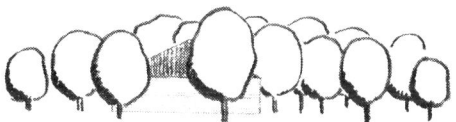

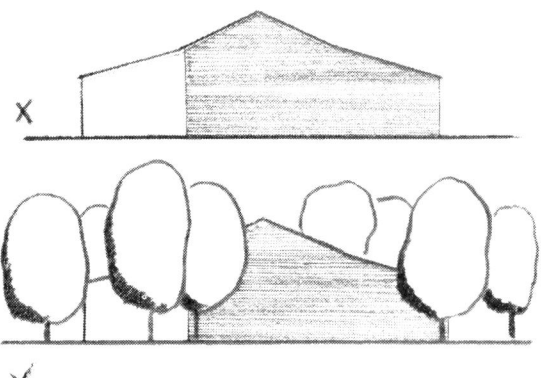

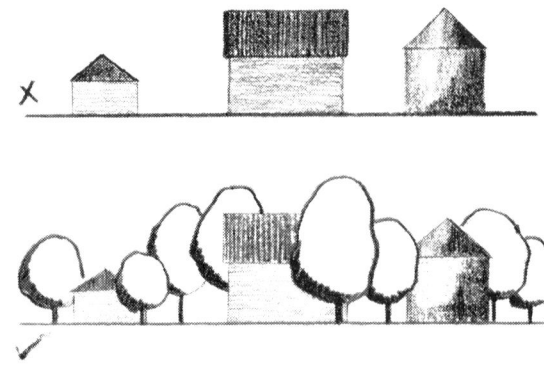

Many new farm buildings, such as woolsheds combined with covered yards, look so enormous that their apparent size needs to be reduced by planting trees to break up the form. Such planting must be tall enough to extend well above roof height. Awkward building forms can be improved by using trees to direct attention away from the form. The trees soften

Plant trees to link various buildings together and co-ordinate the scattered variety of structures that appear on so many farms. Breaking a silhouette is more effective than camouflaging it with creepers, etc. It is not necessary to screen a structure completely; merely soften it by planting to break the outline and reduce its impact.

the angles and edges and create a more appropriate silhouette to relate the building to the surrounding landscape. Buildings of completely different style or scale should not be visible in the same view. Screen-plant with trees so that only the one style is visible from any viewpoint.

Composition

Informal layouts are more likely to look good than formal ones.

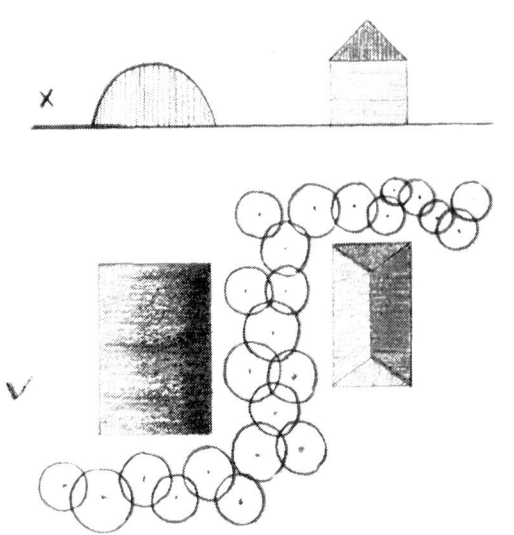

Formal Design

To plant formally — in straight rows at even spacings — is a major decision to take, because the formality will dominate the character of any site. Take care never to use formal patterns which contradict the natural patterns. The steeper a site, the more dominating and inappropriate formal planting will look. For a formal design to be successful, the proportions must be carefully related to the size of the space. Too often formal plantings are too small to frame an area adequately; they are out of scale.

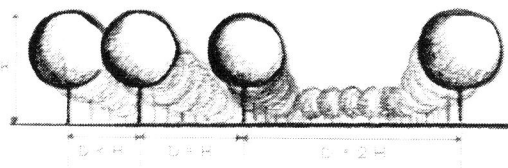

A space can be pleasantly enclosed by planting if the width of the space is no greater than a distance twice the height of the enclosing trees.

Wide spaces cannot be comfortably enclosed by small trees.

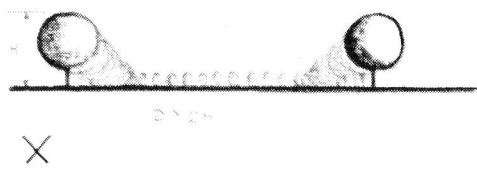

If trees are placed in a row at regular spacings, they must grow evenly or there will be visual conflict. Formal planting layouts are often not successful because of individual tree failures, or variations in growth rates. If one tree fails, the pattern will be upset. To ensure growth rates are even, it is necessary to use just one kind of tree in a formal design. A mixture of species can never create the essential unity.

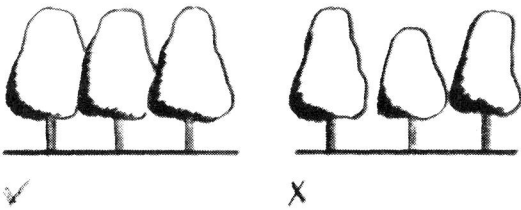

Simplicity is critical for a formal planting to succeed. Use just one kind of tree, and plant them close enough so that their branches intertwine by the time they are half grown. A design dependent on trees of a mature size can look unsatisfactory for many years.

As planting should reinforce the natural patterns of the landscape, formal layouts are very rarely suitable excepting on totally flat and uninteresting topography. Even on an apparently flat site, planting can be used to emphasise natural patterns to make it more interesting and more logical.

Informal Design

Planting layouts which are informal are more likely to complement the landscape, especially where they emphasise the natural patterns. Informal does not mean haphazard. Plan informal plantings involving subtly controlled compositions which appear more natural than contrived. Alternatively, allow the trees to sort out a completely natural pattern through natural regeneration; seeding; or mass planting of seedlings where survival is greatest in the best sites, thinning out toward less favourable areas, thus giving natural transitions.

Have a look at plants that have colonised naturally — whether native trees or shrubs, or exotic weeds such as gorse — observing the spacings between the plants, from dense to sparse in relation to the site conditions. Use this type of grouping in planting design.

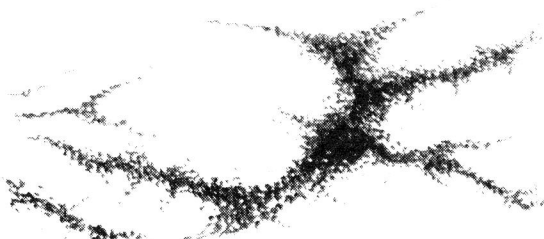

Mixtures of different tree species need to be treated in the same way, with dense groupings of one kind, thinning out as another kind mixes in, and gradually merging into a dense group of the second kind. The groupings should always vary in size. This basic design technique can be applied equally to drifts of trees out in the paddocks or along drives and to mixing plantation species as well as in the more controlled situation of narrow shelter planting.

Basic Principles for Grouping Plants

When using trees, shrubs or even herbaceous material, to achieve a balanced composition that may be viewed from any angle:

1. Do not place one tree on its own. It would be too vulnerable and usually appear out of scale at least for the first few decades. A group is far more likely to be successful and each tree does not need to be a perfect shape.

2. If only two trees are to be planted, then they must be of the same kind and should be planted so close together as to appear to be growing out of the one hole. They should appear almost as one tree with their branches intertwining.

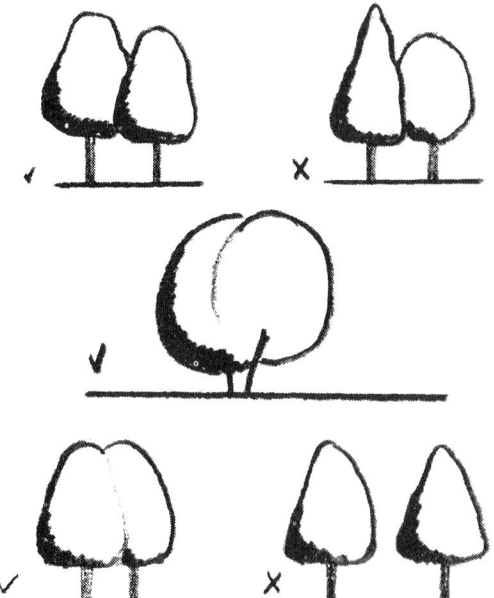

3. Vary the spacings between trees.
   a. A group of three trees should have two close together so that their branches intertwine, and the third slightly further away.

b. For a group of five, have three close together, a fourth just slightly further away and a fifth further away still to appear as a transition out from the main group.

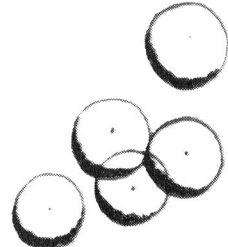

c. For groups of seven or eight or more, increase the spacing from the centre outwards.

4. Do not have strongly contrasting trees within a group. If there is to be contrast in form, then be sure that the scale, habit, colours, and textures are not very different.

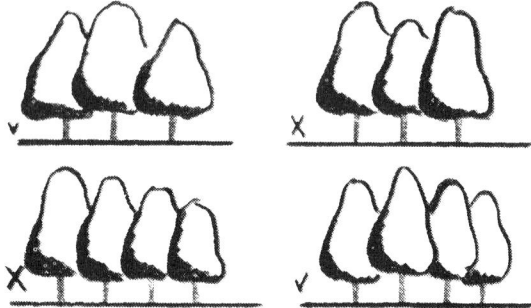

5. Have the tallest-growing tree(s) near the centre of the group. Do not step heights from tallest to shortest, but step up to near the centre of the group, and down again. Do not step up and down symmetrically.

6. Where deciduous and evergreen trees are to be included in the same group, have evergreen species mainly towards the centre.

   The greatest density should be in the middle of a group. Therefore to ensure the group appears balanced in winter, keep the open deciduous trees to the outside of any evergreens.

7. Where both broadleaf (hardwood) and conifer (softwood) species are to be included in the same group, generally keep the conifers toward the centre.

   Conifers are usually more formal and dense than broadleaved trees. The broadleaved trees need to be placed on the outside of the group to soften and "round down" the overall form of the group.

8. Mix trees within groups:
   a. In a group of three trees, have them all the same type, perhaps varying only in size through planting trees of different ages.

   b. With a group of four, have all of one type; or one of a larger growing species, and three of a slightly smaller type.

 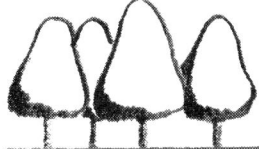

   c. In a group of five, have all of one type; or three of one type and two of another.

 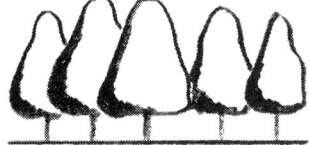

   d. For a group of seven, have all of one type; or four of one type and three of another.

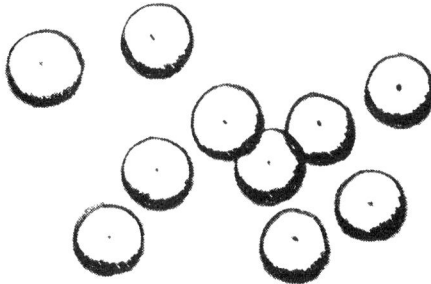

   e. A group of 10 trees is the minimum size for having as many as three different species within a group. A group of 10 trees can be beautiful if all of the one type; or a mixture of two species

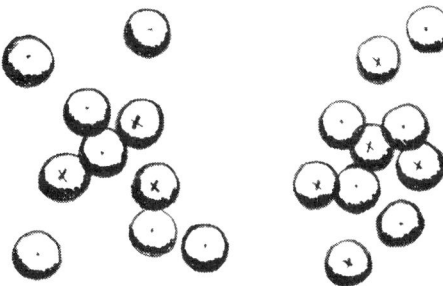

   —perhaps seven of one type and three of another, or five and five, or six and four; but three different types could be used in a group of 10 trees — four of one type, and three of each of the other two types.

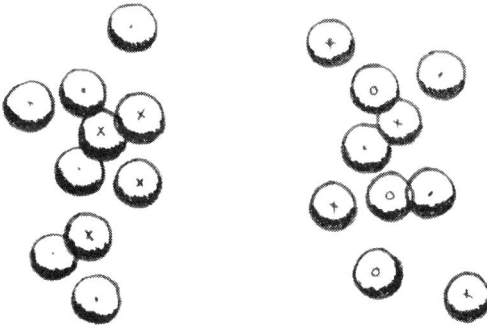

9. Any group of trees should not be a separate composition, but should link into the surrounds — relating to the landform patterns, landuse patterns, and to other vegetation.

   Each group of trees should relate to any other planting nearby, mainly by repeating some of the same trees, or at least trees of very similar scale, form, texture and colour.

10. Where several tree groups are planted, continue at least one type from a group into the next group.

This visually links the groups to give some essential unity.

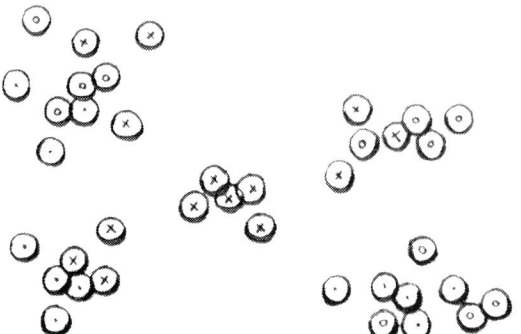

11. Group trees within rows: plant trees in rows only where absolutely essential due to limited space. Grouping can reduce the formality within rows. Never alternate species.

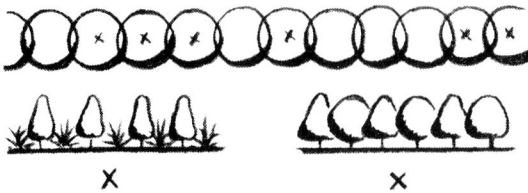

When mixing, use species that do not contrast too much. Vary the form, or the texture, or the colour to a slightly deeper or lighter green. Greater

variation is warranted if conifers must be included in the row. Because of their stronger form it is generally desirable to include a subtle mixture of conifers and also add broadleaved trees to soften them. As in all groupings, it is important to "round down" the edges. Broadleaves informally added to a conifer row will achieve this effect.

Vary rows of trees by planting a few extra trees, of the same kind, outside the line, especially towards the ends of rows. Where two or more rows stand side by side, either mix the species throughout, so that contrasting lines do not eventuate, or group trees at the end to screen this view.

12. If trees are massed together with shrubs underneath, greater variety is acceptable. Trees and shrubs of contrasting form, habit and texture can be grouped and mixed; if closely planted to mass and intertwine. A considerable variety of local and native species can be informally massed to enhance local character.

13. Mixing species:
Whenever different tree types are mixed, make sure the contrasts between the types are subtle. Each type of tree has a particular character which can be defined in terms of its form, habit, texture and colours. These qualities need to be carefully studied to assess the visual compatibility of various tree types.

Form
Look at the forms, or overall shapes of different trees. These can be broadly categorised as round, conical, columnar, horizontal, or weeping.

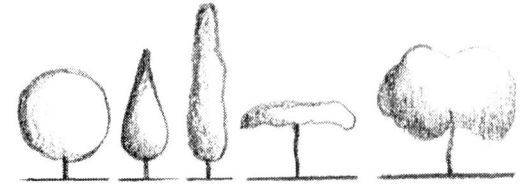

Observe which nestle into a landscape, and which create accent points. The round forms nestle into most landscapes and are most likely to complement landforms. Grouping different round tree forms together usually creates a very restful planting.

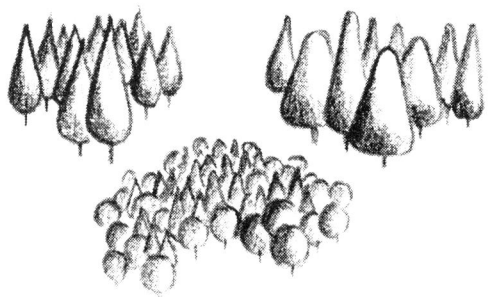

As well as the form of trees, the habit must be carefully considered when deciding which species are visually compatible. Habit, the branching structure, provides the character of the tree within its total form.

Trees generally have either ascending, horizontal or descending (weeping) branching patterns.

In addition, the strength and detail within the branching pattern give individual character to a tree species, eg the rugged, elbowed branches of the English oak; the fine pendulous branches of the birch; and the sweep of the Wellingtonia branches.

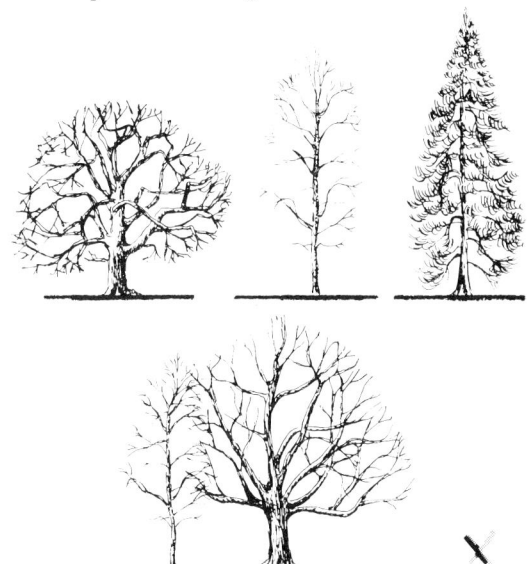

Conical trees can be appropriate. With their height much greater than the width, they emphasise the vertical scale. With the wide base they appear well anchored in the landscape. Groups of just one species of conical tree, or mixtures of several conical types, can look very effective. But unless the conical trees are leafy and soft-looking (generally broadleaves rather than conifers), it is often preferable to use them as accent trees within a group. Have round form trees towards the outside.

The more extreme forms such as columnar (fastigiate), weeping and horizontal, are very difficult to integrate. They are dominating forms, and thus are best avoided. The columnar form of the lombardy poplar has become part of the distinctive character of some districts. Occasionally it may be desirable to continue this character down within a valley. If this strong columnar form of the poplar is to be used, several should be placed centrally in a group, with tall rounded trees grouped around to soften their forms. Lombardy poplars should neither be placed in a row nor in a group on their own.

 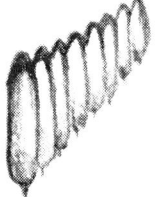

Do not alter the form of a tree by pruning, topping or other mutiliation — it is preferable to let it grow into its natural state. If tree surgery is required, be sure to carefully retain the natural form and habit of the tree.

It is important to have only subtle contrasts in habit within any tree group. Never group strongly contrasting habits together — not dainty pendulous with strong vertical. Within a tree group the habits

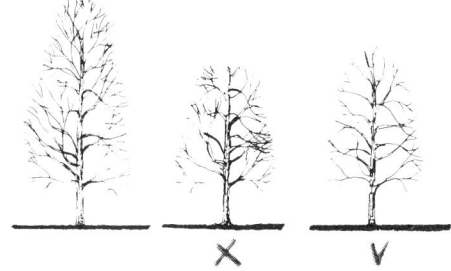

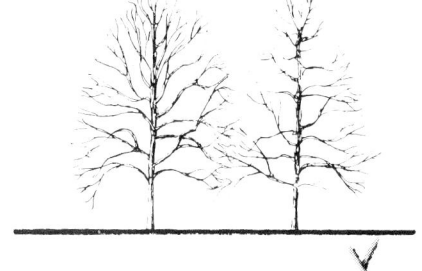

should be of similar boldness, even if the branching is in differing directions. A strong vertical and a strong horizontal may be quite acceptable together, but a dainty horizontal and a strong, angular horizontal may conflict. For example, although a silver birch is basically of descending form, and the Wellingtonia has branches sweeping downwards, they should not be used together as the birch is very dainty whereas the Wellingtonia is very strong.

Group trees of similar habit for a restful, pleasing composition. Although some contrast can be included for accent, this must be carefully controlled to avoid conflict and chaos.

For many tree species the form and habit vary at different ages, perhaps from a pyramidal form with ascending branches when young, to a rounded (or almost square) mature form with horizontal to descending habit.

Texture

In addition to the overall form and habit, each tree has a pattern formed by the leaves and twigs. The play of light and shade on leaves and twigs creates the pattern, or texture.

Texture results from the size and spacing of leaves and twigs; the shape and division of leaves; surface quality of leaves (smooth or wrinkled, shiny or dull); and the length and stiffness of petioles (leaf stalks).

These qualities together give either a coarse, medium or fine texture which is significant from both near and distant views.

A coarse texture results from large leaves (eg sycamore) and will be more coarse when the leaves are widely spaced giving shadows between the leaves (eg catalpa). Small leaves give a fine texture. With cut leaves they appear finer (eg South Island kowhai). Coarse, strongly textured trees (eg horse chestnut, *catalpa*) create focal points, and must be carefully sited. Dense, medium-to-dark coloured foliage which is not so coarsely textured is well-suited as background or general frame-work planting (eg English oak).

The density of the foliage is important. Fine foliage can be set so close together that instead of appearing fine and delicate the tree appears heavy and solid. Dense coarse foliage has the appearance of strength. Short stiff petioles emphasise this strength.

In planting design, aim for subtle contrasts in texture. Use stronger contrasts if the trees are very similar in other ways — similar in size, form, habit, and colour. Or the contrasts could be related to time — the texture of a tree can vary between the seasons, and with age.

Colour

All farm planting should look as though it really belongs to the landscape. To achieve this, summer-green foliage is essential. In recent years, planting for dramatic contrast has been so overdone that garish mixtures have resulted. Contrasts in foliage colour have destroyed the beauty and restfulness of many landscapes.

There are a number of reasons for completely avoiding non-green foliage forms in any planting design. Pale cream, variegated, and golden foliage is so much lighter and brighter than the usual green foliage. It visually dominates other green vegetation, attracting attention away from the subtle contrasts within and between plants.

Seasonal change and interest is important in any landscape. The changes in foliage, flowers and fruits allow different plants to demand more attention and become more dominant at various times of the year. But this happens only during their display of flowers, fruits or autumn foliage.

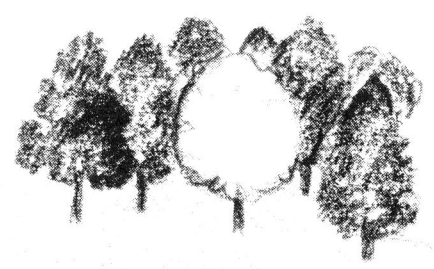

Many golden foliage trees are evergreen, and dominate all year round. Because the clear light that we have throughout New Zealand is much brighter than in most other countries, any light or bright foliage stands out.

Variegated and golden forms can also give the impression of being unhealthy. They do not have the fresh appeal of green foliage. For these reasons it is considered advisable that all golden or variegated trees be completely avoided. Removal of existing ones is usually necessary. Foliage which is red, purple or russet in summer can also be very distracting — it appears almost as autumn colour in the wrong season. Generally avoid such coloured trees.

Although coloured forms may have initial appeal for many people, usually this wanes as they come to appreciate the subtle visual values of plants. Contrasts in texture, in the different tones of green, and particularly the changes with the lighting and the seasons, provide so much interest they can really be appreciated only if there are no variegated or coloured foliage forms in view. The garishness of the latter overpowers the subtleties of the former.

For the same reason that coloured foliage is undesirable, so too with bright flowers and fruits that completely cover a tree. Bright flowering trees, such as pink flowering cherries, and bright fruits, should be kept in the garden, not out in farmland views. If they must be used, ensure there is an ample background of rich green foliage all around. Strongly coloured stems of deciduous trees (eg red, orange, yellow) usually appear too strong for the rural landscape in winter.

If for some reason coloured foliage is required (for floral art, specialist horticulture etc) then such plants need to be grown within an enclosed space where they can only be viewed close by. They should never be part of the general scene.

References

Brian Clouston (ed.), *Landscape Design with Plants*. The Landscape Institute. Heinemann, London, 1977.

Sylvia Crowe, *The Landscape of Forests and Woods*. Forestry Commission Booklet 44. H.M.S.O., London, 1978.

D.S.I.R., *Land Alone Endures: Land Use and the Role of Research*. Discussion Paper No. 3, Government Printer, 1980.

Boyden Evans, *Revegetation Manual: Using New Zealand Native Plants*. QE II National Trust, 1983.

Diane Lucas, *Landscape Guidelines for Rural South Canterbury. 1980-81*.

B. Mollison, D. Holmgren, *Permaculture One: A Perennial Agriculture for Human Settlements*. Corgi, Australia, 1978.

B. Mollison, *Permaculture Two: Practical Design for Town and Country Permanent Agriculture*. Tagari, Australia, 1979.

New Zealand Forest Service, Landscape Section, *Creative Forestry: A Guideline for Forest Managers*. 1982.

Diane Lucas is a landscape architect who was nurtured in the Central Otago high country. She took a science degree at Otago University and a post-graduate diploma in landscape architecture (Dip.L.A.) at Lincoln College before working for four years for the Ministry of Works and Development in Christchurch, Dunedin and the Hamilton districts. After overseas travel she returned to New Zealand overwhelmed by the beauty and diversity of the country but concerned at the tenuous understanding of rural landscape values and the complete lack of guidance available for farmers wishing to develop their land in line with these.

In 1979 she established a rural landscape practice based in Geraldine, South Canterbury and since then has worked mainly as a consultant to farming people. She is also active in developing greater public awareness of landscape values and has published a booklet *Landscape Guidelines for Rural South Canterbury* (1980-81) which is widely used.

Landscape designer Ines Stäger works with Diane and has been involved in the preparation of the drawings for this chapter.

2
Privately Owned Indigenous Forests

Because of increasing concern being expressed at the continuing inroads into non-State forests, the Forestry Council published in 1980 Bulletin No 8 "Policy Guidelines for Private Indigenous Forests". The document notes that loss of private indigenous forest is not generally spectacular — it is an inexorable process. Many unique indigenous forest types have now almost entirely disappeared due in no small part to land development for farming. Deterioration is still taking place on private farms where stock are allowed into bush, thus making regeneration impossible and aggravating losses through attrition, until eventually the stand disappears. Many landowners are conscious of the need to reverse this trend by fencing off the bush and some local bodies do encourage this action by making a remission of rates according to various formulae. (Usually in proportion to the amount of land fenced off, based either on area or valuation.)

For those who wish to go further by taking legal steps to preserve the stand for all time there are a number of options open.

Using the Queen Elizabeth II National Trust Act 1977 is a very practical way of providing effective protection. This act provides for open space covenants which protect areas of land or water which are of aesthetic, cultural, recreational, scenic, scientific or social interest or value. Such areas may be forest remnants, wetland, river or lake verges, or important geological features.

An open space covenant is a legal agreement between the Trust and the landowner or leaseholder, and any subsequent owners, to maintain and protect an area for a specified time, or in perpetuity. The owner retains ownership and the concomitant sense of involvement with the land, while enjoying the security of the formal protection afforded by the Trust.

The Trust actively respects the rights and wishes of the owner, who manages the land in accordance with the terms negotiated for the convenant. The Trust can offer management advice, assistance, and specialist services.

The Trust undertakes to survey and register the covenanted area at no cost to the owner. The Trust may help with management of the area, such as contributing towards the cost of fencing.

Public access to covenanted land is generally encouraged, but it is not always in the best interests of the land, or the owner. For example, where the purpose of the convenant is to provide and protect scenic views from the roadside or other public area, then direct public access may be neither necessary nor desirable. Similarly, public access may be inconvenient at certain times of the year, in which case the covenant can provide access by arrangement with the owner, whose rights against trespass are unaffected.

Open space covenants often cover particular features on a farm. In other cases they cover entire properties where normal farming operations continue, subject to the protection of specified areas.

The owner and the Trust may vary the terms of the covenant by mutual agreement, and if circumstances change in such a way that the covenant is no longer useful it may be revoked, with the consent of the Minister of Lands. However, open space covenants are intended to provide sound protection of valuable landscape in perpetuity while maintaining the owner's traditional link with the land.

The relevant extracts from Bulletin No 8 set out the position as at the time of publication of this book, and may be found in Appendix 2.

Readers wanting to do something a little different might like to grow native trees for timber. Choose a sheltered site and select trees that grow well in your locality. Make sure the soil type and moisture are appropriate and plant the trees about 2.5 m apart, adding a handful of blood-and-bone to encourage growth. If you have cover such as manuka, kanuka or gorse, cut tracks between trees and keep these tracks open constantly. A long bamboo stick put in each planting hole helps to locate any trees not attended to regularly. Prune side branches off as the young trees grow, to retain a knot-free core of about 10 cm. Keep young trees well watered for their first two summers, and if dry spells occur in autumn or spring.

The Queen Elizabeth II National Trust's Revegetation Manual gives lots of helpful hints on establishing native plants and every reader should have a copy.

It also contains an excellent list of further reading references.

Planting natives may seem a somewhat pitiful attempt to redress the present imbalance between the loss of New Zealand's indigenous forest and its available annual increment, but the consequences of not planting should also be considered. In due course most indigenous stands will either disappear or be protected in some way, though some will be managed on a sustainable basis. Considering the wonderful wood values of some of these trees it would be regrettable if they were no longer available to consumers. Certainly there will be a limited supply but present policy is to substitute natives with special purpose-planted exotics. This will provide a supply of high-quality timber within half a century, but should thinking not be for a longer term? Certainly to plan over a period of 50 years is quite a step forward from the *Pinus radiata* regime of 25 years which tends to dominate local thinking. The suggestion to land holders that alternatives to softwoods should be planted is so often met with the question, "How old do they have to be before I can cut them down?" The thought of growing trees on a regime which cannot be seen to have a beginning and an end in a person's lifetime is anathema to many.

New Zealand could well learn from the older European countries which accept that several generations are required to grow trees to harvestable size. In England beeches are on an 80-year rotation and oaks on 150. Sweden, a country not much larger than New Zealand, has 23 million hectares of forest (using 57% of the land) and the shortest rotation for softwoods is 70 years in the south, extending to 140 years in the north, the trees then being 15-20 cm in diameter. They have learned to live with these growth patterns, so why can't we? Many of the New Zealand natives can do better than these, especially when planted and maintained under a managed regime (eg kauris can reach 50 cm in 80 years).

That there is a place in forestry for growing natives is now recognised by the Government: the Forestry Encouragement Grants Scheme gives consideration to any species which have proven, within New Zealand, to have a commercial wood production use, and grants are available for the tending of indigenous regeneration areas.

The authors would like to see more planting of indigenous trees to save bush which would otherwise be felled. Farms with well-tended accessible wood-lots of native trees could increase greatly in value over the years. The owner could eventually cut the trees down with a clear conscience, knowing that that was their intended ultimate use.

3
Trees, Pasture and Soil

Agroforestry may be a new word but the concept of mixing pasture and trees goes back to when the first crops were sown by primitive man (in those unenlightened days the work was usually done by women). Since he tended to destroy the forest to make room for cropping, it was more by accident than design that some trees survived. Older civilisations soon learned that food-bearing trees could be grown as a complementary crop. They also learned much later that land going through the cycle of forest, field and plough often finished up as a desert, as the removal of topsoil by wind and rain became inevitable. The world is full of such disaster areas and in spite of the knowledge available to us now, there are many examples in New Zealand of flat-land agriculture practices being applied to steep hill country. It may not be through cropping, but the effect of forest removal and heavy stocking has resulted in enormous quantities of precious topsoil being lost.

Consider that on average a 5-tonne truckload of sediment flows down the Manawatu river every minute, or 3 million tonnes per year. During the annual flood, a 5-tonne truckload goes down every second for 24 hours — a total of some 432 000 tonnes. The highest flow on record is twice this figure, ie two 5-tonne truckloads every second.

The Waipoua River in Poverty Bay has been responsibly estimated to have transported 37 million tonnes out to sea in one day! It is fair comment to say that much of this sediment is not topsoil but comes

Poplars used to prevent hillside slumping.

43

from the tops of the ranges and from landslips. It is also fair to say that had this process not taken place in the past there would today be none of the rich plains that are the basis of high productivity in Manawatu, Gisborne, Canterbury and elsewhere.

These figures are mightily impressive, but what do they mean in terms of actual loss? Studies being carried out in the Wairarapa include measurements of pasture production over a period of three years on land which has been heavily eroded in the past. They show that:

(a)   Pasture growth on 1977 scars is about 80% down, on average, compared with uneroded ground and

(b)   even after 50 years the pasture growth on old regrassed scars is about 23% down, on average.

By integrating the proportionate areas of eroded ground with the reductions in pasture growth, the loss in "potential productivity" is obtained. Results so far show that the overall loss in potential pasture growth of these hillslopes to date is 16% on average. Further work is expected to show that this figure is somewhat optimistic, ie the reduction may be more serious than this. This figure could increase significantly however with future erosion events.[1]

Trees are natural crops for steep lands for they can store water much better than grasses; their deep-rooting system also seeks out moisture well below the surface. They can withstand drought much more effectively, but above all the trees' widespreading roots hold the land together. Crop-bearing trees are a permanent agriculture so we should be looking much more closely at this form of land use: trees holding together topsoil which continues to grow pasture on which livestock can be grazed.

We tended in the past to grow a forest as a first objective and then to use it for what grazing could be eked out from under it; not primarily for the benefit of the animals and their owners, but more to keep the forest floor clean, with easier access to trees, less fire risk and quicker breakdown of pruning and thinning slash. (Plus of course some useful income for the forest owner.) Recent thinking has been directed to a managed form of trees and pasture whereby the two become fully integrated and given equal status in the planned objectives. The Tree Crops Association has pioneered work in promoting a permanent cropping asset which can be utilised with only minimal loss of pasture production. Side benefits are shade and shelter. Much has yet to be learned as to the species of trees which are best suited to New Zealand conditions and which will produce a quality crop acceptable to overseas consumers. The indications are that chestnuts, walnuts, pecans, persimmons and suchlike

A high yielding honey locust will produce more than 100kg of beans each year.

could play a worthwhile role in land use economy. An oak tree produces acorns by the sackful, honey locust can produce beans with a dry weight of over 2.5 tonnes per annum to the hectare off about 120 trees, willows can produce 15 tonnes of edible dry matter per hectare per annum and some of the stock can continue to graze under these fodder trees. They are some of the permanent trees of agroforestry, but there is also a place for timber trees grown on a rotation basis.

Over the years a few venturesome farmers have put stock amongst their pine trees from a very early age, and perhaps even more farmers have seen stock amongst their newly planted trees as a complete surprise. There are many factors which affect the behaviour of stock towards trees, some of them being most unpredictable. It is probably safe to say that livestock are capable of being managed in such a way that pine trees are not at risk even when quite small. This is particularly so when the same cattle are constantly exposed to pine needles, right from the time they are calves; similarly with sheep. Stock tend to damage trees more in the spring, when they have an urge to find some roughage not present in pasture, but bark stripping can often be attributed to different social

Pines, poplars, totara and sheep all doing well together.

and behavioural patterns. What needs stressing is that the management of two-tier farming has to be of a very high calibre, special skills being required. The dedicated stockman will give preference to his animals, the forester to his trees. There will frequently be compromise decisions to be made and as always the seekers of the best of both worlds are bound to have disappointments.

Much has been written on the subject and a 30-year trial at Tikitere, near Rotorua, is still only one third of its way through its life. After the first 10 years the summary of findings is as follows:
— Successful integration of farming and forestry requires clear objectives and a high standard of management.
— Trees grow faster on farmland than on comparable forest sites.
— A high standard of silviculture is essential to produce high value sawlogs.
— Slash and tree competition are the major effects on agricultural production in the first 10 years.
— Livestock performance is little affected by trees up to 100 stems/ha. Above 200 stems/ha livestock performance declines.[2]

This book is no place to try and cover the subject in any depth, although much of its content is sympathetic to the philosophy of multiple land use, incorporating the concept that trees and farming are complementary, not competitive. In New Zealand less than 5% of forestry is in the hands of small private growers compared with more than 50% in Scandinavian countries such as Sweden and Finland. Throughout the 1981 New Zealand Forestry Conference there was an emphasis on the role of farm forestry which was a reflection of the importance placed on dual-purpose and multipurpose exotic forests. Agroforestry should now be incorporated in the management planning and decision-making of all landowners, to ensure that all the options for land use are fully considered. Growing trees can thus become part of New Zealand's much vaunted and highly valued family farm ownership and so increase the portion of forest resource in the hands of the small grower.

The loss of topsoil is such that protection forestry is vital to retain what is still left, but the opportunity for forest grazing is still there. Widespread planting on marginal country appears to be a viable prospect if the demanding silvicultural regimes can be adhered to. Evidence from the Radiata Task Force is that the best economic returns are obtained from large logs which

Pruned pines and eucalypts on a Northland farm.

are produced from early thinned plantations, or wide-spaced plantings of trees, particularly those possessing superior genetic qualities. While the main thrust of research is on radiata pine, other species respond well to such regimes. For instance poplars are very happy growing in isolation from one another. They can produce fine quality veneer logs, they can help to dry out a wet spot, the grass grows right up to their trunks, their prunings provide edible stock fodder,

they give summer shade, colour up well in the autumn and then allow sunlight onto winter pastures. On steeper country they do all this and as well control land movement. (There is even a suggestion that the leaves can help prevent facial eczema.)

In the summer of 1978 there was a serious drought in the Wairarapa. Former National President of the Farm Forestry Association, Jim Pottinger, was desperately short of food on his Tinui farm. After wean-

Cows and calves enjoy poplar prunings in hot dry weather.

46

High-pruned poplars provide shade for animals and will make good veneer logs.

Widely-spaced eucalypts on a King Country farm.

ing calves at the end of January, for two months he fed his nearly 200 mixed age in-calf beef cows on a diet of poplar leaves, small twigs and branches. Nothing else: young stock had already taken all the grass. The total area used was 45 ha.

These trees are still doing their original job of controlling erosion and providing shade and beauty with potential as a timber crop. It may also be worth noting that in 1979 Jim Pottinger won the award for the best North Island farm forester, while in 1983 he was selected best Wairarapa Hill Country Farmer!

Wide spaced planting can be carried out with almost any of the timber or nut- or fruit-bearing trees, but if high quality logs are one of the end objectives, then regular and systematic pruning is absolutely essential.

Agroforestry is just another form of diversification which enables farmers to maximise the production of the land in line with its particular qualities and poten-

tial and the skills and wishes of the owner. It need not take up much space. A few black walnuts on a choice site will hardly be noticed and yet in 50 years each one could yield a couple of cubic metres of timber — worth on today's values the equivalent of about 10 prime steers. There will be no loss of productivity yet a few small stands of high-quality trees will certainly add to the value of the farm. Even if it is someone else's children who cash up, the present landowner will get his share through capital gain. In the chapter on shelter there is a section on production of timber from shelterbelts: another multiple use of trees on the land.

Because research is making available new information at a very rapid rate, this form of diversification should be carried out only after doing lots of homework and seeking out the best advice and latest techniques likely to give the most worthwhile results. Such diverse use of trees will benefit not only the farmer, but the whole landscape and so the community will be the final beneficiaries. And what is wrong with that?

In a speech given at the opening of the Canterbury Environment Centre in 1983 the Minister for the Environment, Dr Ian Shearer, brought the erosion problem closer to his audience by mentioning that wind stripped 67 tonnes of topsoil per hectare from a cultivated field in mid-Canterbury during a north-westerly blow in 1981. This alone represented 3 percent of the depth of the topsoil. Early in that year 21 mm of rain, over a period of four hours, washed 92 tonnes of topsoil per hectare from a newly sown paddock in South Canterbury. A study by the Otago Catchment Board assessed that wind erosion on the

Maniopoto was taking topsoil at the rate of 20 cubic metres per hectare per year — a rate which would mean there would be none left in 200 years.

Surface erosion (sheet, wind and scree) has been recorded on 74% of the South Island and 24% of the North Island. Soil scientists consider that 13.8 million hectares or 52% of New Zealand's land is affected by surface erosion.[3]. Loss of topsoil should be the concern of every landowner, but especially those who are making a living from their land. They have a responsibility to think in the long term, but unfortunately most do not give much thought beyond 20 years. Even when it comes to tree growing we have been conditioned to the 25-year rotation of *Pinus radiata*. Erosion is a severe and extensive problem. Both prevention and repair are needed to ensure that rates of soil loss are held to or below those which took place before development. This can be achieved by adopting wise land-use policies; only then can we look to productivity being maintained for centuries rather than decades.

Good land management must include preservation of the resource, and the wise use of trees is a management option open to all landowners.

References

1. *Streamland 3*. National Water and Soil Conservation Organisation 1982.
2. *Forest Farming Research at Tikitere*. NZ Forest Service Handbook 1983. (This handbook includes a full list of relevant literature on the subject).
3. G.O. Eyles, Distribution and Severity of Present Soil Erosion in New Zealand. *NZ Geographer* Vol 39 No. 1. Apr. 1983.
4. *NZ Farm Forestry Journal* Vol 20 No. 4 1978.

4
Shelter

New Zealand is a windy country and can be considered as having a maritime climate where the huge surrounding ocean areas largely influence the short-term weather situation. It is often subjected to strong, damaging winds, especially along coastal sites. Although winds are generally less frequent in inland areas they are just as strong and cold as those on the coast. The hill country with its topographical extremes causes marked changes in wind behaviour: rounded hills and sharp ridges and valleys affect the winds differently, increasing speed, funnelling and turbulence.

Until the start of the horticultural boom interest in shelter was fairly limited in agricultural fields. The recent surge in production has confirmed that good effective shelter is critical.

Because New Zealand enjoys such a diverse range of climatic conditions and endemic site situations (soil type, fertility and drainage) it is extremely difficult to present a practical and useful guide to cover the entire country without becoming too specific or too general. The intention is to present general principles in the planning, choice and establishment of shelter to provide a sound area base for further discussions with local advisers.

On a very exposed Wairarapa hill country farm flax
protected by electric fences makes effective low shelter.

Importance of Shelter

The importance of shelter has been well demonstrated over recent years by the expansion of successful crops such as kiwi fruit. The sheep farmer also knows the benefits of 'protected' areas during times of lambing and late shearing. Unexpected gale winds and even light zephyrs can cause stock losses which are often considered 'acts of God' when in fact they could have been avoided through proper use of shelterbelts.

Damage to export-quality horticultural crops, and stock deaths, are obvious results of insufficient shelter, but the insidious wind effect on crop growth and yield is much more difficult to quantify. Plant growth processes are a complicated matter although most growers understand the necessary balance of light, moisture and temperature. Transpiration (water usage) losses from a plant are greatly reduced when wind speeds are lowered. This has a double advantage of ensuring that leaf stomata remain open (enabling photosynthesis to continue with the potential for increased yield) and that the plant is warmer which increases the rate of photosynthesis. High rates of transpiration caused by the wind will accentuate drought stress.

There is little information on the response of grasslands to shelter despite their importance to world agriculture. Nevertheless in a review of world literature Radcliffe shows that yields from tree-sheltered areas are increased by percentages ranging from 15 to 100 and more. The author emphasises the need for grassland shelter research in New Zealand to quantify the benefits which are known to be provided by shelter. Uncompleted research trials indicate that increases in dry matter yield at distances of 3-5 times shelter height compared with 12 times are very substantial — accumulated pasture growth tDM/ha were 5.51 at 3h, 5.40 at 5h, only 3.28 at 12h from a mature shelterbelt. [1]. Many farmers in windy situations are convinced of the effectiveness of shelter on grassland production. On stony drought-prone soils in mid-Canterbury Smail estimated that 20% of his farm production was directly related to his tree planting and the total area of trees occupies only 5.6% of the property. This does not include the residual value of the trees which when well grown and managed can provide both shelter and quality timber. [2].

A 1981 trial under actual farming conditions gave dramatic crop increases on a Methven, Canterbury,

Left: A two-row shelterbelt: slow-growing *Cupressus arizonica* on the windward side and pruned *Pinus radiata* on the leeward side. This carefully managed shelterbelt, about 18 years old, is in South Canterbury.

farm. The crop of oats was partially protected from hot dry north-west winds by a single-row shelterbelt of Douglas fir 550 m long and a mean height of 7 m. The belt had been side trimmed twice and was reasonably permeable. The worth of the shelter in economic yield was very evident at full crop maturity. The yield from the sheltered area averaged 35% increase over the average from the unprotected area with the maximum of 51% coming from crops situated at 4 times shelter height. Yields from 1-6 times shelter height were significantly greater than at 10-30h. [3]

Apart from the wind's effect on the productivity of a crop there are many other undesirable results that can occur under exposed conditions. It is perhaps more positive to summarise the benefits of shelter. It can reduce mechanical damage to foliage, flowers and fruit, thus increasing crop yields
— reduce severe burning from salt-laden winds
— improve market value by ensuring better fruit quality
— encourage flight of pollinating insects and so improve fruit setting
— limit staking of trees to prevent root damage
— reduce topsoil erosion and protect newly seeded crops
— reduce crop flattening (eg hay) and seed loss
— protect stock, especially newborn animals
— improve stock comfort and reduce animal heat-stress in summer
— reduce feed requirements during the winter months
— control snow drifting
— create a warmer working environment in winter
— improve the microclimate, thus widening the range of land use options
— improve spraying conditions, thus minimising drift.

In almost all exposed situations the farmer plants shelter around the house, knowing that family and pets will appreciate the benefits and that the garden will be the better for the improved environment; yet more often than not the same farmer is reluctant to plant shelter over the rest of the farm.

Extracts from some Australian reports on the benefits of shelter are worth quoting in full:

"Previous research in Armidale (Australia) has shown that vertical shelter increased plant and animal production on adjacent areas . . . . Present experiments have confirmed the increase in plant growth and suggest that the growth is not achieved by increased growth per day when there is adequate moisture, but by availability of moisture for a longer period in the sheltered areas. Increased animal production results from the greater plant production."[4]

"Significant differences in water use and evaporation were noted between sheltered and unsheltered plots. Green plant availability is generally higher in sheltered paddocks — about 30% at stocking rate of 10 sheep/ha, and with shelter regeneration of pasture is faster.

"The effect of shelter with varying stocking rate shows:
At 10 sheep/ha liveweight gains were higher in paddocks without shelter.
At 30 sheep/ha there was little difference.
At intermediate stocking rates the sheep with shelter were up to 16% heavier.
At *all* stocking rates more wool was grown by sheep in sheltered paddocks."[5]

Good shelter can minimise spray drift.

There is growing awareness among farmers and orchardists of the benefits of planting trees that can supplement the nectar and pollen sources, particularly during the spring period when nectar and pollen production are low. Some shelter timber species are favoured by the bees, such as *Eucalyptus* (*E.mellio-dora, E.regnans, E.leucoxylon*) *Acacia, Robinia, Gleditsia,* etc. Shelter provides a favourable working environment for the bee, increasing its activity as well as encouraging the growth and flower production on the pollen and nectar-bearing plants. Bees hate wind.

During winter months feed requirements are reduced when there is good shelter.

This row of *Eucalyptus botryoides* in the Manawatu would be more effective if underplanted with a low growing secondary species.

Principles of Shelter

The principles applying to shelter are well described by J.M. Caborn *(Shelterbelts and Windbreaks, 1965)* and have been summarised in MAF Aglink leaflets. The invisible flow of wind has very similar properties to water where the fluid takes the line of least resistance; flow rates and turbulence are largely determined by surface irregularities of the area passed over.

There are four main contributing factors relating to effectiveness of shelter: height, porosity, length and uniformity.

Height of the shelter directly influences the area of wind reduction on the leeward and windward side. The greater the height the greater the area influenced. Generally, good wind shelter is provided for 10 with some effect up to 20 times the shelter height on the leeward side and up to 5 times on the windward side;

where a high degree of protection is required, eg some horticultural crops, belts are repeated at a factor of about 8 times the shelter height.

Porosity of the shelter belt determines the wind behaviour on the leeward side and to a lesser extent on the windward side. Practical experience has shown clearly that belts of medium porosity (40-60%) produce a much more even windflow over a much wider area. Good porosity can be achieved by correct species choice and subsequent management. When porosity is low, the wind profile is changed; a very sheltered area occurs close to the belt but turbulence occurs at a factor of about 5 times the shelter height. An important advantage of live shelter as compared with artificial is that the leaves on the natural shelter respond to changing wind velocities, opening up as the speed increases, thus retaining the filtered air flow

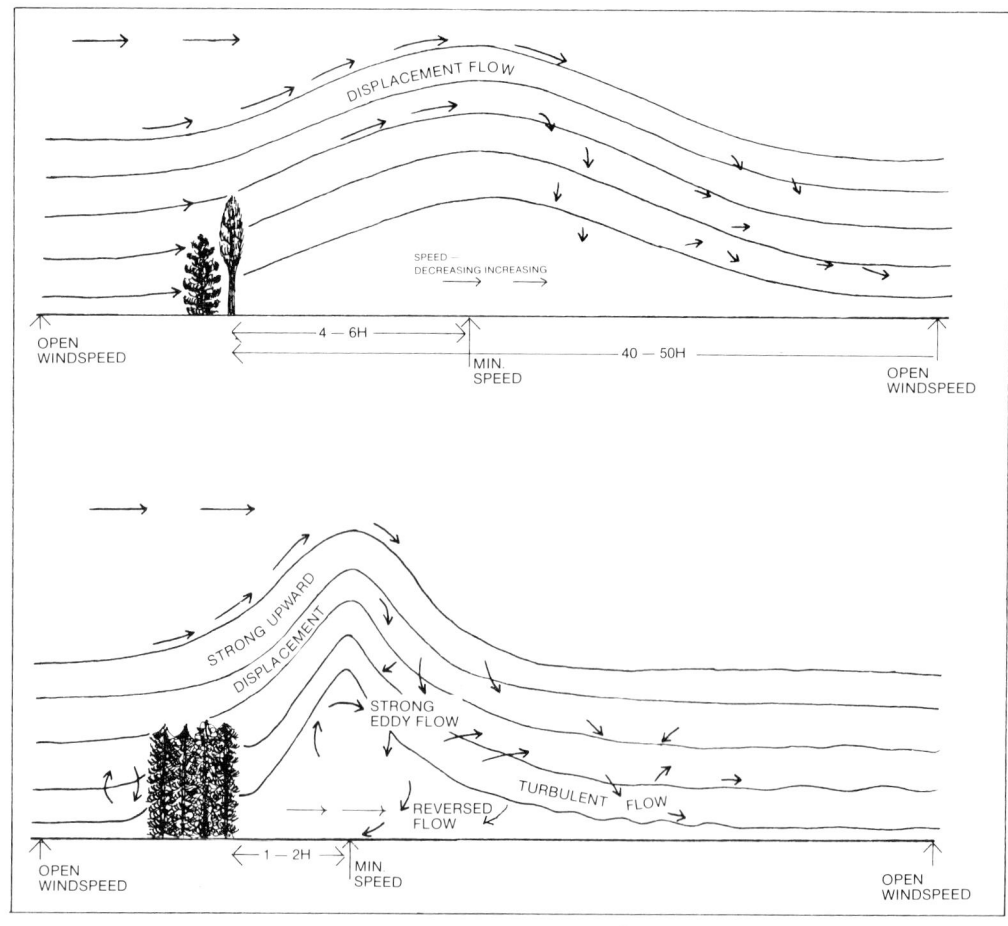

Diagrammatic representation of wind flow through a
permeable barrier (top) and an impermeable barrier
(below).

54

through rather than over the top.

A minimum length of about 20-25 times the ultimate height of the shelterbelt is desirable in order to maintain protection when the wind veers away from right angles to the belt, or when velocities are high, to avoid high wind movement around the ends of a short belt.

Gaps in a shelterbelt cause the wind to funnel through at excessive speed. This can happen where there are missing trees or when there is a draughty space at ground level. It is for this reason that a high standard of establishment and management is required; because of the very nature of the wind patterns through the gaps it is extremely difficult to fill them in later. Any early failure must be replaced as soon as possible.

To summarise, the ideal shelter can be considered as a tall narrow belt of trees with a wind permeability of about 50%, relatively uniform in height, no gaps and consisting of fast-growing, stable, disease-resist-

ant trees with a reasonable life span. However many factors must be considered before such a belt can be obtained as each belt must be matched to the particular site requirements.

Poplars underplanted with pampas make a most effective windbreak.

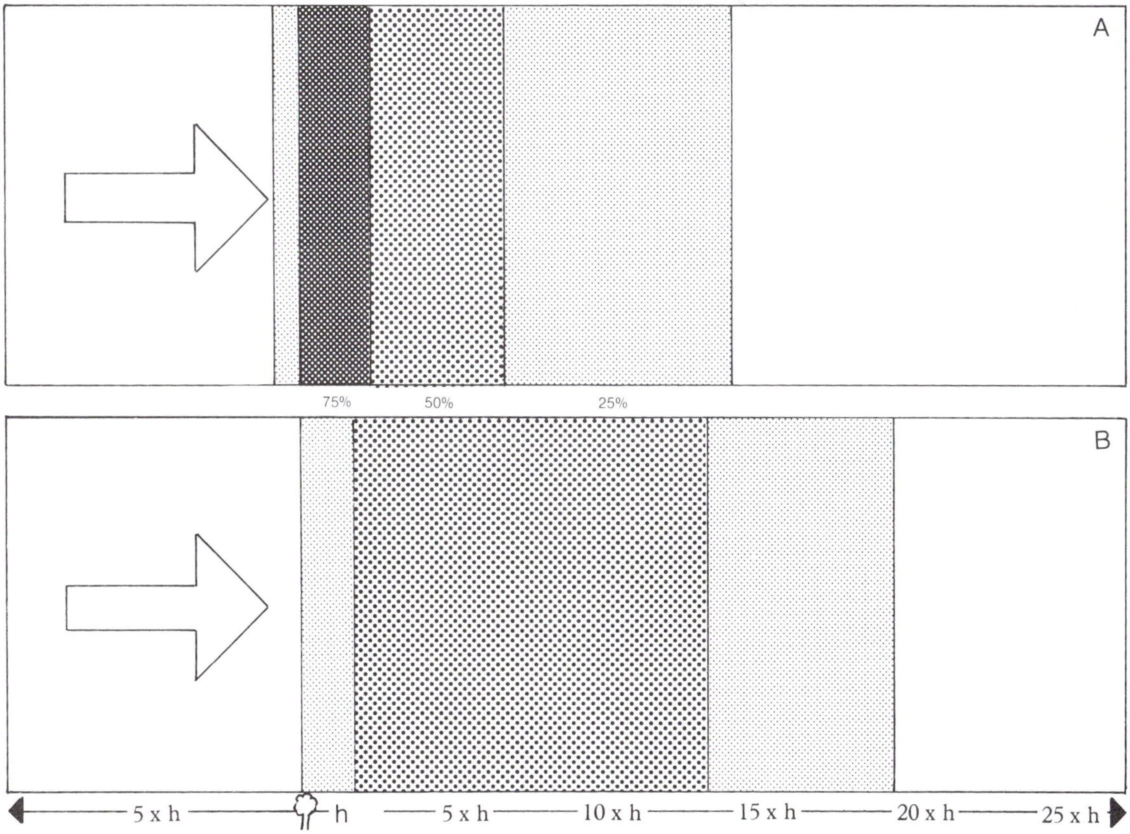

A

75%   50%   25%

B

← — 5 x h — h — 5 x h — 10 x h — 15 x h — 20 x h — 25 x h →

Distribution of zones of shelter at ground level, expressed as a percentage reduction of the wind velocity in the open. h - sheltered height. A — zones of shelter for belts of maximum density throughout their height. B — zones of shelter for belts of medium density throughout their height.

Planning

Because there are distinctly different needs from region to region and even within regions, shelter may require very special design and species choice to be effective. In planning future shelterbelts it is critical to decide what land use protection is intended. For example, a different degree of intensity in shelter establishment is required between arable farming and horticulture. Have a detailed look at what grows well in your area — visit old homesteads, talk to local landowners (farmers and orchardists) and to agricultural and forestry advisers and nurserymen. You will then learn what shelter designs have proved most suitable, and the various alternative tree species which have adapted well to local climate and soils.

The layout and planning of shelterbelts is an important exercise initially for the whole block. Future land use based on soil and topography will determine the intensity of shelter establishment and will highlight any constraints on choices. Once you have decided land use then planning requires decisions on orientation of belts, site problems, species choice, stock ordering, fencing and how much financial investment is needed.

Orientation: To maximise sun on both sides of the belt it should run in a north-south direction, so some compromise will often be required to achieve the best wind protection without harmful crop shading.

Deciduous species should be considered for east-west belts to allow penetration of winter sun. Poor siting of belts can produce very wasteful land use — losses in production due to shading, competition to the crop and frost pockets — resulting in lower crop productivity. In general, existing fences will be along major ridges or drains and so cost of refencing may be a factor in the choice of shelterbelt location. Belts, where possible, should be aesthetically pleasing and so compromises in some situations (eg near homestead blocks) may be necessary between having ideal shelter or retaining views — shelter should harmonise with the existing features of the landscape. Planting along natural watercourses (careful of species choice) can produce a very attractive landscape blending with the natural topography.(See Planting Design.)

Site Constraints: Having decided where the belts are to be established it is necessary to check on site peculiarities that will influence belt design, species choice and future management. Such features are proximity to buildings, overhead wires, landscape value, severity of exposure and proximity to salt-laden winds, natural fertility levels, presence of compacted subsoils, and natural soil drainage levels. All these constraints require noting before selecting the most suitable species and establishment methods required.

Shelter of Leyland cypress runs north and south down a
ridge. On the eastern side are planted various oaks
whose brilliantly coloured leaves show up in autumn
against the evergreens.

Species Choice: Knowing the objectives for the shelter and the site constraints it would seem an easy task to select the ideal tree species. The best choice can be considered as:

— cheap to establish and manage
— fast-growing without excessive root spread
— maintaining desired height and density
— having a compact habit and being windfirm
— requiring minimum maintenance
— not harbouring pests and diseases
— providing nectar and pollen for bees
— and possibly the production of high quality timber, or animal fodder

Most of the current choices available meet only a few of the above requirements and therefore a certain level of management, eg pruning and trimming to maintain porosity, has to be carried out.

The disease risk associated with planting only one or two species has been highlighted by the effects of the poplar rusts discovered in 1973. The planting of several different species on the same property is now common practice in many areas. Anyone planning shelter should study the MAF Aglinks which are available to assist in choosing the best species for the job and to suit the conditions in which it is required to grow. Given a range of trees suitable for shelter every individual will choose differently according to his or her personal interests whether they be timber, bees, aesthetics, or wildlife habitats. There is no one choice but there is a choice for everyone's needs.

Ordering: When the species has been selected and quantities calculated it is very sensible to order shelter and any other required trees well in advance of the planting season. By ordering at least six months ahead stocks will be assured, and your local nurseryman will be able to plan his stock movements too. This will ensure that good seedlings and service are available. Buying "off the shelf" at the last minute can be a disaster both in availability and quality.

Fencing: There can be no short cut to fencing out areas to plant and this requires careful organising before shelter establishment. Stock proofing is essential to uniformity as once tree tops are eaten out trees are severely set back and subsequent growth is uneven and trees malformed. Fencing is expensive but costs can be reduced by using electric fences where appropriate.

Financial commitments to other management priorities will determine the level of shelter establishment for any one year. The most exposed areas should receive priority, but it is acknowledged that while horticultural shelter is essential, farm shelter is merely desirable. In the long term shelterbelt ages should be staggered so not all belts mature at the same time.

Site Situation: In shelterbelt establishment we are looking for 100% survival, optimum growth for the species and tree stability. To achieve this four factors

The result of poor fencing — draughty and uneven shelter.

have to be taken into account and all four are essential: proper site preparation, selection of good quality stock, correct planting technique, and adequate maintenance. The skill is in achieving a sound root system with a strong tap root and well distributed laterals, like a naturally regenerated tree from seed. Good forestry practice also recognises these four factors, and much can be learned from experience in this field.

Site Preparation

There are very few sites where shelter can be established successfully without some form of preparation such as weed control, ripping, drainage, cultivation or animal control.

Weed Control: To enable sufficient light and moisture to be available to the tree weeds must be eliminated. When dry conditions occur in late spring and summer tree deaths are often not directly due to shortage of rain, but more through weed and grass competition for the available moisture. All planting should have some sort of weed control. Development of herbicides over recent years has simplified this task.

The use of the correct chemical for the job at the recommended rates cannot be overemphasised. Desiccant sprays give a quick knock-down effect but do not penetrate to the root system, so some grasses such as paspalum and kikuyu will regrow. For these a spray with a translocation ability will be required (ie a systemic chemical which will be readily absorbed and transported through the plant system). Residual chemicals can also be used to prevent regrowth but it is of course necessary to ensure that the residue retained in the soil will not affect tree growth. Advice on correct use of weedicides is available from manufacturers and advisers and should be sought during the planning stage. Preplanting spraying can be applied as a continuous one metre strip or as a spot application around each planting position. Minimise spray drift by doing the job on a calm fine day.

Ripping: (to 50-70 cm) should be standard practice on problem soils, with compacted subsoils, hard pans or very stony sites. Even on clay soils ripping to a moderate depth has proved worthwhile. Ripping gives improved aeration and drainage thus allowing roots to penetrate a larger volume of soil than would have been the case without treatment, thereby increasing vigour and stability. Correct ripper design should ensure that a reasonable volume of soil is shattered. If a single tine ripper without wings is used, at least two lines 30 cm apart should be ripped to give a greater shattering effect. (Plant between rips.) A single tine

rip can cause instability by roots following the line when there is no soil shattering associated with the rip. Ripping should be done in the dry season: not when the soil is wet.

Drainage: Poor drainage is always an inhibiting factor in achieving good plant growth and the same general principles apply for shelterbelts as for other trees (see page 85). Planting of belts alongside a drain because it saves fencing often seems an easy option. As the root system will not develop on the drain side instability is almost inevitable especially in soft ground such as peat. This practice is a sure way of building up future problems. If you must plant alongside a drain always plant on the windward side.

Cultivation by rotary hoeing is often carried out as a means of incorporating extra fertilisers within the soil prior to planting and for weed control. It is often a window dressing and does not greatly help subsequent development if drainage, weeds or soil pan have not been adequately dealt with.

Animal Control: Standard fencing practices used on the farm will suffice for stock but there is no easy way to control feral animals. The most effective way is to eliminate them, otherwise some of the suggestions made on pages 81-83 may be useful.

Selection of Tree Stocks: This is another crucial area —if tree quality is poor then survival and subsequent tree growth will also be inferior regardless of other techniques used. Remember that in proportion to all other costs (preparation, planting, fertilising, etc) tree costs are very small and therefore it is unwise to look for tree stock "bargains": there is no such thing in shelter stock.

There are several factors you can check on when ordering stock: firstly, stem condition which includes height, stem diameter, foliage colour, damage by insects and fungi and degree of hardiness; and secondly, root condition, including fibrous root development and root balance. Mycorrhizal and root damage are observable at the nursery: stock should be checked for these. Thirdly, size of plants: be careful of buying large seedlings as this stock can easily desiccate and may swivel in the wind, causing stem damage. Large seedlings in small containers will have serious root distortion which may lead to strangulation or "hockey stick" root formation with resulting instability.

Sturdy seedlings with a good stem diameter in relation to height do better in terms of survival and subsequent growth than tall seedlings.

The choice of whether to use bare-rooted or container-grown plants will depend on the farmer's personal preference. The merits of each option are discussed on pages 85-86. Since fairly large quantities are being handled it must be stressed that good pre-planting preparation and a well organised planting programme are essential if bare-rooted plants are to be used.

Effort is required to ensure good packaging, fast transport and sensible precautions to protect trees from damage or drying out.

Planting

Planting usually commences in late autumn once the soils are moist and goes through to late spring for some varieties. June and July are the best months for bare-rooted stock and for cuttings such as willows and poplars. If the area is subject to hard frosts then planting of trees should be delayed until the worst frosts are over. Non-suckering bamboo is a species that should be planted as late as October, although because of its shallow rooting it must be irrigated regularly throughout the first summer.

The spacing will determine the speed with which effective early shelter is achieved; it will adversely affect stability, uniformity and height if planting is too close. Cuttings of poplars and willows are generally spaced at 0.5m to 1m whilst internal breaks (*Pittosporums, Casuarinas*) are often planted at 1.0m. The slower growing evergreens such as *Cryptomeria japonica, Thuja* and *Cupressus* are best planted at about 2-2.5m. Fast-growing *Pinus* and *Eucalyptus* for long-term tall shelter should be planted at a minimum of 2m. Multiple-row planting will modify these general spacings and shelter experience in one region may dictate particular spacing requirements. The actual planting technique varies from site to site, but the greatest success will be achieved when the soil is generally broken up; the seedling is placed upright at a depth no less than the root collar; the roots are evenly spread without cramping and the soil gently firmed about the plant.

Distortion and cramping of the root system may reduce both growth and stability. Deeper planting is recommended where the soils tend to be drought prone, for example sands, volcanic ash and gravelly soils. However, deep planting on often wet, poorly aerated deep clay soils could be disastrous. A spade or mattock is normally used to prepare each hole for planting; however a post-hole borer may also be used providing the sides are well spaded out to allow future root penetration.

Should container-grown plants exhibit any root distortion simply cut off any coils and make four vertical slits to enable roots to be freed. Trim off any damaged roots as these can allow pathogens to enter and cause root rot.

In the Bay of Plenty willows are closely planted as shelter for horticulture. With irrigation they grow extremely fast.

59

Cuttings are usually driven into the ground or alternatively a crowbar can be used to make a hole. A black polythene mulch can be employed to create a warmer soil temperature, to conserve moisture and to prevent weed growth around the cutting. An angled cut at the base of the cutting will make penetration through the plastic and into the soil much easier. Shoot growth from the cutting depends on moisture and nutrient reserves held within the wood until roots are sufficiently well developed to sustain shoot growth. Therefore standing cuttings in water for 7-10 days before planting can contribute to survival. The more of the cutting inserted in the ground the better the early root development and reduction in dehydration. Generally cuttings should be planted with about two-thirds of their length firmly in the soil.

Fertiliser can be incorporated at time of planting, applied either in the last cultivation prior to plastic mulching (if used) or as a slow-release fertiliser placed in the planting hole and thoroughly mixed into the soil before planting. Most plants will benefit from a well-balanced fertiliser such as blood and bone or crop mix 6:6:5. However, soil tests or advice from agricultural advisers will be able to confirm a suitable fertiliser programme for a particular locality. Fertilisers applied too close to the stem or in contact with the roots will cause root "burn" and often death to the seedling. Remember that most shelterbelts are planted on land previously in production and manured in the past. It is not to be assumed that fertiliser is required.

Maintenance

Factors adversely affecting growth after establishment are lack of moisture, infertility, disease and animal damage.

Moisture competition is a major reason why many shelter lines never become effective. Proper weed control after planting, undertaken by hand, by mulching or with herbicides may be necessary for a number of years depending on the growth rates of the species used.

Mulches of untreated sawdust, bark, or both, about 10-15 cm thick along the shelter line after killing all perennial weeds, can be a very cheap form of weed control. A scattering of blood and bone applied before mulching replaces nitrogen used in decomposition. Care should be taken not to heap mulch about the seedling stem as abrasion damage and stem rot may occur.

Weeds can still be controlled by herbicides even after planting, but these are dangerous to young trees if applied incorrectly. Avoid drift onto trees by using low-pressure applicators with a shield to the spray boom, or cover plants at time of spraying. (See also earlier recommendations on weed control.)

Where moisture is limiting to good growth, proper weed control should ensure survival but the addition of irrigation will increase growth. Low-pressure systems such as trickle irrigation are now commonly used throughout the horticultural industry. The effect of irrigation is greatest in the initial years of establishment when the developing seedling requires good moisture availability. Different species have varying sensitivity to moisture stress; for example *Eucalyptus* will tolerate high moisture stress whereas willows and poplars need abundant rates of available moisture to maintain good growth rates. Trickle irrigation requires clean water together with good design to ensure correct pipe sizes, positions and flow rates, and these factors should be considered at the early planning stage.

Depending on the natural soil fertility and how much basal dressing has already been applied, side dressing may not be required. There is some benefit in notching the fertiliser into the soil to reduce nutrient losses and ensuring application is about 15 cm away from the seedling to prevent any burning effect. Don't overdo it — get good local advice as various soils and tree species have markedly different requirements.

Control of lateral spread by regular side trimming, especially in poplars, willows and *Casuarinas* will keep trees narrow, porous, windfirm and prevent gaps developing underneath. Evergreen varieties are best trimmed in late summer or early spring at times of vigorous growth. Trimming little and often will maintain internal shelter and reduce the risk of dieback. In horticulture blocks deep root pruning is now being found necessary to counter lateral expansion of the root system into the productive areas.

Disease

Nearly all shelter species can be affected by various pests and diseases, although if healthly seedlings and good establishment techniques are used then any disease problems will be minimal. The types of diseases that are relatively common among shelter trees can be corrected without too much trouble providing precautions are taken before serious loss occurs.
— Black beetle and grass grub are major pests on farm-land, affecting roots and causing severe losses. Post-planting treatment with organophosphates will

control them.

— White crown canker will affect most shelter trees although some species are more resistant to canker than others. It will kill clusters of trees, spreading to adjacent trees to produce serious gaps. Plant resistant species.

— Root diseases such as *Phytophthora* and *Pythium* cause death by killing fibrous roots. These can be a problem where the site is poorly drained and where plants have been physically damaged at planting time. Proper site preparation and careful planting will restrict this problem.

— Cypress canker, result of a fungus attack, causes severe dieback (eg Lawson's cypress and Leyland cypress). Avoid planting susceptible species in areas where this disease is endemic.

— Needle Cast disease in pines is less common in shelter planting than in a forest situation, however spraying with copper based fungicides to control the disease in the first 3-6 years may be required.

— Leaf Roller damage can severely limit growth of *Cryptomeria* and some *Eucalyptus* species by chewing out branch and leader tips. Spraying with insecticides during spring and autumn may be necessary for control.

Other disorders such as leaf spotting fungi (*Cryptomeria*), silver leaf disease (poplars, willows and *Eucalyptus*) and mite damage *(Cryptomeria)* can all be easily controlled if noticed early during routine health inspections.

Cold

If you lose enough heat from your body core, you die. So do animals. Strong winds accompanied by low temperatures cause rapid cooling of exposed surfaces of the body in both people and livestock. A strong wind combined with a temperature slightly below freezing can have the same effect as a temperature which is nearly 20°C lower.

Anyone who is outdoors during low temperatures and strong winds will find he or she becomes exhausted easily and is more subject to frostbite or even death. Stockmen and stockwomen likewise should consider the effect of the wind chill factor on unprotected livestock during cold strong winds.

Table showing effect of wind on temperature

°C	calm	Wind Velocity 24 km/h	48km/h	64km/h
-1.1°C	-1.1°C	-11.7°C	-18.9°C	-20°C
-6.7	-6.7	-21.1	-27.8	-30
-12.2	-12.2	-27.8	-36.1	-37.8
-17.8	-17.8	-36.1	-45	-47.7
-23.3	-23.3	-42.8	-52.7	-56.1
-28.9	-28.9	-51.1	-61.1	-66.1
-34.4	-34.4	-56.7	-70.0	-73.8
-40	-40	-62.2	-78.3	-82.2

Wind speeds greater than 64km/h have little additional chilling effect.

If they lose enough heat from their body core, animals will die.

Snow Shelter

Snow storms in much of Otago and Southland are accompanied by strong south-west winds. This is due to the absence of a mountain barrier to shield these southern areas from storms originating in Antarctica. Upland areas above 400 m in altitude are capable of quite high levels of production — up to 10 stock units per hectare, but are subject to heavy falls of snow from April to October. One major limiting factor in farm production is the lack of shelter.

Shelter in these situations has to be designed to cope with drifting snow. A fall of only 10 cm accompanied by strong winds can cause major drifts. Even when the storm has passed the wind can still cause drifting. A conventional one or two row shelterbelt has the effect of collecting the snow in the sheltered area. These belts are then of no value — when needed most they become deathtraps for livestock.

There are two ways that the snow can be stopped before reaching the sheltered area:
1. by having a multi-row belt, wide enough to trap all the snow in the actual belt.
2. by having a gully fenced into the belt on the windward side. The snow drifts into the gully, and the trees downwind provide the shelter for the stock, hay feeding area etc.

The second method is preferred because as well as taking what could be a dangerous gully out of the paddock, the whole shelterbelt area can be grazed over the summer months once the trees have reached a suitable height.

While these shelterbelts do not follow the design of the permeable windbreaks that are in vogue further north, they are appropriate and necessary in these colder southern areas. The windchill factor increases dramatically once windspeed gets above five kilometres per hour. As well as controlling the snow, these wide belts also provide an area where windspread is near zero and where newborn lambs and newly shorn sheep can survive the roughest weather.

When winter storms are over and lambing is finished these shelterbelts are still working for the farmer — increasing grass and animal production and conserving soil moisture.

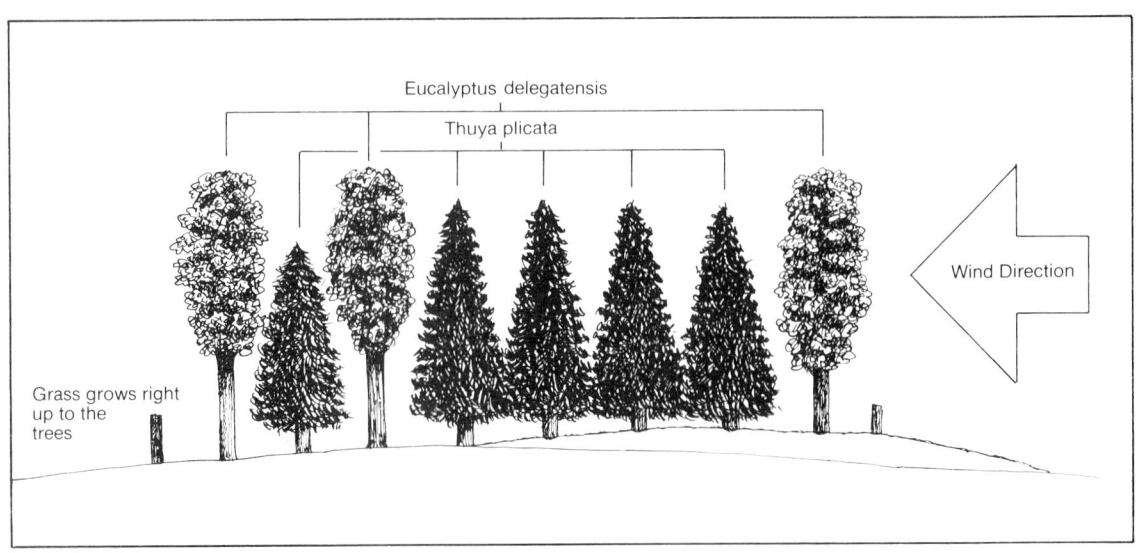

Eucalyptus delegatensis

Thuya plicata

Wind Direction

Grass grows right up to the trees

In this multi-row shelterbelt snow cannot drift on to the leeward side. The inside trees are the woodlot component and could be Douglas Fir, *Pinus nigra* or *Pinus radiata*.

Only a light layer of snow rests on this, the leeward side —
drifting snow has been caught in the shelter belt.

Wind Direction

The gulley traps drifting snow and good shelter is
provided on the leeward side of the trees.

Multiple use of Shelter

Shelterbelts can provide useful timber and fencing material for on-farm use as well as providing valuable stock/crop shelter. There has been an increasing awareness of multiple land use over recent years and timber production is just one extra reward with minimal additional input. Timber from shelterbelts is by no means a new concept as large timber volumes were removed from shelterbelts up and down the country during the log export drive during the 1970s. However, most of that timber was unmanaged and production was an unexpected bonus.

By proper selection of species and correctly applied management techniques a shelterbelt can be designed for timber production. Because timber-producing species are suitable for shelter planting, long-term management (30-40 years) will produce a valuable wood resource. Just how valuable depends on the level of management, that is selective pruning and thinning. In managing a shelterbelt we need to maintain porosity and prevent any serious gaps developing — a pruning technique must ensure the maintenance of the shelter design. The simplest plan is to establish multiple rows, using two different species. Slow-growing trees planted on the side of the prevailing wind become ultimately tall primary shelter, replacing the faster-growing trees when these are harvested.

The choice of the faster-growing species will include known high-yielding quality timber species such as *Pinus radiata, Pseudotsuga menziesii, Eucalyptus* spp., *Cupressus* spp. and *Acacia melanoxylon*. Selection of both categories will relate to the region and various site characteristics.

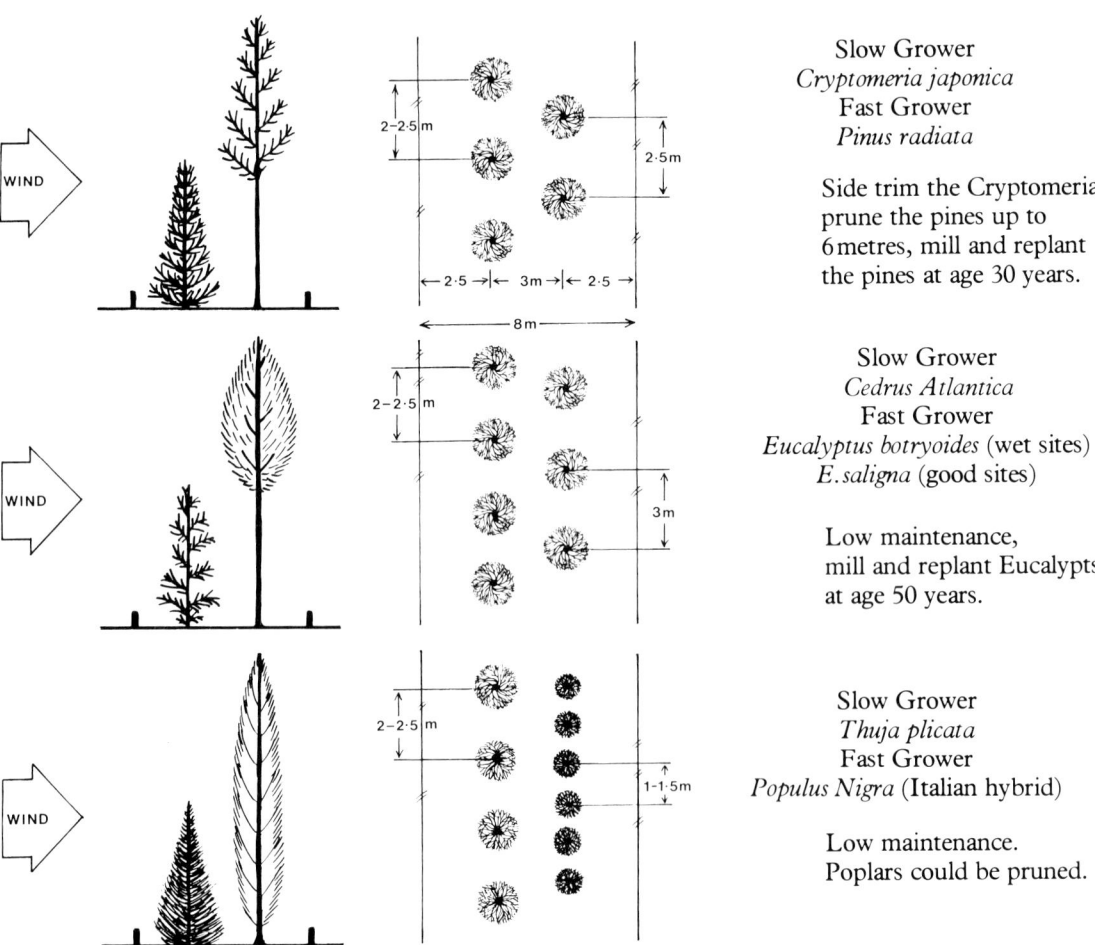

Slow Grower
Cryptomeria japonica
Fast Grower
Pinus radiata

Side trim the Cryptomeria, prune the pines up to 6 metres, mill and replant the pines at age 30 years.

Slow Grower
Cedrus Atlantica
Fast Grower
Eucalyptus botryoides (wet sites)
E. saligna (good sites)

Low maintenance, mill and replant Eucalypts at age 50 years.

Slow Grower
Thuja plicata
Fast Grower
Populus Nigra (Italian hybrid)

Low maintenance.
Poplars could be pruned.

Examples of two row general purpose permeable shelter belts. Species choice and spacing will depend on region and local site characteristics.

Allowing for site and soil limitations, the aim should be to produce timber of a quality acceptable to the market. The higher the quality, the better return to be made at harvesting time. However, quality timber is generally associated with defect-free (clearwood) timber which is usually a result of wood grown outside a core of pruned branch stubs. But the principles of pruning (removing all branches up the stem of the tree to a determined height) is in opposition to the principles of good shelter, ie maintaining a gap-free belt. Therefore if pruning is to be considered, the design and management must compensate for the effect of such pruning.

The following diagram suggests methods for the production of timber from shelterbelts.

When two species are considered for planting, by

Management of shelterbelts for timber

(a) Plant timber species, no management. This system will provide timber of lower quality than the following options.

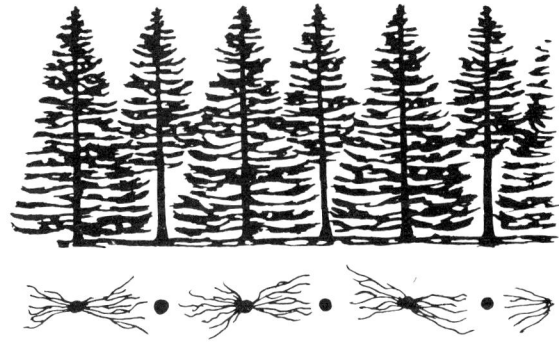

(d) A combination of (b) and (c).

(b) Prune every second tree. Every second tree will produce a proportion of defect-free timber, while branches from neighbouring trees will overlap to provide even porosity.

(e) Prune all trees. All trees producing clearwood butt logs but the design must allow for the holes to be filled by another unpruned row and/or another species. An alternative (less intensive management) is using a recognised self pruning species such as eucalypts (although these still need some pruning of persistent branches in a shelterbelt situation) with the gaps filled in by another species.

View from above

(c) Fan prune all trees. (Fan pruning is the pruning of branches growing at right angles to the line of the shelterbelt.) This system is akin to trimming but branches are removed flush with the stem. Shading over the fence is reduced while good porosity is maintained. Some increase in timber quality is also gained.

(f) Prune every second set of branches up to the stem to create long clear lengths of timber between whorls. A method of increasing porosity as well as some improvement to timber yield.

the careful selection of a fast- and slow-growing species, timber production is made easier. The fast-growing species can be pruned for clearwood production while the second species should have grown enough to fill the gaps, either by planting alternately with the fast-growing species if in a single row, or as a second row. (N.B. Secondary species should always be planted on windward side.) The more rows of timber-producing species planted, the closer the management comes to that of a woodlot. Also, the more rows planted, the denser the belt becomes. This requires more management to maintain a porous shelterbelt and thus effective shelter.

It should be noted that the Forest Service has a stated policy on special-purpose timber trees (see Appendix 1). This recommends the planting of only a limited number of species other than *Pinus radiata* so as to reduce future marketing problems.

Firewood production is another management alternative. To maintain optimum structure multiple rows of say *Pinus radiata* or *Cupressus* spp. will produce thinnings which can be used as a fuelwood. Fast-growing species such as wattles *(Acacia dealbata)* and coppicing *Eucalyptus* species *(E. saligna* in the north) may provide high-volume returns as a short-term shelter harvest.

Soil Erosion

Sediment from Whitianga River after a storm.

The top few centimetres of soil are usually richest in nutrients and organisms which make the nutrients available to plants, as well as being the most physically suitable for seed germination. Hence any removal of this soil by wind depletes the cropping capability of the site.

In a speech delivered to the Royal Forest and Bird Protection Society in 1983 the Minister for the Environment, Dr Ian Shearer, stated that more than 75% of New Zealand's land area now shows signs of erosion. He went on to say: "Some 3.4 million hectares of land in New Zealand is affected by wind erosion, or 13 percent of our total land area.

"Tests of a cultivated paddock in mid-Canterbury in 1975 showed that wind was stripping away five tonnes of soil per hectare per day. Over a two-day period in 1981, 67 tonnes of topsoil per hectare were lost to one of the fierce north-westerlies that often sweep the Canterbury Plains. Similar losses of soil to erosion occur in Hawkes Bay. For example, a 10 square kilometre catchment in the Ruahine Ranges is eroding at the rate of 7000 tonnes a year.

"Add to all this the 2.6 million tonnes of silt and soil a year that wash into the hydro lake behind the Roxburgh Dam, and the fact that the Clutha Dam will inevitably face the same problems. New Zealand is prone to high natural rates of erosion, but the past destruction of our native forests and overgrazing of our hill country have accelerated the problem dramatically.

"We are working to contain erosion by planting to stabilise hillsides, planting shelterbelts, retiring high country land in the South Island, and using direct drilling techniques for planting crops. If we fail, New Zealand will itself see a major and permanent decline in its capacity to produce food and fibre, and in the export markets they sustain.

"The land is our greatest asset, and our economic survival depends on it."

These alarming examples of soil erosion emphasise how necessary it is to plant trees not only to shelter man, beast, and crop, but also to protect the very substance of this country's productive capacity.

Willows being used to start controlling serious erosion of volcanic soils.

References

1. J.E. Radcliffe, Grassland Responses to Shelter — A Review, *NZ Journal of Experimental Agriculture,* Vol 11: 5-10, 1983.
2. P.W. Smail, Trees for Shelter, *Farm Forestry,* Vol 21-1, 1979.
3. J.W. Sturrock, Shelter Boosts Crop Yield by 35%, *NZ Journal Agriculture,* Sept 1981.
4. J.J. Lynch, CSIRO Division of Plant Industry Annual Report, 1972/73.
5. J.J. Lynch, CSIRO Division of Plant Industry Annual Report, 1973/74.

See also:

J.M. Caborn, *Shelterbelts and Windbreaks,* Dept Forestry and National Resources, University of Edinburgh, 1965.

C.G.R. Chavasse, Management of Shelterbelts for Wood Products, *NZ Journal of Forestry 27* (2), 1982.

R.L. Hathaway, New and Potential Horticultural Shelter Species, *NZ Agricultural Science 16* (1), 1982.

R.L. Hathaway, Back to Basics on Shelter, *Growing Today,* July 1983.

Ministry of Agriculture and Fisheries Information Service M.A.F. Aglinks on Shelter, FPP 385, 390, 441; HPP 62, 120, 121, 130, 131, 137, 167, 169, 170, 184, 205, 227.

NZ Forest Service, NZ Forest Service Policy on Exotic Special Purpose Species (1981).

I. Nicholas, Timber Production from Shelterbelts, Forest Research Report, 1982.

J.W. Sturrock, *The Control of Wind: The Roles of Research and Farm Forestry,* DSIR, Lincoln.

5
Shade

A happy horse under his plane tree.

It was Noel Coward who drew attention to the peculiar behaviour of colonials when he sang of mad dogs and Englishmen going out in the midday sun. New Zealanders still do it today, and subject their farm animals to the same conditions. Few farms have adequate shade for the comfort of their stock whose distress on really hot days is plain to see. You will have observed the pathetic attempts of sheep seeking relief from the hot sun in the shade of a solitary power pole, or settling into the minute cover given by an unwanted and unloved nodding thistle. So little research on the effect of shade under New Zealand conditions has been done that reliance has to be placed on overseas information. Has it been neglected here because it involves no obvious economic gain, the measuring stick required to justify most research?

If livestock are happier and more contented when provided with shade, this is surely justification for providing it. People use it around their homes and occasionally a tree or two is grown to provide more comfortable conditions in the stockyards — not usually for the benefit of the stock, but rather for the worker. Contented stock make for contented stockmen, and stock suffering from stress — whatever form it might take — tend to transmit that stress to the stockman.

Humane considerations aside, overseas research suggests that there can be an economic gain from shade.

"All farm animals, sheep, cattle and pigs, are homeotherms. They attempt to maintain their body temperatures within the range most suitable for their

optimum biological activity. Under hot conditions an animal's ability to regulate its body temperature depends on an effective evaporative heat loss mechanism. In European cattle no demands are made on the temperature-regulating mechanisms between 0° and 15°C. After this there is a rapid increase in respiration and vapourisation rates. At about 27°C these mechanisms begin to fail as shown by the abrupt rise in rectal temperature, decline in food production, milk production and body weight. Heat stress in cattle is reflected in lowered food consumption and as a result productivity is affected in cows and adverse changes occur in yield and composition of milk. The critical temperature for milk yield decline appears to be between 21°C and 27°C for Holsteins and Jerseys.

"The deleterious effect of hot weather on farm animals necessitates sheltering them from heat including sun radiation. This is best done by trees because their leaves are cooled by vaporisation from their surfaces.

"With air temperature ranging from 15-32°C Jerseys and Holsteins sought shade at about 27°. On days when shade temperature was 29° they spent only 11% of their time grazing. At night when

Contented stock make stockmen contented.

Above 15°C there is a rapid increase in respiration and vapourisation rates.

temperature was 27°, 37% of their time was spent grazing."[1]

"The difference of 0.14 pound daily weight gain in favour of steers having access to shade was 'significant' (mainly steers of British breeding). Shade had no effect on carcass grade or dressing percentage and there were no significant differences in feed required for gain."[2]

"Shade increased summerlong gain of yearling Hereford steers on rangeland by a profitable 19 lb (8.6 kg) head in a 4 year study. High summer humidity depressed steer gains much more than did high summer temperature. The combined effects of humidity above 45% and temperature above 85°F (29°C) were especially harmful. Each 'hot muggy day' reduced summer long steer gains by 1 lb (.45 kg). Cattle eagerly sought shade during hot summer days. By manipulating shade, cattle were drawn to under-utilised areas of pasture to reduce damaging spot grazing. Shade was nearly as effective as water location and supplemental feeding as a tool to promote uniform grazing within a pasture. South facing, open sheds used as winter shelters did not increase steer gains, nor would the steers use them even during storms."[3]

"At temperatures above 70° (21.1°C) milk yield decreases slowly at first, but after 80° (26.7°C) there is a sudden drop."[4]

"On the basis of the reviews written over the last 20 years the conclusion that high environmental temperature reduces productive and reproductive efficiency of livestock seems well justified."[5]

The greatest economic benefits provided by shade appear to be to the dairy farmer because milk yield and quality start to deteriorate at 21°C, but as temperature climbs the beef rearer also benefits.

Well-shaded yards by a well-painted shed.

Two herds of deer need two trees.

Of concern to many who have studied the situation is the stress to which deer are being subjected with their removal to unsheltered and unshaded environments. They have similar regulatory mechanisms to other ruminant domesticated animals but are less equipped to handle the farm situation because they have not had generations of conditioning to it. They are accustomed to living on forest fringes where they can duck for cover or seek shade and shelter at their convenience. Farmers pluck them from this natural environment and force them to live in small open paddocks where they spend their lives in an almost perpetual state of tension, running for non-existent cover at the slightest alarm and sheltered by nothing more than a netting fence.

This handling of deer reflects a degree of insensitivity almost equal to factory farming of pigs or hens. It might be difficult to change the latter situations, but we can do much to alleviate deer stress by planting trees. Fenced-off corners not only allow the tree to be protected but the longer grass which will grow around it will provide cover for newborn fawns, provided the bottom wire or board is fixed high enough off the ground. The huge financial investments being made in deer surely justify a greater consideration for their welfare.

There are a number of diseases in which the skin of affected animals becomes unduly sensitive to sunlight. The most common of these is facial eczema which affects sheep and cattle of all ages over much of New Zealand, occurring from January to May. The extreme discomfort suffered by affected animals which are forced to stay in the sun is a most distressing sight. There is no cure for facial eczema but the unhappy lot of the sick animal will be relieved if it has access to shade and this may well help in its eventual recovery through its own natural processes.

The relevance of what has been written can best be illustrated by reference to the meteorological records. However it should be borne in mind that it is not temperature alone that triggers off adverse effects. A mid-west (U.S.A.) trial[6] indicated that there are four environmental factors that can stress feedlot cattle if these factors are at a high level: average minimum air temperature; average maximum air temperature; average radiant heat load; number of hours above 29.5°C.

It is fairly clear that once air temperatures go above 21°C there are adverse effects on most farm animals. If these temperatures are coupled with other undesirable environment factors then the effect is compounded. It is a commonly held belief that tempera-

In a treeless paddock dairy cows seek shade from afternoon sun.

ture as measured in the sun is higher than that in the shade. There is in fact no difference. It is the difference in the radiation absorbed by the animal in the two different situations which determines the degree of stress.

There are only a handful of areas in New Zealand where the number of days when the temperature exceeds 27°C is above 10 a year. It is a very different story for above 21°C. From official records taken over periods of 20-40 years the number of days when the Daily Maximum Temperature exceeds 21°C is given for a representative group of places:

Average Days per Annum		Average Days per Annum	
Kaitaia	132	Levin	72
Kerikeri	164	Blenheim	111
Tauranga	123	Ashburton	95
Taupo	104	Christchurch	80
Ruakura	118	Moa Creek	74
Masterton	108	Alexandra	140
Gisborne	133	Roxburgh	96
Napier	130	Invercargill	31

When trees are used to provide shade, there is no reason why the same trees cannot also provide timber and beauty too. Evergreens are normally unsuitable as they result in less winter sun and loss of too much pasture; they also encourage stock camping. Typical of appropriate tree types are the black poplar hybrids which are quite happy without the company of others. Pruned up to 6 m they can eventually provide peeler logs and will during the intervening years give excellent shade. Grass grows right up to their base and during the winter, sunlight will be allowed onto the pasture. The high pruning of any shade tree is important for it results in the area of shade moving around the paddock as the day goes by. Thus there is no over-use of any one area by the animals and the grass sward remains undamaged.

(*The Encyclopedia of Organic Gardening*, Rodale Books Inc., describes accumulator plants as those which have an ability to collect trace elements from the soil with storage in their tissues of several hundred times the amount contained in an equal weight of soil. It lists poplar and hickory leaves and peach tree clippings as accumulators of zinc. Used as shade trees it might be possible that they could contribute enough zinc to influence the incidence of facial eczema.)

Relief from the sun's heat during a Northland summer.

References

1. Shingoro Moda, The Feeding and Management of Farm Animals under Hot Weather Conditions. Extension Bulletin No. 27, Food and Fertiliser Technology Centre, Taiwan.

2. Peacock et al., Influence of Shade on Fattening Cattle in South Florida. Bulletin 700 (Technical), Agricultural Experiment Stations, Institute of Food and Agricultural Sciences, University of Florida.

3. E.H. McIlvain and M.C. Shoop, Shade for Improving Cattle Gains and Rangeland Use. Study conducted on the Southern Plains Experimental Range, Woodward, Oklahoma, by the Crops Research Division, Agricultural Research Service, U.S. Department of Agriculture. *Journal of Range Management*, Vol. 24 No. 3, May 1971.

4. J. Hancock, Direct Influence of Climate on Milk Production. Commonwealth Bureau of Dairy Science 16, 1954.

5. J.W. Fuquay, *Journal of Animal Science*, Vol. 52 No. 1, 1981.

6. T.E. Bond and D.B. Laster, Influence of Shading on Production of Midwest Feedlot Cattle. Transactions of ASAE Paper No. 74.4536, Aug. 1975.

6
Trees for Birds

In a foreword to Bruce Harvey's *Portfolio of New Zealand Birds,* the late Professor Gordon Williams, sometime Director of New Zealand Wildlife Service, wrote: "As our heritage of nature is endangered so our appreciation of this unique and shrinking asset increases; and we should be grateful to anyone who draws our attention to what we are in so much danger of losing for ever." It seems important to include in this book a few suggestions as to how the rural land-owner can help preserve the bird population, both native and exotic, although the latter seem in little danger since those that have survived since the years of introduction are now well adapted to New Zealand conditions. We tend to take birds for granted and it is sometimes necessary to be in a place entirely devoid of birdlife before it is brought home just how much we accept as part of our normal life the birdsong of night and morning.

The Wildlife Service has issued a pamphlet "Tree Planting for Native Birds" from which the following extract and list of recommended species is taken:

"Profound changes in the New Zealand landscape during the last hundred years or so have made life impossible, or precarious, in a great part of the coun-

try, for many native birds.

"The preservation of original habitat, as in National Parks, Wildlife Sanctuaries, and various forms of reserves has, in many cases, halted the decline, but total reliance on this form of protection puts our birds in the same category as specimens in zoos or museums. We shouldn't have to go to some special area to see the natural wild inhabitants of our country.

"Like all living creatures, birds rely for their existence on the availability of certain requirements. Should any one be lacking, no matter how abundant the rest, life is impossible.

"The scarcity of native birdlife in New Zealand's populated and developed areas, town or country, indicates that essential requirements are missing. In some instances a whole range of requirements may be involved, in others perhaps only one. If we are to encourage native birdlife therefore, we have to see that these requirements are available or, in other words, provide suitable habitats. We don't have to return the country to its original state. The fact that a few native birds are seen in urban areas, even in the heart of cities, shows that they are adaptable and can live in situations far different from their original habitats provided that the alternative conditions are suitable.

"Of the various things that we can do to make conditions suitable, the planting of suitable trees and shrubs can be the most effective. Directly or indirectly, trees and shrubs provide many of the basic requirements — food, shelter, escape, cover, and suitable nesting places.

What to Plant:
"Any tree or shrub will have some value to some bird but to get the best possible results from our planting we have to be selective. A year-round supply of food is often the most serious limiting factor. If we provide this, particularly for fruit and nectar feeders, the same trees in sufficient variety will also provide most other requirements, including food for insect- and seed-eaters. Selection must of course be influenced by local climate and conditions, and the advice of local horticulturists should be sought. The following list is intended as a general guide to the more important food species, ranging from tall trees to prostrate shrubs.

Native

Aristotelia serrata (wineberry) 6 m: Blackish-red current-like berries in late summer.

Clianthus puniceus (kaka beak) 2 m: Attractive spreading shrub with masses of vivid red flowers Nov.-Dec.

Coprosma spp: Tall or prostrate shrubs that fruit profusely over an extended period. Of the taller species 3-8 m *C. lucida*, *C. robusta* (karamu) and *C. repens* (taupata) are particularly valuable. *C. rhamnoides* grows to 2 m and has crimson berries. The cultivated hybrids *C. x kirkii* and *C.* 'Prostrata' are useful prostrate forms.

Corokia spp: Shrubs growing to 2.5 m. *C. buddleioides*, dark red berries. *C. cotoneaster*, orange-red berries. *C. macrocarpa*, large yellow berries.

Dysoxylum spectabile (kohekohe) 13 m: Flowers directly from trunk or branches in creamy white sprays up to 0.3 m long. Fruits ripen Jul.-Aug.

Fuchsia excorticata (tree fuchsia) 12 m: One of the few native deciduous trees. Flowers Aug.-Dec. Berries (konini) ripen Dec.-Mar. Likes damp situations.

Fuchsia procumbens: Prostrate trailing shrub, bright rosy pink berries.

Fuchsia perscandens: Climbing shrub with dark purple berries.

Hedycarya arborea (pigeonwood) 12 m: Aromatic tree, flowering Oct.-Dec. Berries (red) ripen Oct.-Dec. the following year.

Hymenanthera crassifolia: Coastal compact shrub. Green, yellow or pale blue fruit ripen Oct.-Mar.

Hymenanthera obovata 4 m: Dense shrub with purplish berries.

Hymenanthera chathamica 3 m: Erect shrub with white, purple-flecked berries.

Knightia excelsa (rewarewa) New Zealand honeysuckle: Slender tapering tree, flowers provide nectar Oct.-Nov.

Macropiper excelsum (kawakawa) 6 m: Suitable for shady situations. Orange-yellow fruit favoured by pigeons.

Melicope ternata (wharangi) 6 m: Greenish flowers Sep.-Oct., black shiny seeds.

Melicytus ramiflorus (mahoe, whitey wood) 10 m: Small greenish yellow flowers and violet blue berries. Flowers Nov.-Jan.

Metrosideros excelsa (pohutukawa) 15 m.

Metrosideros kermadecensis ((Kermadec pohutukawa): Extended flowering season, including winter.

Metrosideros fulgens: Climber, orange-red flowers, winter flowering.

Metrosideros robusta (northern rata) 30 m.

Metrosideros umbellata (southern rata) 20 m.

Myrsine australis (red matipo, mapou) 6 m: Small white flowers Dec.-Feb. Black berries.

Phormium cookianum (mountain flax): Smaller than *tenax*, suitable for dry hillsides.

Phormium tenax (New Zealand flax): Red flowers producing copious quantities of nectar Nov.-Jan.

Pittosporum spp: Attractive small trees and shrubs supplying nectar and seeds. *P. tenuifolium* (kohuhu, black matipo), *P. crassifolium* (karo) *P. eugenioides* (tarata, lemonwood), particularly recommended.

Podocarpus ferrugineus (miro) 25 m: Large red berries ripening in winter.

Pseudopanax arboreus (five-finger) 8 m.

Schefflera digitata (pate) 6 m: Flowering Feb.-Mar., purplish black fruit ripening Mar.-Apr. following year.

Sophora microphylla (kowhai) 10 m.

Sophora tetraptera (kowhai) 13 m: The kowhais are an important source of nectar in the early spring.

Tetrapathaea tetrandra (New Zealand passion flower): Climber, handsome orange-coloured fruit in summer and autumn.

Vitex lucens (puriri) 20 m: Pink or red flowers and fruit for much of the year.

Introduced

Many introduced trees and shrubs are attractive to native birds. The following are particularly recommended:

Arbutus unedo (strawberry tree)

Banksia species (Australian honeysuckle)

Callistemon citrinus 'Splendens' (bottlebrush)

Chaenomeles species (japonicas)

Cotoneaster species

Cytisus proliferus (tree lucerne): a favourite of native pigeons

Erythrina crista-galli (coral tree)

Eucalyptus species, particularly *E.leucoxylon* 'Rosea' which flowers in autumn and winter.

Grevillea species

Homalanthus species

Lambertia formosa (honey flower)

Melaleuca species

Prunus species

Viburnum japonicum.

(End of extract.)

Generally it will be found that deciduous trees tend to attract and hold birds more than evergreen, although planting of any tree which can provide a food source for birds should be worthwhile. Look to berried trees and shrubs if you want to encourage the birds to stay around your farm.

Apart from trees you can also establish feeding stations handy to the house. These can be supplied with mutton fat, lard, nectar or sugar liquid and household scraps which will provide additional food for birds, particularly during winter when natural food resources are low.

Once again it is pertinent to point out that so many trees can serve a dual purpose, and should you decide to plant a tree specifically for birds it will be unlikely that you cannot find one which will serve another purpose on the farm, be it long-term timber, shelter or beauty.

Ministry of Agriculture and Fisheries Aglink FPP26 is worth reading. It sets out the advantages of establishing trees on effluent pond surrounds so that birds are attracted to the site and there is an improvement in the appearance of the area.

7
Tree Sources
of Nectar and Pollen

This section is included because many farmers have a special interest in bees and are conscious of the fact that it is in the national interest that there is a plentiful supply of their food as they are essential to the reproduction of plant species. In New Zealand approximately one-third of our diet comes directly from plants requiring insect pollination or indirectly from animals which are fed largely on insect-pollinated crops. Honey bees are by far the most important and numerous of these pollinators.

Honey bees need protein which they obtain from pollen, and carbohydrates which they obtain from nectar. The critical period in the beekeeping cycle is the spring, when the hive is expanding but the main flow of nectar is not usually available.

A healthy honey bee colony will rear in one year between 110 000 and 200 000 bees. This requires 30-50 kg of pollen and to collect this amount each hive will have to bring in 2-4 million bee loads of pollen. It has also been calculated that it requires 144 000 - 160 000 bee trips to gather and produce one kilogram of honey. The bee requires a large amount of energy to carry out this self-imposed task, and since the energy is provided by the carbohydrates the provision of nectar is vital.

In some areas, eg Canterbury, land development has produced a sterile environment which will no longer support enough bee colonies to carry out all the pollination that is required. Elsewhere too, removal of noxious weeds such as gorse and nodding thistle has aggravated the scarcity of food sources. Willows along stream banks have been an excellent source of early pollen and nectar but in the interests of flood control these are being cut down. The more the natural food supplies disappear the greater the dependence there is on artificial feeding and the higher the cost of maintaining a hive, provided it even stays in the area.

The planting of nectar- and pollen-bearing trees is therefore important and there is every possibility that such a programme can be compatible with and complementary to other planting objectives. Many trees used for beauty, timber, erosion control and shelter can provide bee fodder at a time when it is most required, ie when pasture flowers, which provide most bee requirements, are not yet in bloom, or when drought has taken its toll.

In addition to offering a food source, shelter also creates a better environment for bee aeronautics, and if there are no headwinds to battle against (especially tiresome with a load on) the bee may well increase the number of daily trips. The necessity of providing bees for pollination of kiwifruit has dramatically illustrated the important role of this most energetic and productive insect and how essential it is to pastoral and horticultural economies.

Left: Lime trees provide summer food for bees.

Bee Food Sources

The information below is taken from MAF Aglinks FPP 529 and 530.

Np   Used by bees more as a nectar than pollen source

Pn   Used by bees more as a pollen than nectar source

P   Pollen source only

NP   Equally valuable for nectar and pollen

Spring/Early Summer
(October-Nov.)

Acer pseudoplatanus (sycamore)	Np
Aristotelia serrata (wineberry, makomako)	Np
Cordyline australis (cabbage tree)	Np
Corynocarpus laevigatus (karaka)	NP
Elaeocarpus dentatus (hinau)	Np
Fuchsia excorticata (kotukutuku, konini)	NP
Knightia excelsa (rewarewa)	NP
Ligustrum vulgare (privet)	Np
Malus domestica (apple)	Np
Pittosporum crassifolium (karo)	Pn
P. eugenioides (lemonwood, tarata)	NP
P. tenuifolium (kohuhu)	Np
Pyrus spp. (pear)	P
Quintinia serrata (quintinia)	Np
Robinia pseudoacacia (robinia)	NP
Weinmannia racemosa (kamahi)	Np
W. silvicola (tawhero, towai)	Np

Summer
(December-March)

Eucalyptus ficifolia (red flowering gum)	Np
E. viminalis (manna gum)	Np
E. melliodora (yellow box)	Np
Melicytus ramiflorus (mahoe)	NP
Metrosideros excelsa (pohutukawa)	Np
M. robusta (rata)	Np
M. umbellata (southern rata)	Np
Gleditsia triacanthos (honey locust)	Pn
Ixerba brexioides (tawari)	Np
Leptospermum ericoides (kanuka)	Np
L. scoparium (manuka)	Np
Ligustrum sinense (Chinese privet)	Np
Schinus molle (Peruvian pepper tree)	Np
Tilia spp. (lime, linden)	Np

Autumn/Early Winter
(April-May)

Eucalyptus delegatensis	NP
E. leucoxylon 'Rosea' (winter-flowering pink gum)	NP
E. regnans	NP
E. viminalis	Np
Hoheria populnea (lacebark, houhere)	NP

Winter/Early Spring
(June-Sept.)

Acacia baileyana Cootamundra wattle	P
A. decurrens green wattle	P
Albizia lophantha brush wattle	Np
Banksia integrifolia	N
Hakea sericea spiny hakea	NP
Prunus persica peach, nectarine	Pn
Prunus sp. ornamental cherry	Pn
Pseudopanax arboreus five-finger	Np
Salix babylonica weeping willow	NP
S. caprea goat willow	Pn
S. fragilis crack willow	NP
S. matsudana Pekin willow	NP
Sophora tetraptera *S. microphylla* kowhai	NP

8
Handling and Planting of Trees

Nothing kills enthusiasm quicker than a succession of planting failures, so it is important that correct procedures be followed if success is to be assured. There are many unavoidable factors affecting survival without adding failures caused by shoddy or careless planting. You are making an investment in labour and money so it is worth taking a little extra care right at the beginning.

Techniques of establishing shelterbelts and woodlots are the subjects of publications by the Ministry of Agriculture and Fisheries (Aglinks) and by the Forest Service. It is advisable to obtain up-to-date information from these sources if such planting is contemplated. If you are planting in large numbers you will find it worthwhile reading the chapter on shelter for many of the same principles apply.

Protectors

The rural landowner has special problems to cope with. Of all of them the most important is protection from animals, be they domestic such as cattle, sheep, deer, goats and horses (the worst enemies) or feral animals such as opossums, hares/rabbits, pukeko and goats. The first piece of advice that can be given is to get your protector up first and plant your tree later. It is too easy to get carried away when in a nursery and buy more than you have planned for. You must resist the temptation to plant out trees intending to put up protectors later or before you move your stock in.

Stock protectors come in a great variety of styles, but there is one feature they all have in common — they are unattractive and do nothing to enhance the beauty of a tree. Some very expensive and imposing wooden structures are to be seen, especially on horse farms, but to the landscape lover these are unattractive. Protectors should be as unobtrusive as possible. The use of electric fences makes it feasible to have very lightweight, effective, cheap protection with the minimum of visual impact. Suitable electric protec-

tors have been devised to deter almost all animals and because of their cheapness, ease of erection and effectiveness they are probably the best choice. To be sure there will be accidents, with the inevitable damage or even total loss of the trees, but this risk must be offset by the probability that the use of electric fences will enable many more trees to be planted in a season than if reliance is placed on mechanical protection. The odd loss out of a large planting is tolerable, and on balance more will be accomplished over the years by the use of electric fencing than by any other means. In any case there is plenty of evidence to show that many structures built of timber in one form or another merely act as convenient rubbing points for stock, eventually collapsing under the constant pressure being exerted by animals weighing half a tonne or more.

Landholders must make their choice according to their own experience and inclinations, so there are no firm recommendations on what the protector should look like. There are however a selection of photos of various methods which have been used and these can be seen on the following pages. They are reproduced without comment in the hope that they offer guidance as to how to go about designing your protector, together with some of the things you should not do.

Special mention should be made of the best use of land so that grazing loss is minimal; in this respect corners should not be overlooked. There are already two fences erected and it is little effort to wire up between the two to complete the triangle. If the line is taken across from points 7 metres from the corner, it will be approximately 10 metres long. This enclosed area will be .0025 of a hectare (about 1/120 of an acre). Each such area could hold anything from three to six trees and would hardly be missed on even the smallest farm. This is especially so in paddocks which are mostly used for cropping, where the headlands are lost to production anyway.

Some protectors provide excellent scratching facilities.

Site Preparation

Trees do not thrive in competition with grass — especially farm pastures which tend to be well established and vigorous. A new tree can get away to a good start if planting is carried out in accordance with principles set out in this chapter, but may well succumb to summer stress if it has to compete with grass for moisture. Even before summer small seedlings can be overwhelmed by spring grass flushes; these will have long been awaited and needed on other parts of the farm but in the planting area may well result in the seedlings never being seen again. Farmers are busy people in the spring and even with the best of intentions often never get back to planting sites to release trees from competitive growth. So plan your plantings in such a way that they can cope without assistance for several months, for your animals will, and certainly should, take priority.

Before planting, the grass sward should be removed by scarfing or preferably spraying with a non-residual herbicide which with the addition of Simazine will be effective for several months. This may in itself not be enough, since at planting time in the winter such vigorous grasses as kikuyu and paspalum are dormant and will appear again during the summer. Small plants do not stand a chance against these fast, tall-growing species. Post-planting treatment is therefore necessary for at least the summer following planting, and with slower growing species it could well be necessary for some years after planting if best results are to be obtained.

Having selected a suitable tree for your site, or vice versa, and erected a protector, you then have to plant the tree which you have bought to match those conditions. Ideally you should follow the guidelines set out here. Farmers must pay special attention to new trees for they are not planted in the sheltered suburb of some city; on the contrary, a farmer is transferring a plant from a protected and pampered nursery environment to the exposed and often harsh conditions of the fields. It cannot just be dropped in a hole and forgotten for months on end. Like a young animal it must be nurtured if it is to become strong and healthy

Peat moss improves texture of heavy soils and provides fibre to assist moisture in light soils.

and grow rapidly to maturity.

If you can think far enough ahead it is good sense to dig your holes before collection of the plants from the nursery: cut off the turf, dig a hole, chop up the turf, and replace all back in the hole making sure you do not bring the subsoil up to the surface. It will break down with the colder weather and will be easy to handle at planting time. If you have the opportunity it is helpful to mix heavy subsoil with peat moss, sand or old farm manure to help make it more acceptable to the new root system. Adding fibrous material to very light soil improves moisture retention. Just before planting is a good time to use your herbicide to knock down any regrowth.

If conditions are very wet it is better to wait until they have improved (unless it is permanently wet when the problem has to be handled on a permanent basis) and if conditions are unduly windy some artificial shelter such as plastic mesh, old straw bales, etc will help early establishment.

Drainage

If a planting hole cannot drain it will act as a tank, keeping soil in the root zone saturated and shutting off air. Failure through root rot is almost inevitable. Commonsense will dictate the most appropriate methods of overcoming the problem; these include penetrating the impermeable layer with a posthole digger or crowbar, adding a side drain, cutting a series of straight lines radiating from the planting hole, digging an oversize hole and backfilling with half to two-thirds of soil mixed with coarse material, or just giving up and building a pond instead.

Bare Root Planting

In winter and spring bare-rooted trees are usually available from nurseries and are cheaper than container-grown plants. Bare-rooted trees are usually easier to handle and more vigorous, so winter planting is not only of benefit to the plants but usually coincides with the quieter time on the farm. When bare-rooted trees are planted the hole is back-filled with a uniform soil mix similar to the surrounding soil. By contrast a container-grown plant has two different mixtures in the hole, often making it unfirm and water penetration difficult, as well as forcing the roots to adapt to a radical change of environment.

Bare-rooted plants need to have fresh plump roots which are not dry and withered, looking as if they have had a long day out! If they do not look fresh and healthy do not buy them, but if you have the misfortune to have them in such a condition then give them a good soaking.

Whenever you are planting care in handling is vital. Do not let the roots or the foliage dry out and at all times protect the whole plant from the wind. If you allow foliage to get in the wind, desiccation will result at a time when the roots are dormant and total

Deep cuts will help disperse moisture into the surrounding soil.

All trees should be soaked in water for about 5 minutes, or at least until bubbles stop rising, prior to plantings. Drain off surplus water.

loss is more than likely. Don't just heave your new purchases on the back of the pickup along with the posts, wire and bags of stockfeed, for they will surely suffer physical damage. Out of the nursery into an 80 km/hour gale is no fun for young trees. Put them into some sort of container and make sure it is big enough, for young roots are easily damaged.

The planting hole should be large enough to accommodate all the roots without cramping, bending or cutting them. The tree should be planted at the same level as it was in the nursery and this is clearly indicated by soil marks on the stem. Soils should be firmly compacted around the roots (this does not mean jumping up and down on the backfill using your heel in like manner to a post rammer). Leave the top surface soil loose as this helps to absorb water. An after-planting watering is a good idea if this is practical.

For the forest species such as pines, eucalypts, blackwoods, etc it is equally important that seedlings be of the highest quality — more so in fact since once planted they are likely to receive less attention than the amenity species, since they are planted in such large numbers.

Preconditioning in the nursery is now a highly specialised technique. Land owners establishing woodlots should ensure that nursery handling, uplifting and transport to site are of the highest standards. Literature and advice are available from the Forest Service, and you are recommended to make purchases only from established and reliable nurseries experienced in growing such species.

Container-Grown Trees

These are popular because they extend the planting season and can be held over between nursery sale and planting time without any adverse effect. When buying make sure the plant looks healthy, has a vigorous robust appearance and good foliage. Watch for root-bound plants and avoid those where roots can be seen growing through drainage holes or above soil level. Plastic bags, cans or pots must be removed with minimum disturbance of the root ball. Plants in solid containers can be tipped upside down on the hand, with the tree stem held between the fingers, and the edge tapped on a post or spade. Hessian should not be removed if young shoots are strongly growing through it. If this has happened cut the twine, pull the hessian away from the bark only and leave it to rot in the ground.

Dig a hole twice the size of the container. Container plants are often grown in a light fast-draining mix that favours rapid root development, and if set into small holes the roots may well find it difficult to penetrate the surrounding material. This will make them shallow rooted and liable to dry out. Your large hole should be back filled with good friable easily penetrated soil mix which will make life easy for the plant which has just had to suffer a major change in its

Carefully remove containers without damaging the roots.

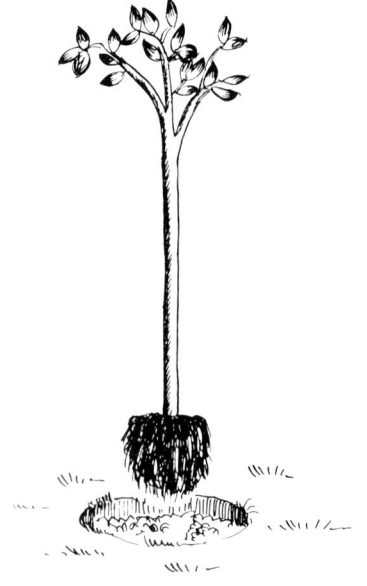

Do not disturb the root ball except as necessary to straighten out and disentangle roots which have spiralled around the container.

environment.

Basic planting technique is similar to bare-rooted and again you should not plant too deeply — the top of the root ball should not be more than 3cm below the soil. After removing the container have a good look at the roots. If they are crowded or all coiled up straighten them out with a knife just before insertion in the hole. Surplus roots which have spiralled round until they look like the inside of a clock should be cut off so that any new growth will go sideways and downwards into fresh ground. Plants which are grown in peat pots can be planted container and all, but make sure that the bottom of the pot is broken apart to facilitate easy root penetration. It is also most important to remove the lip of the pot or cover it with soil, otherwise it will act as a wick and allow moisture to evaporate into the atmosphere with disastrous results.

Transplanting

Sometimes a tree larger than is usually handled needs to be moved; for instance a *Cedrus deodara* might have grown too large for the home garden and has to be moved out on to the farm.

Plan to move the tree during winter when it is dormant. Several months beforehand dig around the tree with the spade vertical, cutting downwards near the drip line. This will shorten the outer roots and encourage the growth of more compact feeder roots.

A few days before moving, soak the whole root mass with water and spray the leaves. Prepare the planting hole as described earlier, making quite sure it is large enough. Choose a calm cloudy day if possible.

Dig a trench around the tree, then gradually sever the roots under the root ball, being careful not to crumble the soil away. An alternative method of wrenching is to cut the roots on three sides only about a month before moving the tree. At transplanting time the remaining roots are cut. This method could be used if the tree is to be moved at relatively short notice. Tie a rag or something similar on to a branch facing north.

Wrap sacking around the root ball, draw up tightly and secure firmly, especially underneath where the soil is liable to fall away from the roots.

When replanting in the new site ensure that the rag is positioned to the north. This reduces one cause of stress to the tree by not altering its orientation.

Work as quickly as possible following earlier planting directions. Larger trees require thorough watering several times during the first year after moving.

Staking

For larger specimens a stake will stabilise a tree and will help establishment since it prevents the movement that breaks off new roots, and assists in training the tree to a good shape. In wetter spots it is essential if a larger specimen is to stay even reasonably upright. The stake should preferably be placed in position

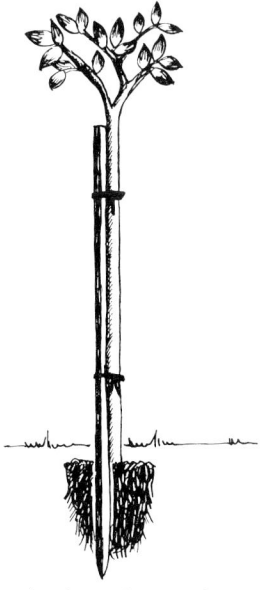

Do not plant too deeply — the top of a container-grown species should not be more than 3cm below the ground surface.

Staking stabilises trees during establishment period. Place in position before planting to lessen root damage.

prior to planting to prevent root damage. The tree should be placed on the leeward side and secured firmly with a flexible tie — don't buy one as there is no more useful end to the life of pantyhose than to support a tree in its infancy. Old bicycle tyres can be made into good ties, but periodic checks should always be made to ensure that there is no strangling.

Tie-on labels attached at the nursery can cause ringbarking so always remove them and retie them to the stake if on-site identification is desired.

Mulching

This is a great help to young plants and consists of a 6-8cm layer of material around them. It acts as an insulator, prevents evaporation of moisture and keeps roots at an even temperature. It also stops the soil surface from baking into a hard pan, but most importantly it acts as a weed control. The ground should be soaked before applying mulch. Ideally peat moss could be applied around specially valuable specimens, but this is hardly feasible on large-scale plantings on farms. On the other hand the person on the land often has access to many suitable materials such as old hay, sawdust from the mobile mill, post peelings from post thinning, hedge trimmings from the home garden or horticulture block, or garden compost and leaf mould. Mulches must be kept away from the trunk as excess heat and moisture contained in the material can destroy the bark.

Mulching is one of those tasks which is avoidable and seemingly of doubtful worth at the time of application since there are many other things which seem more important, but it will pay very handsome dividends.

Fertiliser

Excessive feeding at planting time is both dangerous and unnecessary. A natural fertiliser such as blood and bone can be incorporated into the soil before planting, but the safest way is to scatter a couple of handfuls on to the surface after planting. By the time it reaches the roots it will be in soluble form and readily available. The farmer however can usually find organic manure about the farm and what better than animal dung, which serves as a mulch as well as manure? For centuries trees have grown very adequately without any artificial manures — seeds have simply germinated and grown, so why hurry to grow at accelerated speeds? One must learn to accept that if a tree is planted on a site resembling its natural conditions, then it will grow fast enough to be quite rewarding to the planter.

We are very fortunate in New Zealand that trees grow quickly compared with most other countries, where the inhabitants accept that tree planting is done not only for their own generation but for others to come. A New Zealander can see trees grow to maturity in a lifetime, without any artificial aids

Mulching prevents weeds growing and evaporation of moisture is lessened. Soak the ground well before mulching.

Avoid excessive feeding at planting time. A couple of handfuls on the soil surface will be in soluble form when it eventually reaches the roots.

through a combination of soil and climate. Perhaps where there is a proven deficiency artificial manure can be applied, but otherwise it is hard to justify.

Watering

It is quite impracticable for the farmer to keep up a regular watering programme so it is even more important to take steps at planting time to minimise competition for moisture. Elimination of weeds, good site preparation and mulching are the answers. There will be however some specimen trees which deserve that extra bit of attention and which may well be planted near the home or sheds where there are watering points. These should be given some additional water during that first summer when stress is likely to be greatest.

"A little and often" may fill the purse but it's an adage that can kill the tree when applied to a watering programme. The water will never penetrate to the lower levels and the result will be a shallow root system. Water moves very little laterally so enough must be used each time to give coverage of the whole root zone, ie water out to the drip line. Over-watering, particularly in heavy clay, will be worse than not watering at all, for the roots will "drown" through lack of oxygen.

A useful guide to frequency of watering is the following table which suggests days between applications:

	Sand	Loam	Clay
Shallow Rooted	4-6	7-10	10-12
Medium	7-10	10-15	15-20
Deep Rooted	15-20	20-30	30 or more

Conditions other than those in the soil will also influence the degree of moisture stress, a major one being the desiccating effect of wind, which will increase water demand.

A system used in Israel for centuries can be effective when stones or small rocks are available. These are put into a layer or two in a depression around the base of the young tree, acting as a mulch and through condensation providing that extra drop of moisture.

A recent arrival on the market is a plastic bag which can trickle feed water at a preset controlled rate. It also acts as a mulch and can be reused — just the job for a busy farmer or anyone who fancies a little yachting during the heat of the summer.

Water may well come from the farm bore, but to most people putting it on plants is the bore and should be avoided if possible. The plant will be stronger and more independent if it is grown in conditions which will enable it to cope on its own. Make that extra effort at planting time and so lessen your post-planting work.

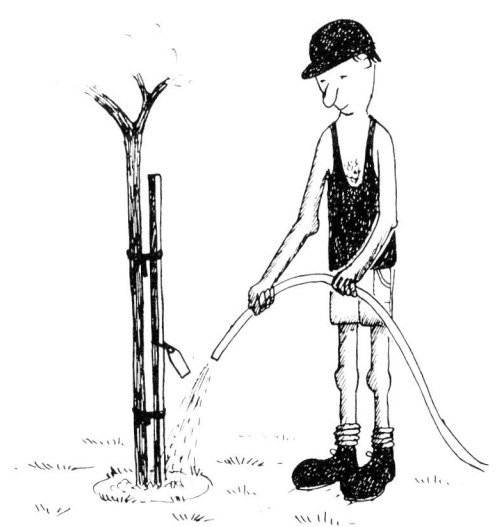

Give a thorough watering at planting time and regular soakings during dry weather.

9
Exotic Species

The early explorers frequently commented on the heedless use of fire by the Maori — a practice described as "all forest that was easy to burn was burnt". This indiscriminate firing resulted in the loss of many forests in the relatively arid zones, so by the time the first settlers arrived a good proportion of New Zealand's tree cover had already disappeared. The first objective of these pioneer forbears was to subjugate nature to their will by cutting down or destroying in some way the rest of the vegetation which occupied the land. They saw it as an impediment — which it was — to developing productive farm lands. Few felled the bush with discretion; mostly it was wholesale destruction without thought to the long-term effects. In any case there was always another valley clothed in bush next door. Following the requirement of land for farming came an increasing demand for timber for the new towns and this resulted in even greater destruction of trees. 1000 years ago forest covered three-quarters of New Zealand; 850 years later the Polynesians had destroyed 30% of it; in the last 150 years, Europeans have destroyed another 40%.[1]

Having achieved this first objective, the landholders took a deep breath and stood back to admire their handiwork. They found themselves in a grassland devoid of trees except for an odd pocket of native bush which had escaped the firing, but that consisted of evergreens. The emigrants from England had left behind them a legacy of trees which were a dominant feature of the landscape. Perhaps they were a little surprised to find that they had lost touch with one of the things they didn't value until it had disappeared, as well as being nearly bowled over by the wind.

They missed the everchanging colours of the deciduous trees reflecting the changing seasons. There is a significant response to these patterns from those who live and work on the land. The colouring of autumn leaves suggests a battening down for winter and as the winds sweep the trees bare, revealing their interesting shapes, farmers wonder if they have adequate hay for their winter requirements. The new growth of spring reflects the end of the cold season and spirits lift accordingly.

So a touch of homesickness and a draught around their necks prompted the early settlers to import those species which were so much a part of their surroundings before leaving for faraway shores. It was not only farmers who had attacks of nostalgia: missionaries too began the importation of seeds, and today many of the old mission sites are surrounded by trees dating from a century and a half ago. Norfolk pines still standing as majestic sentinels in warmer parts of the North Island were brought into the country in 1840 and planted by Bishop Selwyn. The oldest living exotic tree in New Zealand is alleged to be an English oak near the Waimate North mission house. Samuel Marsden was sending from Sydney fruit trees for the missionaries in New Zealand as early as 1819.

Mr A. Ludlam of Lower Hutt started gardens in 1840 and set up an exchange system, sending plants back to England and receiving others in return. He later published the first paper on the establishment and growth of exotic trees in New Zealand, this being presented to the NZ Exhibition in 1865.

Writing of her arrival in Auckland in 1842 Lady Martin said, "There was hardly a shrub to be seen then, though a few years later we were embowered in a wealth of trees, English and native, so rapid is the growth in that genial climate."

The demand for deciduous trees and others which could counter the effect of the desiccating winds encouraged entrepreneurs to start up business. In 1850 a Mr McVicar advertised "Scotch firs, Stone pines, Italian poplars etc". In 1853 William Hale had established such a successful nursery in Nelson that he could offer for sale 10000 fruit and forest trees including many of the well-loved English broadleaves.

In the South Island it had not been necessary to be quite so destructive as there was not much indigenous forest to start with. The large station-owners were foremost in planting up the countryside: many of the first conifers (*Pinus radiata* late 1850s, *Cupressus macrocarpa* 1864) were planted at Mt Peel station for specimen and shelter trees. Lady Barker in 1866 wrote of the "large English sorts of trees" which had been planted in Christchurch. Eucalypts soon made their way all over the country and made a big impact on the general scene. Many varieties were imported as seedlings which were to provide quick shelter. Lumped together under the blanket title of gums, they were frequently planted on sites quite unsuitable to their requirements, but many of those that did survive could still be growing today.

The gold miners too were responsible for planting, possibly bringing the seed from California, for they often planted trees indigenous to that part of the world. Canterbury was so short of timber that supplies had to be brought from Australia and America, and this led to the passing of legislation in 1871 to encourage tree planting. Under the Forest Trees Planting Encouragement Act settlers who planted 500 trees per acre (1 250 per ha) could apply for extra land in the ratio of 2:1 once the trees had reached 2 ft (60 cm) in height. Some excellent stands of Douglas fir, sequoiadendron, eucalypts, cedars, cypresses and some other broadleaf species were established as a result of this first forestry incentive scheme.

The extent of the growth in numbers and varieties of exotic trees is indicated by a record made in 1878 by Mr T.H. Potts. That year he measured in Governor's Bay, near Lyttleton, a stand which included 77 different varieties of conifers. The Selwyn Plantation Board in Canterbury, still in existence, was formed in 1879. The first government department to do much planting was the railways. Evidence of this initiative remains and some fine oak stands can be seen near railway lines in both islands. From this time there was a steady progression towards the eventual establishment in 1919 of the State Forest Service, although other state agencies carried out extensive planting in various parts of the country from 1896.

Exotic trees do well in New Zealand. Confidence in the future of the forest industry is such that the millionth hectare of exotic forest has just been planted (1983). These are mainly softwoods but many species of hardwoods have been tried out, providing useful information on which to base the current policy of planting selected species of exotics to replace native hardwoods. Readers interested in planting these trees for commercial purposes should refer to the Forest Service Policy on Exotic Special Purpose Species (Appendix 1).

For those who look to trees only to provide diversity in the landscape and pleasure to all, there is plenty of evidence that this is achievable. New Zealand is blessed with the most favourable of conditions which allow exotics to grow to best advantage, providing the species and the site are reasonably well matched. But we must never undervalue the cranky enthusiast who in spite of all the contrary advice he or she has received, succeeds in establishing a tree which according to the experts would not have a hope. We need such people.

S.W. Burstall writes in his *Historic and Notable Trees of New Zealand* of trees that have reached dimensions not attained in their country of origin (eg cypresses, pines and eucalypts). He predicts that in 50 years time a large and impressive international list could be compiled of 'Notable Exotic Trees of New Zealand'. He has measured thousands of trees and has plenty of evidence to back up that prediction.

References

1. J.L. Nicholls, New Zealand Forest Service Reprint 1371 ODC 902 (931).

Abies

Abies alba (silver fir) in the Taihape district.

The *Abies* (firs) are evergreen conifers. There are many of them and they come from the temperate countries of Europe, Asia and America. They are handsome trees varying in size from about 15 m to over 90 m. They yield non-durable soft, light-weight timbers which are used in the countries of origin for general carpentry work, indoor fittings, pulping, boxing, matchwood, etc. The trees will grow in most friable soils, but they are moisture-loving and prefer damp, fertile soils in areas of high rainfall where winters are prolonged and temperatures are cold. In warm or humid conditions they are likely to attract the attention of destructive insect enemies; as ornamentals under such conditions they are not successful and become most unsightly. They are hardy and while dormant can stand any low temperature to be encountered in New Zealand, but late frosts can damage spring flushes. Rainfall 1 000-2 000 mm desirable. Most are very windfirm and will retain branches right to the ground.

Apart from *A. pinsapo* and *A. nordmanniana* the species are not at all common in New Zealand and *Abies* have not been grown to any extent for timber production; they have however been used for ornamental planting in parks and on some farmlands, usually with conspicuous success. *Abies,* by developing into fine specimens, will reward the tree lover who is patient and can take a long term view.

Species most likely to be suitable for cultivation in this country include the following.

A. alba (silver fir) is a straight-growing, tapering tree which can reach a height of 30-50 m. It is an important forest tree in France and Germany and grows well in Great Britain. Its wood is of considerable value in those countries and turpentine is obtained from its foliage. It is the species most likely to respond well in heavy clays, but it will also grow in loams and in light sandy soils where rainfall is adequate. Not common in New Zealand its form is very variable.

A.amabilis (Pacific silver fir) is popular for landscape work in Europe and the U.S.A. because of its lustrous, silvery-blue-green foliage and its handsome, spire-like crown. It will grow to about 30 m in any free soil; but like all *Abies,* it thrives in areas where winters are cold and rainfall is high.

A.cephalonica (Greek fir) is a large stately mountain species which will grow well in limestone country. Similar to *A.nordmanniana* and *A.alba.* Leaves spread all round branches, but not as noticeably so as *A.pinsapo.*

A.concolor (white fir) is a medium-sized tree which will grow to about 30 m in somewhat drier conditions than most other *Abies.* It is variable and hybridises with *A.grandis.* Inland in Colorado it will endure very harsh conditions.

A.grandis (grand fir) in western U.S.A. can grow to 90 m on ideal sites and yields a somewhat inferior timber. Probably the fastest in New Zealand with growth up to 1 m per year. Resembles Douglas fir and likes similar conditions.

A.magnifica (Californian red fir) averages about 30 m, developing a narrow conical crown. It will grow in poor soils if they are free-draining, but it does best in moist, well-drained, fertile loams in cold localities. The timber is one of the exportable Pacific coast softwoods and is the heaviest of all true firs. Chief characteristic is shortness of branches — in outline the tree is like a Lombardy poplar (fastigiate). It is a useful form in landscaping especially since rust disease has hit the Lombardy poplar: there are not many trees with similar habit. Flushes very late so a good

Above: Abies magnifica (Californian red fir). *Right: Abies Concolor* (white fir).

94

tree for cold climates. A slow starter and then perhaps 400 mm a year.

A. nordmanniana (Caucasian fir) is a big, handsome tree which comes from the mountain regions of the Caucasus where it reaches 50 m; best trees in New Zealand have reached 30 m. Second most common fir

Spring growth of *Abies nordmanniana* (Caucasian fir).

Abies nordmanniana (Caucasian fir) in high central North Island country.

in New Zealand and likes moister and softer site if it is to do really well with growth of 600 mm per annum. Large handsome cones 150 mm long x 40 mm. Easy to grow and usually healthy.

A. pinsapo (Spanish fir) originates from the mountains of southern Spain and is a comparatively small (25 m) tree of pleasing habit. Most widely planted fir in New Zealand. Very tolerant of harsh conditions and a wide variety of sites including limestone and proximity to the sea. Probably tolerates as dry conditions as any and insects do not bother it. Grows at rate of 250-450 mm per annum to about 8 m and is one of only two species with radially spreading leaves.

A. procera (noble fir) grows to large size in its native habitat in the mountain ranges of north-west U.S.A. Its timber is strong and close-grained and it is regarded as the best of the American silver fir woods, suitable for all carpentry purposes. The tree grows best in cold localities and in cool, damp soils of some fertility; it can also grow in poor soils provided they are free and the roots have access to water. Noble fir is one of the best for ornamental planting, but as the tree can exceed 60 m in suitable conditions, it should be given plenty of room to display its natural attractiveness. Cones are the largest of the species, 250 mm long x 100 mm. Still rare in New Zealand and easily confused with *A. magnifica.*

A. religiosa (sacred fir) comes from Mexico and was introduced into New Zealand by the Forest Service in 1957. It is a fast grower compared with most firs with height increases of up to a metre in a year. It tends to develop double leaders but with one pruned off it becomes a fine straight tree growing to 10 m. It flushes early and is susceptible to late frosts. It is a good fir for the milder districts of this country and will tolerate lime conditions.

A. vejari also comes from Mexico and is therefore suitable for New Zealand's warmer climates. Young specimens resemble *A. religiosa* but in most respects *A. vejari* is a superior tree with a straight leader. It is a fast and vigorous grower and could reach 20 m although specimens here are still relatively young and have not yet shown their full potential. It flushes later than *A. religiosa* and therefore avoids unseasonable frost damage. It is often a good blue colour.

Propagation is by seed which is generally of low viability and even when sown not later than the spring following collection, germination is not likely to be higher than about 50 per cent.

Acacia

This very large evergreen genus - there are something like 900 different species - is scattered throughout many lands. In some countries the trees are known as mimosa, but in New Zealand and in Australia they are known as wattles. Many of the species are prized for their attractive foliage and for the abundance of their golden-yellow blossoms. The majority are small, shrubby trees or bushes, more suited for garden planting and particulars of these can be found in most nursery catalogues.

The timber-yielding *Acacias* are quick-growing and most of them thrive in poor and dry soils. Their wood makes excellent firewood. Those listed below are all natives of Australia.

A. baileyana (Cootamundra wattle) is one of the most popular and easily grown of the ornamental flowering species. It is a small tree, rarely exceeding 10 m in height, hardy and short-lived, which blooms prolifically in mid-winter when colour of any kind is scarce.

Acacia baileyana covered in flowers in winter.

Acacia dealbata (silver wattle) grown with other trees as a windbreak. Note the electric rabbit fence.

Its silver-grey foliage makes a pleasing contrast when the tree is sited among green-leaved trees. It will grow in any reasonably drained soil, but it is prone to wind damage and should not be planted in exposed situations.

A.dealbata (silver wattle) has been fairly extensively grown, mostly for firewood, sometimes for quick temporary shelter or for the beautiful gold of early spring blossom. The tree grows rapidly and easily almost anywhere and yields good fuel woods. Neither dry nor poor soils are detrimental to vigorous growth but the tree is unhappy in poor drainage. It reaches 15 m with a spread of 12 m in Australia, but specimens up to 25 m can be found in New Zealand's Whaka forest. The timber has no commercial value.

A.decurrens (green wattle) is larger than *A. baileyana* and can grow up to 17 m with a spread of 8 m. Not so attractive, it is easier to establish and prefers a sunny well-drained position. It has feathery foliage, and flowers in the spring — after *A. baileyana* but before *A.mearnsii.*

A.mearnsii (black wattle) was at one time extensively planted in parts of New Zealand for the tannin which was extracted from its bark, but the ravages of gall fungus rendered its cultivation uneconomic. The tree is still grown on some farms, mostly for fuel, the timber being sometimes used as temporary fencing material. Logs split readily into posts and battens, posts usually giving service for from eight to ten years. *A. mearnsii* is hardy and will grow in clays and poor soils. In good soils it is a very rapid grower and can reach 30 m.

A.melanoxylon (Australian blackwood) is the largest and most important of the timber-yielding *Acacias.* It is often not recognised at first glance by the layman as a 'wattle', possibly because its compound pinnate leaves change very early in life to firm, broad phyllodes. In its best form, *A. melanoxylon* is a tree which, when grown in properly stocked and managed plantations, will attain a height of 35 m or more with a good, clean bole yielding a handsome, golden-brown, medium-weight timber of considerable value. When grown in the open as an individual, it will develop a heavily-foliaged crown on a short, stout bole and become an efficient, wide-spreading shade or ornamental tree.

A.melanoxylon is quite a common tree in many parts of New Zealand, but few farmers appear to place a true value on its timber worth; until recently no serious attempt seems to have been made to cultivate it for timber production. Its timber is, in fact, one of the best of the world's cabinet and furniture woods. It is also used for panelling, for the manufacture of gun stocks, for piano tuning boards and for many other exacting purposes. In Australia, when the trees were more plentiful than they are now, it was also

Above: Acacia mearnsii (black wattle) undamaged by livestock, on a farm near Cambridge. *Right:* A fine *Acacia melanoxylon* (Australian blackwood), open-grown near Te Poi.

Young blackwoods stabilising a steep roadside near Hunterville.

growth and form, although trees do respond well to fertile moist sites. Studies indicate that trees will reach a diameter of 60 cm at 40 years of age. Silvicultural treatment and manner of growing are important, so readers should seek out the latest information available from the Forest Service. Unlike most *Acacias* the young plants are amenable to wrenching and transplant without trouble. The tree is a soil improver and when grown in conjunction with eucalypts the practice appears to be beneficial to both.

A.verticillata (prickly moses) has needle-like phyllodes with sharp points. It will stand salt wind exposure and is sometimes used as a hedging plant. It grows to about 6 m and has been used for farm shelter because stock dislike its spiny leaves. Subject to gall fungus.

There are other Australian species which are widespread over inland areas of that country and which frequently arouse the interest of visiting New Zealand pastoralists. They yield extremely hard and ground-durable timbers and have a value as fodder trees in dry years. All are shrubs or small trees, rarely exceeding 10 m in height and able to endure very dry conditions. The handsome, dark-brown timbers of the group are exceedingly hard and tough and in localities where the trees grow they are used as fence posts. It is not suggested that these species would have a general interest for New Zealand farmers, but planters who like to experiment with unusual trees may like to try some of them. The most important of the group are *A. aneura* (mulga), *A. cambagei* (gidgee) and *A. pendula* (myall).

The trees are propagated from seed which usually has a hard outer casing and needs to be soaked in near-boiling water for an hour or so before sowing. The seedlings do not take kindly to transplanting, and unless the grower is skilled in wrenching techniques it is better to sow seed *in situ* or in containers. Suckers taken from suckering species will usually grow readily.

used for building purposes. The timber is easily worked, turns and bends well and dresses to a smooth finish which takes a high polish. Farmers are encouraged to plant this tree, which along with other special-purpose trees is expected to supply high-quality hardwoods to replace the dwindling supply from indigenous and imported sources.

The tree is very hardy and able to grow in most soils but to produce a good timber tree it must be sheltered. Rainfall, altitude, aspect and soil, compared with shelter, have only minimal effect on

Acer

Most of the maples grown in New Zealand are the small garden varieties. It is only seldom that the larger species are seen growing on farmlands, yet they are conspicuously beautiful trees and well worth the attention of the planter whose aim is landscape improvement. There are more than 100 species, mostly deciduous, the larger ones being spreading, shapely trees, many of them highly prized for the beauty of their autumn foliage. Some yield valuable hardwood timbers which, in Canada and U.S.A., are sought for the manufacture of furniture, for flooring and for many other purposes. The trees are reasonably soil tolerant, and being notably hardy are suitable for cultivation in cold areas where they produce the best autumn colouring.

A. macrophyllum (big leaf maple) is the only commercial species of the four that grow in western U.S.A. It requires moist soils; open grown it reaches a height of 20 m. It has a pleasing shape with a broad rounded crown of dense blue-green foliage and a short trunk. Compared with other maples the leaves are conspicu-ously large, being from 15-30 cm long and slightly broader. They vary in size on the same tree and turn a golden yellow in autumn. Timber is used extensively for furniture and other specialist uses.

A. negundo (box elder) is a very common tree throughout the whole of eastern U.S.A. It has ash-like pinnate leaves and possesses the ability to grow in very poor soils, reaching, depending on soil fertility, heights from 10-20 m. It is often of poor form with timber of little commercial value. Its main virtue is that it is one of the few *Acer* species that will with-stand wind. As against this it has a fairly short life, growing very slowly after 15 years and rarely exceed-ing 60 years.

A. nigrum (black maple) comes from eastern U.S.A. and resembles sugar maple (*A. saccharum*) in most respects. It grows naturally in good, moist country and will reach a height of about 25 m. Its timber is very hard and strong, similar to sugar maple and it gets its name from the deeply furrowed black bark.

An attractive farm entrance with two *Acer negundo* (box elder).

A young *Acer platanoides* (Norway maple) in autumn, on the authors' farm. Note the electric fence.

Acer pseudoplatanus (sycamore) near Pirongia.

A. platanoides (Norway maple) is a native of Europe. It is a hardy tree of graceful aspect with a low, rounded, globe-like crown on a short bole and is commonly planted in Britain, Canada and the U.S.A. It will grow in most soils, including those of poor quality, but is at its best in deep, light loams containing a little lime. It dislikes wet situations but seems to withstand city-type pollution. It will resist salt-laden winds and is therefore a good subject for coastal planting. Its leaves turn a vivid yellow in autumn. The timber is of little importance.

A. pseudoplatanus (sycamore) is the largest of the maples, a deep-rooting, quick-growing tree which will grow to well beyond 30 m in deep moist soils and to somewhat smaller size in poorer soils or in clays. Given the right conditions it becomes a weed species. A native of Europe, it is hardy and will resist salt winds. Its foliage has no autumn appeal. The timber is medium-weight, usually straight-grained, and is used for many purposes including the manufacture of furniture and for veneering, turnery and panelling. Sometimes the grain is curly or wavy, producing a fiddlebark figure; this is the traditional wood for violin backs. It makes good fuel.

A. rubrum (scarlet maple) is a hardy American species with a wide geographical range extending over the whole of eastern U.S.A. and parts of Canada. It grows rapidly and in most soils, but prefers those that are on the moist side. In its natural state it is often found inhabiting swampy sites. The tree will grow to 15-20 m with a narrow crown. It is shallow-rooting and prone to wind damage in exposed situations. It is one of the most sought-after species for ornamental planting. Its leaves turn a brilliant scarlet with the coming of the first winter frosts. The timber is used for many purposes where hard wood is required and is made into charcoal.

A. saccharum (sugar maple) is a shapely tree of 15-30 m with a round or egg-shaped crown and a rather shallow and wide-spreading root system. The species is one of the longest-lived of the maples, ranging over a large area of the U.S.A. and Canada. It is of considerable value in those countries for its production of maple sugar and syrup. Its timber is used for flooring, shoe trees, musical instruments and many purposes where a firm close-grained hard wood is required. Accidental forms with contorted grain and known as birdseye maple are prized for cabinet making. It thrives under a variety of conditions but grows especially well on gravelly, slightly alkaline soils.

Propagation is normally by seed and nearly all species are easily transplanted.

The many scores of small ornamental maples suitable for garden cultivation do not come within the scope of this book. Full particulars of these can be obtained from most nursery catalogues.

Aesculus

There are about twenty *Aesculus* species. They are widely distributed throughout the northern hemisphere and are known in European countries as horse chestnuts. They are hardy, deciduous trees, some of large size and spreading habit. All will grow in free soils that are well-drained.

A. x carnea (red horse chestnut) is a tree almost identical in form with the common horse chestnut but smaller in size and somewhat slower in growth. It is a shapely tree seldom exceeding 15 m in height and bearing in spring masses of reddish pink flowers. It grows best in conditions specified for *A. hippocastanum*. There is a variety 'Briotii' which has richly coloured crimson flowers, and needs to be grafted to reproduce true to type.

A. hippocastanum (horse chestnut) is the species most frequently seen in New Zealand. It is the largest tree of the genus and can, in good loams with plenty of moisture and in reasonably sheltered situations, attain a height exceeding 30 m with a crown of symmetrically spreading branches on a short, robust bole.

Its flowers are large, white and attractive, appearing in spring. The tree came originally from the mountainous country of northern Greece, but it has been cultivated for centuries in other lands, especially in Europe, where its white soft timber is prized for numerous woodware purposes including turnery, dairy and kitchen utensils and sports equipment. In England, the horse chestnut is highly esteemed for its

Flowers of *Aesculus hippocastanum* (horse chestnut).

Aesculus hippocastanum (horse chestnut) in full flower in December.

Foliage of *Aesculus indica* (Indian horse chestnut) in spring.

been given room to develop its spreading branches it has usually proved to be a very attractive shade tree. The nuts are inedible, but over the centuries before the arrival of electronic games have as 'conkers' given endless hours of enjoyment to children of all ages.

A. indica (Indian horse chestnut) is a magnificent tree originating in the Himalayas and growing to 30 m. Produces panicles of pink flushed flowers sometimes up to 40 cm long and 13 cm wide. New spring growth is particularly attractive.

About half a dozen Aesculus species come from North America where they are known as buckeyes. The white flowers of some of these trees are flushed with pink or greenish-white.

ornamental appeal and some famous avenues exist in that country — the one at Hampton Court, near London, being world famous. Some of the older New Zealand estates possess fine specimens; where it has

They are readily propagated from seed provided the nuts are sown as soon as they fall or else stratified in damp sand over winter.

Ailanthus

The species most commonly grown in New Zealand is *A. altissima*, sometimes called *A. glandulosa* and usually known as the Tree of Heaven. This is a rather aggressive, deciduous tree, a native of China, which grows rapidly in light soils and somewhat more slowly in heavier soils. It reaches a maximum height of approximately 20 m with a thin, loose crown of branches bearing large compound leaves which on young vigorous trees can be up to 1 m long, and small greenish flowers. In summer the female bears bright red fruit in propellor-like keys. Its chief claim to attention lies in its ability to withstand air pollution. It can be found in many of the largest cities in the world and there is a fine avenue of them in Bowen Street in the heart of Auckland. In congenial soils the tree will sucker freely; these suckers are sometimes difficult to deal with and can prove a nuisance.

The colloquial name is apt to mislead because the smell of the male leaves when bruised, and of the flowers, is decidedly disagreeable. Planters who wish to avoid this distressing emanation should plant only female trees.

Propagation is from seed or from root cuttings.

Vigorous *Ailanthus altissima* (tree of heaven) near Auckland.

Albizia

A genus of about 30 species native to warmer parts of Asia, evergreen and deciduous and closely related to *Acacias* with which they are sometimes confused. Some are fast-growing — *A.lophantha* (brush wattle) was often used to establish a quick shelterbelt in warmer parts of New Zealand. The species sets seed profusely and in some of the lighter soils has assumed pest proportions.

Another species (*A.lebbeck*) is known in the Philippines as 'woman's tongue' because the large flat seed pods rattle in the breeze.

A.julibrissin (silk tree) is the species most seen in New Zealand. It thrives in dry hot districts with light sandy soil, is quite hardy and deciduous. Its home is the Middle and the Far East where it will survive very severe winters. Under favourable conditions it grows to 15 m with a trunk diameter of 0.5 m. Its head is often as wide as it is tall. The elegant, finely divided foliage is a most attractive rich green and folds up at night. The flowers in large white or pink pompoms are set on top of the leaves and are in evidence over the

Albizia julibrissin (silk tree) in flower in January.

summer months after which they are replaced by light-brown papery pods which hang on the branches for a long time.

Plant in a situation below the viewing point so flowers can be looked down on.

Increase is from seed and specimens are easily shifted.

Alnus

This is a genus of about 30, only some of which reach tree size, originating in the colder parts of the northern hemisphere and in South American mountain country. They are hardy, deciduous trees which usually grow in moist or wet soils, although certain of them also grow well on high land. The timbers of a few species are commercially valuable, that of red alder being the most useful. The genus could be used on New Zealand sites where it is difficult to establish other trees, eg areas subject to salt-water flooding.

Alnus is one of the fifteen or so non-leguminous genera which are nitrogen-fixing. Their root nodules fix atmospheric nitrogen at rates comparable to those of legumes such as clover. Male and female parts are separate on the same tree; males are in long hanging catkins produced in early winter; females are tiny erect catkins produced in spring which ripen to form green woody cones. This combination makes it a fascinating tree during the deciduous period.

Alders are natural colonisers of disturbed and infertile sites. The decay of their roots and litter, which breaks down rapidly and is comparatively high in nutrients, enhances the fertility of the soil particularly with regard to available nitrogen compounds; by

building up the organic fraction decay also improves soil structure.

Alders have been widely used for revegetation of infertile and industrially disturbed sites in Europe, U.S.A. and Japan. Black and grey alder are consistently among the best performing trees for revegetating acid mine spoil and tolerate soil pH as low as 3.5. In its homeland, Italian alder is planted to consolidate landslips.

In gully control plantings or woodlots alders may be interplanted with other trees such as Douglas fir or poplar. Soil amelioration by the alders greatly increases the growth rate of its associates. In forestry generally alders can fulfil successive roles as soil enricher, nurse and early crop.

Current interest is focussed on alders for horticultural shelterbelts. Whilst alders can be damaged if fully exposed in districts subject to strong winds, they are very suitable for internal east-west shelterbelts where their deciduous habit admits the winter sun. They respond well to being trimmed by leafing out and retaining their lower branches, and with their moderate growth rates trimming is required less frequently than for more vigorously growing species.

Owing to their nitrogen fixing ability, roots of alder shelterbelts compete less with economic crops for available nutrients.

A. cordata (Italian alder) is a fast-growing, handsome tree which reaches around 25 m. It is largely indifferent to soil type, growing in both boggy and dry soils. It is one of the best for ornamental planting, being notable for its bright green glistening foliage. Under water the timber is extremely durable and was used for the piles on which Venice was built.

A. glutinosa (black or common alder) is a hardy European species seldom exceeding 25 m in height and of somewhat bushy appearance. It grows best in wet areas along river banks, typical examples being seen beside the Waikato River. It can be used in situations subject to strong salt winds and occasional saltwater flooding, on wet clays and marshlands; it is sufficiently versatile to be used also for ornamental planting on dry land. The timber, which is warm and soft, is used for furniture, firewood and the manufacture of clogs, and is claimed to be extremely durable for any underwater purpose, traditionally being used for bridge piling in Europe.

A. incana (grey alder) and *A. rhombifolia* (white alder) are two species used in the U.S.A. for planting boggy areas and in stream beds to slow down the rush of water during floods. Neither of their woods has any value except as fuel. Both trees reach a height of 15-25 metres.

A. rubra (red alder) is a North American species inhabiting a coastal strip from northern British Columbia on the borders of Alaska to southern California. It can attain a height of 25-35 m, according to site. It is a vigorous grower, capable of yielding millable logs in about 30 years, its form being as a rule reasonably good, with a clean, tapering bole and narrow crown, the branches sometimes drooping. It grows naturally only within 80 km or so of the sea and where soils are moist and fertile, particularly favouring river banks and gullies. Trees growing in drier soils do not possess the same vigour nor do they grow to the same size. It flushes early in spring and is therefore unsuitable for areas where late frosts occur. The timber is light in weight and of fine texture, being used in America for many hardwood purposes, particularly turnery, furniture-making and veneering. In New Zealand small quantities have been milled from State forests where planting started in 1904.

Alders are propagated from seed which ripens in late autumn and should be sown in spring. The seedlings require light shade from direct sunlight for a month or two after striking. They transplant readily as either one- or two-year-olds.

Alnus glutinosa (black alder) on a river bank.

Alnus glutinosa (black alder) in winter.

Angophora

There are several *Angophora* species, all evergreen Australian natives closely related to Eucalyptus.

Angophora costata flowers in early January.

The uncommon *Angophora costata* near Tauranga.

A. costata (smooth barked apple gum, rusty gum) is the species most frequently seen in New Zealand. It is a handsome tree from New South Wales where it grows in both coastal and inland areas, often in poor and rocky soils. In these latter conditions the limbs of the tree often assume contorted shapes which, although verging on the grotesque, nevertheless leave an impression of gnarled and noble beauty. It can reach 25 m with a 20 m spread. The red coloured timber is not ground durable, but it is hard and extremely strong and is used for construction work above ground where exceptional strength is required.

Specimens of *A. costata* can be seen in warmer parts of the North Island invariably fulfilling the role of shade or ornamental tree. These specimens have clean, smooth stems and substantial, wide-spreading branches. The colour of the bole changes according to the season of the year. It is always smooth, but varies from whitish or grey to salmon or a rusty colour, and even at times assumes a mottled appearance. The young foliage is very beautiful, fiery red at first, then changing to rust colour, later to dark and glossy green. It is this foliage, cut in spring when the red colour is at its best, that meets with such ready sale as 'gum tips' from the flower stalls in Australian city streets.

Those seeking a large, evergreen shade tree of unusually handsome appearance will find *A. costata* a rewarding subject.

Propagation is from seed. The seedlings are frost tender at first, able to withstand temperatures of only -4 °C or so, but if nursed during the first winter they grow hardier with age. The tree will grow in any reasonable soil.

Angophora costata has fascinating bark which changes with the seasons.

Araucaria

There are about 14 *Araucaria* and as many, or slightly more, varieties. They are evergreen trees of the conifer family and are related to the New Zealand kauri. Native to South America, Australia and various Pacific islands, they yield softwoods of varying usefulness (those of Bunya pine and hoop pine being the most valuable) and are capable of growing to heights of 30-40 m.

A.araucana syn. *A.imbricata* (monkey puzzle tree) originates from Chile and Argentina where it grows at elevations up to 1 200 m. The hardiest of the *Araucarias*, it has thick, spirally arranged scale-like leaves which are sharp pointed. These grow on widely spaced branches which are slightly drooping at the bottom but upwards pointed on the higher parts of the tree. Once very popular in New Zealand,

although older trees tended to die off after severe droughts, it prefers a cool root run and should not be planted in very dry areas. Its common name derives from a remark made in 1834 by a prominent English lawyer who observed, when inspecting a specimen in Cornwall, that it would puzzle a monkey to climb it.

The tree will grow to 30 m or more with symmetrical form, in old age becoming flat-topped. Each spring it puts out four or five side branches; one authority, referring to the characteristic geometrical branching pattern, suggests that it must have been designed by an unimaginative engineer working for a hidebound government department. In its topmost branches the female tree bears large yellowish-brown cones resembling pineapples which eventually produce an edible seed. The timber is a useful general-purpose softwood, the heartwood having a pink tinge.

Araucaria araucana (monkey puzzle) in a country garden.

A. bidwillii (Bunya pine) comes from Australia. It grows to large size (30-45m) and like all Araucarias is of symmetrical form. The bole is usually straight and branchless, except when grown in the open. In its Queensland home it prefers moist soils of some fertility, but it will also grow in poor soils provided rainfall is adequate. It also produces an edible seed. The tree is fairly hardy and in New Zealand has been seen growing as far south as Cambridge where temperatures of -8 °C are sometimes recorded. The timber is a good milling subject and is used for building, flooring, joinery, etc. It is fairly soft and is not durable.

A. cunninghamii (hoop pine), another Australian species, is a very good milling softwood, much like Bunya pine. The wood product of the two trees is marketed by the timber trade under the name of Queensland pine and is in demand on account of uniform grain, toughness and strength. Uses to which these timbers are put range from matchwood and furniture making to the deckings of sheep trucks. Hoop pine is a handsome, tall-growing, clean-boled tree. It comes from the high rainfall coastal areas of northern New South Wales and Queensland and although it will grow over a wide range of soils, it is unfortunately extremely frost tender and would be likely to prosper only in warm, moist coastal localities in New Zealand. Healthy young saplings have been seen in the Gisborne area.

A. heterophylla (Norfolk Island pine) is the best known *Araucaria* in New Zealand. The tree is a fairly common feature of many North Island beach resorts. It grows best in sandy soils where in favourable conditions it can reach a height of up to 45 m. The young seedlings are frost tender and can be grown with

The striking form of *Araucaria bidwillii* (bunya pine).

safety only in warmer areas. Its branching habit is horizontal, its form symmetrical. The tree is able to stand exposure to strong salt winds without burning and is sometimes planted as windbreaks in northern coastal areas. Norfolk Island pine never seems to depart from the perpendicular; the tree is always symmetrical, no matter in what exposed situation it is grown. In strong winds its trunk and branches bend and lash but have a resilience which enables them to return once again to perfect positioning. This resilience is possibly due to an elastic outer bark. Little is known of the timber, but it is said to be useful to a limited degree.

All species can be grown from either seed or cuttings.

Many settlers planted *Araucaria heterophylla* (Norfolk Island pine) on the skyline.

Betula

Some of the birches — there are between 30 and 40 species, all deciduous — are regarded in other countries, especially in Scandinavia, as useful timber trees; they yield serviceable hardwoods which are used for flooring and for the manufacture of furniture. Birches are very hardy trees, most of them coming from cold latitudes. The more graceful and elegant species are widely used for ornamental planting, and it is almost exclusively in this role that they are seen in New Zealand. A copse of birches against a dark background is most effective. Those with the greatest aesthetic appeal are silver birch, paper birch and yellow birch.

B. lutea (yellow birch), a native of eastern North America, can grow to 25-30 m in most soils, either moist or dry. It carries a branchy top on a well defined central stem and its bark, while the tree is young, is smooth and of an attractive yellow-gold colour.

B. papyrifera (paper birch) is one of the large American species which can attain a height of up to 30 m in good conditions. In poor soils it may not exceed half that height. It is a fast-growing, hardy, but short-lived tree which grows in most soils, preferring moist and fertile loams. Its timber is hard, heavy, straight-grained and strong, and is used for spools and other turnery.

B. pendula (silver birch) comes from Europe and Asia

Minor and is regarded by many planters as the most beautiful of all deciduous trees. Its upright, silvery-white bole and slender drooping branchlets are as familiar to the townsman as to the farmer, for it enjoys universal popularity in suburban gardens and on farmlands. The species is very hardy and will grow in most soils, but has a preference for those of some fertility. It is not drought-resistant nor is it partial to tough or wet clays, but will attain a height of 15-20 m in conditions which suit it. It is naturally of graceful habit and provided it has congenial soils, plenty of light and adequate moisture, it will grow without training or pruning into a shapely tree of great distinction.

B. pubescens (white birch) is frequently accepted as silver birch, but it is definitely an inferior tree. It is common in the poor soils of the Scottish highlands and in the moister soils of the glens, but though its attractiveness is not denied, it does not possess the graciousness of the real silver birch. It can be distinguished from *B. pendula* by its more erect branching habit, more reddish bark and by its downy (or pubescent) young twigs, those of *B. pendula* being distinctly warty.

Birches are propagated from seed which should be sown, as soon as collected in autumn, in a seed-bed of coarse sand and barely covered with fine sieved earth mixed with sand.

Birches make splendid farm trees.

Brachychiton

Brachychiton acerifolium (flame tree) on a Northland property in January.

A young *Brachychiton populneum* (kurrajong) near Tauranga.

This Australian native was formerly listed as *Sterculia*, the name being derived from *stercus,* Latin for dung. The leaves and flowers of the genus have a foetid smell. Three species are of more than ordinary interest.

B. acerifolium (Illawarra flame tree) is a deciduous tree spectacular when in flower, as like most of the species it drops its leaves just before it becomes a mass of rich scarlet bell-shaped flowers hanging in panicles 30 cm long. Seedlings take about 30 years to flower but some grafted hybrids are earlier. The tree grows to 30 m but is slow to start in temperate zones. More suited to Northland and some East Coast areas, where summers are hot.

B. populneum (kurrajong) is the species most likely to be useful on farmlands. It is a handsome, sturdy evergreen which will grow to 10-20 m with a spreading, leafy crown on a short, squat bole. It is extensively planted in Australia as a shade, avenue or stock fodder tree. It will grow in most soils, including clays and limestones and is a noted drought-resister. Kurrajongs are cultivated systematically on many stations in central and western New South Wales as a stand-by feed tree in times of drought, but they do not seem to have been considered for this purpose in the troublesome drier areas of New Zealand. The foliage, which remains glossy green and succulent even in the driest and hottest summers, is highly nutritious. Occasional kurrajongs are seen, particularly in the Auckland, Waikato and Poverty Bay districts, but few farmers seem to have recognised their effectiveness as a landscape improver of shapely and handsome appearance. It can be grown with little trouble in almost any soil and in districts where temperatures go down to -8°C. The timber is of little or no commercial value.

B. rupestre (Queensland bottle tree) is well known by reason of its grotesquely swollen trunk; less well known is the nutritive value of its foliage. It is a semi-deciduous tree that grows 10-15 m in height, but its trunk can have a girth of 10 m, giving the appearance of a large wooden bottle. It is slow-growing and requires a warm climate.

Propagation of all species is from seed.

Callitris

The Australian cypress pines are attractive trees as the generic name (from the Greek *kalos*, meaning beautiful) implies. They are of special importance because of their ability to grow in very poor and dry soils and because of the resistance of their timbers to the attack of wood-destroying pests. There are about 20 species and two or three of these could probably be used in some of New Zealand's inland low-rainfall areas where difficulty is experienced in establishing other trees. Cypress pines cover wide areas in all Australian states. They yield timbers of considerable worth for both milling and fencing purposes. The growth habit of these evergreen trees is pyramidal so they make very pleasing ornamental specimens.

Species most likely to be of interest for farm planting include the following:

C.columellaris (coast cypress pine) is a tall and stately tree of some beauty. It grows usually in barren, sandy soils in coastal areas of lower Queensland and about the Northern Rivers district of New South Wales. It would be likely to grow only in warmer areas in New Zealand. It is slender-branched and of pyramidal habit and will attain a height of about 25 m. It will withstand some frost and can cope with wind. Many people regard the tree as Australia's most beautiful conifer.

C.glauca (white cypress pine) has a wide distribution throughout all Australian mainland states. It is an inland tree and it grows in sandy loams. In poor and very dry areas it is inclined to remain stunted, but in better soils and with reasonable rainfall it will reach a height of 30 m. It is of tall, stately and pyramidal form and is sometimes used for shelterbelts. Its timber is strong and ground durable. Along the basins of the Murray and Murrumbidgee rivers the tree is known as Murray River pine and there, pastoralists regard its timber as equal in ground durability to the best eucalypts. Locally grown seedlings have been undamaged by temperatures of -5 °C.

The seldom-seen *Callitris columellaris.*

Propagation is from seed which should be sown in open beds in the spring.

Calodendron

C.capense (Cape chestnut) is a handsome evergreen tree of about 15 m native to South Africa. It grows well in reasonably free soils that do not dry out unduly, but is unlikely to succeed in districts where winter temperatures fall below about -6 °C and even then it would require some protection in its early years. For those who have the conditions necessary for its successful cultivation it is a rewarding tree, usually of round-headed habit with a crown of dark green leaves and bearing, in spring, spectacular masses of rosy-lilac or flesh-coloured flowers. Many South Africans regard the Cape chestnut as the most beautiful of that country's native trees. In New Zealand specimens are known to be growing well in Marlborough and around Auckland and in some of the congenial coastal districts of both islands.

Propagation is from seeds or cuttings. The seeds take considerable time to germinate, usually about four months and sometimes much longer.

Calocedrus

This genus (formerly included in *libocedrus*) consists of shapely, evergreen conifers, closed related to *Thuyas* and somewhat resembling them. The timbers of the trees loosely termed 'cedars' have a fragrant odour and are strong and durable, useful for a variety of purposes.

C.decurrens (incense cedar) is the most important species from a timber point of view. It is a tall tree which can exceed 30 m in height, with a straight, tapering, widely buttressed bole. It has a narrow, columnar outline with erect branches and flattened branchlets of very dark green scale-like leaves. Native to some of the western states of the U.S.A., its soft, fragrant and extremely durable timber is used there for building purposes, fencing, furniture-making and pencil casings. It is a hardy tree which will grow in most soils, including clays; it prefers good well-drained loams with some moisture. Young trees of the species are often seen in New Zealand, mostly in parks and large gardens, but so far as is known, very little attempt has been made to grow them for timber production or for wind shelter purposes.

Propagation is from seed or from cuttings taken in the late autumn and struck in a cool, moist situation.

A group of young *Calocedrus decurrens* (incense cedar).

Carpinus

The early autumn foliage of *Carpinus betulus* (hornbeam) near Taihape.

Although there are more than 20 *Carpinus* species, only one of them is likely to be of use for farmlands planting in New Zealand.

C.betulus (common hornbeam) is a handsome, very hardy, round-headed little tree of about 15 m which could be useful in situations where a bigger tree is not wanted. It is wind-resistant and will grow in most soils, including clays that are not water-logged. It does not dislike limestone country and will tolerate salt winds. A deciduous tree, its leaves turn a rich autumn brown and sometimes stay on the tree for most of the winter. It is amenable to pruning and in England it is frequently used for hedging in heavy country. The wood is white, very hard, heavy and close-grained.

Propagation is from seed which ripens in autumn and should be sown as soon as possible after collection. It remains dormant during winter, germinating in spring.

Carya

The magnificent *Carya ovata x tomentosa* (hickory)
makes a splendid shade tree.

For some unknown reason the hickories, as *Carya* species are commonly known, appear to have been neglected in New Zealand; they are easily grown, and some of them produce heavy crops of edible nuts. There are about 22 species and all but one or two come from North America. Their timbers are hard, strong, tough, and resilient, being probably the best woods obtainable for tool handles and sports gear. There is little difference in the qualities of the timbers yielded by the various species and all are marketed under the common name of hickory. The sapwood has values equal to the heartwood but the timber is not ground durable. When grown in stands the trees develop long, slender boles clear of branches and with little crown; but most of them, when grown in the open, are luxuriantly foliaged, spreading in habit and shapely in form. They are deciduous and generally are slow growers. They make good specimen trees; if sweet nut species are used the economic gain to the planter can be considerable.

C. aquatica (water hickory) is a species which grows naturally in poor swampy country or on poor, wet flats; it is not as hardy as most hickories and would be likely to thrive only in warmer areas.

C. cordiformis (bitternut hickory or swamp hickory) thrives in low moist soil, near the borders of streams and swamps, but can also grow on drier uplands. In best conditions it can reach 35 m, growing more rapidly than the rest of the hickories. Its timber is somewhat inferior to the true hickories but is used for the same purposes. The tree can be identified by its striking characteristic of bright yellow winter buds.

C. glabra (pignut hickory) grows to 17-30 m and produces an inferior and virtually inedible nut. Its wood is the heaviest of all commercial hickories and is without equal for its shock-resisting qualities.

C. illinoensis (pecan) is a better nut-yielder and is also the largest of the hickories, but it can be grown only in comparatively frost-free areas. It grows naturally in moist but well-drained soils. There is growing interest in this tree in New Zealand and considerable research is under way to establish its commercial potential.

C. ovata (shagbark hickory) is easily grown for sweet nut production and is also a good timber tree. It grows best in good, moist soils and can reach a height of 20-25 m in these conditions. In poorer or drier soils it is likely to be smaller. It is hardy, grows naturally in country subject to heavy winter snowfalls, and in open situations makes a handsome ornamental tree with rich yellow autumn foliage.

C. tomentosa (mockernut hickory) grows to 20-30 m and can tolerate drier soils of good quality. Its nuts are large and edible, but the shells are very thick and the kernels disappointingly small. It is a notably foliaceous tree and its pleasantly fragrant leaves turn a rich yellow before falling in autumn. It can suffer frost damage.

Hickories are propagated from nuts which should be stratified in damp sand over winter and sown in early spring. To secure strong, healthy plants it is essential not to damage the abnormally long taproot which, in a small yearling plant only a few centimetres high, can be up to 1 metre long. It is therefore better to sow the nuts *in situ* or in long, narrow containers especially manufactured for the purpose.

Castanea

There are about ten Castanea species and although they are commonly called chestnuts (sweet or eating chestnuts) they have no botanical relationship to *Aesculus* species which are also known as chestnuts (horse chestnuts). The leaves of the latter are compound and consist of seven leaflets attached in radiating arrangement to the end of a long, stout stalk, whereas the leaves of *Castanea* are simple, long, oblong and pointed.

C. sativa (Spanish chestnut or sweet chestnut) is the species most commonly cultivated in New Zealand. It comes from Southern Europe from where it was introduced to Britain by the Romans. It is a shapely deciduous tree which can attain a height of 20-25 m with a short, stout bole and a widespreading crown of strong, semi-erect branches. It is very hardy and will grow in most soils except those with a high lime content. The fruits or nuts are edible and in some countries they are consumed with relish after being roasted. In France, a special cultivator (*C. sativa* 'Gros Merle') is grown for the abundant crops of nuts it produces. The tree is a favourite subject for shade planting on many New Zealand farmlands. There is growing interest in the establishment of grafted chestnuts for commercial cropping, and evaluation of a variety of trees is taking place with a view to establishing an export market for the nuts.

The timber is a valuable one, being ground durable. In Europe it is coppiced to provide poles. The timber resembles oak in appearance but is lighter and more easily worked. It is used for a wide range of purposes including furniture, coffins, fence palings and casks.

Other chestnuts which yield edible nuts are *C. mollissima* (Chinese chestnut) and *C. crenata* (Japanese chestnut). The American chestnut *(C. dentata)* grows to a large size and yields a timber of some value, but the original stands have largely been wiped out by chestnut blight.

Sweet chestnuts are easily propagated from their nuts which should be gathered in autumn when ripe and sown stratified, fairly deep in friable soil in late winter. They should be grafted or budded to ensure production of a known nut quality.

A widespreading *Castanea sativa* (Spanish chestnut) on a Waikato farm.

Casuarina

The *Casuarinas,* which are evergreen, come mostly from Australia where they are known as 'sheoaks'. The double-barrelled colloquial name refers to the similarity of most of their timbers to the timber of the English oak, and to the peculiar sound produced by a high wind passing through the needle-like foliage.

Sheoaks are of medium size and usually of graceful and decorative appearance. They yield timbers that are hard, moderately strong, tough and handsome and which are used for cabinet, turnery and furniture work. Most of these timbers have an 'oak' figure, the medullary rays being pronounced. They make excellent fuelwood and in the past were extensively used in bakers' ovens.

It is unlikely that sheoaks will be planted to any significant extent in New Zealand for farm timber production, but they will continue to be grown for wind shelter and for ornamental and shade purposes. Some species could be useful for cultivation in inland areas where dry, sandy or poor clay soils make it difficult to establish other trees.

C. cristata is one of the most attractive of the she oaks. It is an inland species which grows best in good soils containing lime; it dislikes clays and usually reaches about 20 m with a clean, cylindrical bole and stiffly erect branches. Only experiment would determine the climatic limits of this tree in New Zealand, but it is suggested that it would tolerate fairly cold conditions. The timber is exceptionally handsome, hard, heavy, close-grained and completely different from that of other she oaks, resembling walnut rather than oak. It is deep reddish-brown in colour and is used for the manufacture of high-quality furniture.

C. cunninghamiana (river sheoak) is the largest tree of the genus. Its height varies from about 17-20 m according to soil and moisture conditions. It grows best in deep, free soils where its roots have access to water, and in these conditions it will develop into a large and exceedingly handsome tree. In its native home it is confined to river banks and river flats, but under cultivation elsewhere it has demonstrated an

Casuarina cunninghamiana (river sheoak) growing in peat.

Casuarina glauca (swamp sheoak) makes a fine golf course tree.

Casuarina torulosa (forest sheoak) growing well at the top of a blackberry-infested gully.

ability to grow (though not so exuberantly) in drier conditions provided the soil is free. It has also shown it can grow well in peat soils. The species is hardy and can endure either cold or warm temperatures in coastal or inland localities. Of handsome aspect, with pendulous branchlets, it is frequently used for shelter, ornament or shade. Its pale coloured timber is hard, strong and durable. It is now being extensively planted for quick shelter for horticultural use and when trimmed it can be formed into a very narrow hedge.

C. equisetifolia var. *incana* (beach sheoak) is a medium-sized tree which, in its natural home along the coastline of northern New South Wales and Queensland, is often found growing right at the water's edge, defying the salt-laden ocean winds. It grows to about 20 m with wide-spreading and pendulous branches. Its reddish-pink timber is hard and fine-grained, but of doubtful worth, except as a first class fuel. The value of the tree lies in its ability to grow in difficult coastal conditions.

C. glauca (swamp sheoak) grows to about 17-20 m, usually developing a shapely form with a reasonably good bole and an erect branching system commencing low down on the tree. It is found naturally on tidal areas and in river swamps but is a very adaptable species. This is a tree that could be employed in low-lying coastal areas either for timber production or for shelter purposes. Its brownish timber is very

hard and close-grained and is used for furniture making and veneering.

C. stricta (drooping sheoak) will grow in dry areas where it forms a tree up to 15 m. It has dense dark green pendulous branches. In spring the male tree is most striking, covered with coppery golden pollen. It could be grown more often in areas where other species are hard to establish.

C. torulosa (forest sheoak) is a hardy tree that will grow in poor and light soils or in good soils in coastal or inland areas, reaching a height of 15-25 m, the greater height being attained in good soils. In parts of its natural home it grows on heavy clays. The species has an erect branching habit with graceful, drooping foliage. Its red coloured timber is of good quality and is used for cabinet and veneer work.

Another species that could be grown in inland areas in dry soils or poor clays is *C. luehmannii*, (bull sheoak or bull oak). It grows to about 16 m and yields good serviceable timber. *C. suberosa* (coast sheoak) will grow in coastal or inland areas and is equally at home in cold or warm localities. Its brownish timber has little commercial value but the tree could be useful for clothing poor or sandy areas where better trees are difficult or impossible to grow.

Propagation of all species is from seed, which should be grown in spring. The seed is contained in cones which ripen in late summer or autumn.

Catalpa

The *Catalpas* are hardy, moisture loving, deciduous trees. There are several species but the two most common are those native to North America. (The name is a Cherokee Indian word adopted by the early settlers.) They are picturesque trees with large decorative leaves and conspicuous flower-clusters, which are followed by long, slender, cylindrical pods containing many seeds each having a tuft of white hair at the end. Like most large-leaved trees they prefer a sheltered site.

C.bignonioides (Southern catalpa or bean tree) is a wide-spreading tree with a roundish top, growing to 15 m with a clean straight trunk. It bears conspicuous white trumpet-shaped flowers, spotted with yellow and purple, in panicles at the ends of the branchlets. There is a close resemblance between this and *C.speciosa* and it is almost impossible to distinguish between them in the seedling stage. This difficulty has led to the distribution of its seed in the belief that it was *C.speciosa*. The tree needs good loamy soil to make satisfactory growth. *C.bignoioides* 'Aurea' has gold leaves and is one of the most attractive yellow-foliaged trees.) It has been commonly believed that the timber from this species is worthless. It also seems that there is some confusion over the taxonomy of the New Zealand material.

C.ovata (yellow catalpa) is a Chinese species which grows to 10 m on a straight bole with wide-spaced branches. The yellowish flowers are smaller than the other two species mentioned and open later in the season. It responds readily to good soil and moisture conditions. No information on its timber qualities has been found.

C.speciosa (Northern or hardy catalpa) has been cultivated in New Zealand for at least 100 years and was known to have been grown near Hamilton where it succumbed to frost. It was also extensively planted (2 million trees) by the Forest Service in the Rotorua district about 70 years ago, but again it is believed to have failed because of frost. There is however reason to believe that this tenderness can be overcome by

Catalpa bignonioides (bean tree) shading stockyards and screening an ugly shed.

Flowers of *Catalpa bignonioides* (bean tree) in January.

clonal selection since the tree grows satisfactorily in Kew Gardens; in the Waikato, 3-year-old trees survived temperatures of -8 °C in 1982. It is probably late, rather than winter frosts that do the damage.

A larger tree than *C. bignonioides*, it is not so graceful in form. Grown in the open the trunk is usually short and crooked, the crown broad and spreading with thick scraggy branches. In rich bottomland soils it can grow to 30 m; it has trumpet-shaped flowers similar to *C. bignonioides* but only faintly spotted with purple. The seed pods are 30-45 cm long and 1.5 cm across. The tree does best in moist loamy soils and is of interest to farmers because it produces a very ground-durable timber which is suitable for fence posts. Its tendency to branch out must be curbed by close planting and any side branches must be pruned off. Such branching will often occur when the leading shoot is killed by frost. As this happens only when the trees are young an alternative is to allow the trees to grow unpruned for three or four years and then cut them off close to the ground in early spring. New coppicing shoots will grow over 2 m in a year if the site is a suitable one.

The timber, which must be well dried before use, is coarse-grained and soft. The bark is reputed to be unpalatable to most animals including opossums and the foliage only slightly palatable for a short period after bud burst.

Catalpas are usually grown from seed, but cuttings will grow up to 40 cm in the first year provided they have very moist conditions to strike and grow.

A 3 year old *Catalpa speciosa*.

Cedrus

There are four true cedars, three of them being readily available to planters in this country. They are long-lived, handsome evergreen conifers growing to large size with spreading, horizontal branches. Their timbers are fragrant and they are durable. They can be used for various carpentry and cabinet purposes and also for ground work. The trees grow best in good deep loams, but any reasonable soil is suitable provided drainage is good. They are hardy mountain dwellers which can withstand severe winter conditions. When cedars are employed for avenue, ornamental or shade purposes they should be given plenty of room to enable them to develop their true magnificence.

The pyramidal *Cedrus atlantica* (Atlas cedar).

A fine row of *Cedrus deodara* (Himalayan cedar) near Cheviot.

C. atlantica (Atlas cedar) comes from the Atlas Mountains in Algeria and Morocco. It is a large, majestic, spreading tree reaching a height in excess of 30 m, not unlike the deodar in general appearance but having a stiffer, more angular look. It is resistant to cold and does best in moderately good, well-drained soils, but is a slow grower. Its variety 'glauca' has attractive silvery-blue foliage. The timber is durable and is useful for milling into general purpose timber.

C. deodara (deodar or Himalayan cedar) comes from the mountains of Afghanistan and the northwest Himalayas. It is a handsome and hardy tree which does best in good, deep soils. It will also grow

Cedrus atlantica glauca.

Foliage and cones of *Cedrus atlantica* glauca.

in light, sandy soils or in friable clays, provided drainage is good. It grows up to 25 m with a spread of 12 m and has a graceful, pyramidal shape with pendulous branches, especially in its younger years, and a distinguishing drooping leader. Its foliage is somewhat paler than that of either *C.libani* or *C.atlantica*. In congenial conditions it can attain a height well over 30 m. Its timber is strongly scented and ground durable.

C.libani (cedar of Lebanon) has a special appeal to many planters because of its association with the Holy Land and the scriptures. The tree comes from Asia Minor and the mountains of Lebanon. It was from the fragrant durable wood of this species that King Solomon built his temple and the adjoining palace, as well as a house for his wife, who was the Pharoah's daughter. The forests were once very extensive but could not survive the exploitation of King Solomon and King Hiram of Tyre. To assist Hiram's slave army, Solomon is alleged to have conscripted 30 000 Israelites and 150 000 slaves together with 3 300 supervisors, all of whom were put to cutting down the forests: today only a few remnants remain. It is a stately tree with handsome, spreading horizontal branches and with age usually develops a flattened top. It can grow up to 35 m with a girth of 16 m. Cedar of Lebanon will grow in most soils so long as they are not too wet and heavy, but it does best in good deep loams. It will not tolerate bad drainage. Once established, it will endure dry conditions in low rainfall areas. Its timber is rather coarse, but durable.

A great number of timbers are loosely known as 'cedars' in the timber trade. The trees from which most of these timbers come are not true cedars. They are included in the genera *Cedrela, Juniperus, Thuya,*

Cedrus libani (Lebanon cedar) on a hilltop near Hamilton.

Cryptomeria, Libocedrus, Calocedrus, Cupressus and *Chamaecyparis.*

Cedars are propagated from seed or from cuttings. Seed should be sown as soon as possible after collection, otherwise it is liable to deteriorate.

Chamaecyparis

Chamaecyparis is a small genus of evergreen conifers, mostly with flattened and spreading branching systems which make them suitable for employment as shelterbelt trees. They grow best in slightly moist but well-drained soils. They are hardy and wind-firm. The two most important farm species are *C.lawsoniana* and *C.nootkatensis*, although dozens of cultivars have been propagated from this genus, covering a wide range of sizes, shapes and colours.

C.lawsoniana (Lawson cypress or Port Orford cedar) was first planted in New Zealand over a century ago and is one of the most valuable introduced wind shelter trees. The many kilometres of shelterbelts planted over widespread areas pay tribute to its worth. Easily grown, easily handled and once established, growing with great vigour, it branches naturally close to the ground and if properly tended makes a very dense wind barrier. It grows best in good, well-drained loams in high rainfall areas, disliking overdry conditions, salt winds and wet soils. It is hardy and will withstand severe frosts. Native to Oregon, U.S.A., it grows there as a timber tree, sometimes reaching heights of 60 m. Its scented wood is milled under the name of white cedar or Port Orford cedar and is durable and easily worked. Little is known of locally grown timber and although claims for ground durability have been made, these have proved difficult to assess. Logs have been milled into satisfactory gate timber and into rails and scantlings. Tests on 30-50-year-old trees from different sites show very little variation in log material. Indications are that New Zealand-grown trees will produce timber similar in density to that grown in U.S.A.

Unfortunately, in recent years Lawson cypress has in many localities suffered from a canker disease which has caused heavy mortality. It is doubtful if there is a single shelterbelt in some areas of the Waikato — and there are scores of such belts, for the tree was a popular one — which is not affected to a more-or-less serious extent. There does not appear to be any effective means of countering this trouble so any farmer intending to plant the tree should first seek expert local advice.

It is the most satisfactory timber for wooden arrows, about 20 million of these being produced annually in U.S.A. It is also used for boatbuilding, canoe paddles, cabinet work, venetian blinds and matchsticks.

C.nootkatensis (Nootka cypress) is a tree similar in general appearance and habit to Lawson cypress, but of somewhat smaller size, seldom exceeding 30m in height and with a marked drooping of its branches. It comes from British Columbia and Alaska where it grows within the influence of the sea. Under cultivation, it responds best to good moist soils, is slow-growing and long-lived. Its timber is yellow, hard, close-grained, durable and is used for similar purposes to Lawson cypress. The pleasing pyramidal shape of the tree makes it a good subject for ornamental planting. So far as is known, it has not been attacked by canker.

C.thyoides (white cypress) comes from eastern U.S.A., where it grows in swamps near the coast. In its natural state it can reach 30m but 15m is a good height for New Zealand. It will grow in almost any soil but is slow on peat. Its timber is very durable and light, and because the trunk is straight and free from limbs it has been extensively used for power poles in U.S.A.

These trees are usually propagated from seed but seedlings, especially of the species *C.lawsoniana*, almost always show evidence of cross-pollination or departure from type. If uniform young plants are required, it is therefore better to propagate from cuttings which are easily rooted in autumn.

A healthy *Chamaecyparis lawsoniana* (Lawson cypress, Port Orford cedar).

Chamaecyparis nootkatensis (Nootka cypress) near Taihape.

Cinnamomum

The laurel family, of which *Cinnamomum* is a genus, provides a wide range of products in the fields of oils, perfumes and drugs. There are more than 1000 members, about 30 of them being *Cinnamomum* species.

C. camphora (camphor laurel) is grown in the warmer areas of New Zealand mostly on account of its ornamental appeal; it is a delight to the eye in every season. Some trees are known to have been milled and these have yielded highly scented woods for chests and cabinet-making. The scent from true camphorwood will last hundreds of years, but as the timber is now scarce the inferior *C. zeylanicum* is often substituted in modern chests and only a small portion of the genuine camphorwood is used to give a modicum of scent. The tree originates in China, Formosa and Japan and is the source of commercial camphor, which is removed from the bark after the tree is over 50 years old.

Camphor has been used as a charm hung around the neck to ward off plagues, and in ointment for relieving muscle pains. So highly was it valued that capital punishment was once the penalty for anyone cutting down such a tree. It is usually of compact form, evergreen, and growing up to 20 m on a squat bole with a rounded head of soft, glossy, light-green foliage tinged with yellow, although spring foliage can be pink, red or bronze. It is somewhat slow-growing, but is wind resistant and will tolerate a fair amount of saline exposure. It prefers well-drained soils that do not dry out unduly. Until it is well established, it will not survive temperatures less than -5 °C. The tree is a useful shade subject for coastal localities.

Propagation is from seed, which should be sown in early spring, or from cuttings taken in late autumn.

A young *Cinnamomum camphora* on a Whangarei sheep farm.

Corylus

Although *C. avellana* does not qualify, so far as size is concerned, as a farm tree, it yields a useful product in the form of edible nuts and therefore justifies itself as a potential revenue earner.

It is a hardy many-stemmed little deciduous tree usually known as hazelnut, or filbert in U.S.A. It comes from Europe and will grow to about 5 m in most soils, but has a decided preference for those that are fertile and well-drained. It bears edible nuts, provided it has a pollinator, and its roundish leaves turn an attractive yellow in autumn.

In England hazel is frequently used as a hedging plant and in this role it develops a dense bushiness which creates effective shelter. But if the tree is to be grown for the production of edible nuts on a commercial basis then good shelter is necessary. The New Zealand Tree Crops Association is evaluating a number of varieties for yield and quality and is also trying to establish which pollinators are the most suitable.

Propagation is from seed, grafting or suckers. Advice on latest research results should be obtained before planting on any scale.

Cryptomeria

Cryptomeria is a genus of evergreen conifers of which *C.japonica* (Japanese cedar) is the only known species. The tree is a native of Japan but is also found in some parts of China. In the former country it grows to large size and is a tree of considerable economic importance, generally regarded as Japan's most valuable timber yielder. The reddish, coarse-grained wood is used for all building purposes and for furniture making. The tree lends itself to decorative planting the *Cryptomeria* avenues of Japan being world-famous for their majestic beauty.

In New Zealand, stately Japanese cedars are frequently seen in the surroundings of some of the older established homes and in parks and public gardens. They are also seen as windbreaks and are now being used extensively for horticultural shelterbelts. Only occasionally are they found in plantations grown for timber. The tree is a very beautiful one which can be used effectively for avenue or group planting on many farmlands.

The species is a tall-growing, tapering tree of low-branching habit in its earlier years, later developing a shaft-like bole. It can grow in cold conditions and thrives in districts where winter temperatures reach -11°C. It does best in good, moist soils and in reasonably sheltered situations but will grow, though not so

A fine pair of *Cryptomeria japonica* (Japanese cedar) in the Reefton Domain.

Cryptomeria japonica 'Elegans' growing on a peat golf course.

vigorously, in most other soils provided rainfall is adequate. It is showing great promise in heavy clays in northern New Zealand and is proving reasonably

tolerant to salt winds. The tree does not object to shade or underplanting. As a shelterbelt subject it is quite satisfactory as long as it retains its lower branches. Just how long these lower branches will persist it is difficult to say, but even in New Zealand, trees which cannot be more than 60 years of age have developed the clean, shaft-like boles characteristic of the older Japanese trees.

A cultivar named 'Elegans', growing to about 15-17m, is quite unlike the species, being bushy with beautiful foliage which turns a reddish-bronze colour in autumn and back to green again in the spring. Unfortunately in warmer districts the autumn foliage can be disfigured by attacks from thrips.

Propagation is from seed or from cuttings. Cones ripen in late autumn and seed should be sown as soon as possible after collecting. Cuttings taken in early autumn root readily.

x Cupressocyparis

x *C.leylandii* (Leyland cypress) is a hybrid or cross between *Cupressus macrocarpa* and *Chamaecyparis nootkatensis*. It is often, but erroneously, called *Cupressus leylandii*.

First bred in Wales late last century, the tree has gained a great reputation in England for general hardiness and ability to withstand very cold conditions. It is an attractive evergreen conifer, a vigorous and erect grower, with feathery foliage resembling that of *Chamaecyparis nootkatensis* borne on compact, wide-angled branchlets. It grows rapidly in most conditions (including moist soils) and it is much hardier than any *Cupressus* species. In the colder parts of England it is being used as a hedging plant as it there displays an ability to stand regular clipping.

The timber has not yet been fully evaluated but in view of the wood qualities of the parents, is likely to be valuable. The tree should be a useful one for farm shelter and timber purposes, especially in cold areas. Its handsome form and attractive foliage make it a good subject for ornamental or specimen planting.

A number of trials have been laid down throughout New Zealand, these including clones of Haggerston Grey, Naylor's Blue and the more widely known Leighton Green. A regular evaluation is taking place so planters should refer to the Forest Service for latest information. It is known that in the Waikato at least the tree is subject to canker.

Propagation is best from cuttings; taken in autumn they root readily, but if grown from seed the plant may not come true to type.

x *Cupressocyparis leylandii* (Leyland cypress) on a sheep-grazed hillside.

Cupressus

The *Cupressus* genus comprises a dozen species and as many more varieties. They are evergreen conifers, mostly of low-branching habit, important as timber yielders and as shelter trees. Some grow to very large size and are of handsome form and these are commonly used as ornamental subjects. Many show a great variation of type within the species, making seed collection something of a gamble. In some countries, notably in the U.S.A., certain *Cupressus* species have been attacked by a canker disease for which there appears to be no effective counter, and this disease has appeared in New Zealand. Planters would be wise to seek the advice of the Forest Service before committing themselves to the considerable expenditure involved in establishing such species as *C.macrocarpa*. It is not suggested that the species should be avoided, but it would be wiser (and cheaper) to find out beforehand exactly what the position is in any particular locality. Cupressus species most likely to be of use include the following:

C.arizonica (Arizona cypress) is a good shelterbelt tree. It grows to medium height only — from 17-20 m —and can withstand warm or cold temperatures and wet or dry conditions. The foliage is a conspicuous blue-green and it sometimes has an offensive smell, especially when bruised. It is widely employed in South Africa for hedges, windbreaks and shelter. As far as is known, canker has not been reported as attacking the species. Considerable variation in types occurs and seed sources are therefore important. The wood which is soft and lightweight is durable and can be used for posts and general farm use. *C.glabra*, often mistaken for *C.arizonica*, has a much greyer foliage with an attractive peeling red bark and will withstand drought and high temperatures.

C.benthamii is a variety of *C.lusitanica*. In the past many seedlings under this name have been sold for use in shelterbelts in country too wet for the successful establishment of other species. It is doubtful if they were true to type and botanists are of the opinion that the name should no longer be used in New Zealand.

C.lusitanica (Mexican cypress), a tree with several good varieties, will grow to a height of about 30m in

Foliage and fruit of *Cupressus arizonica* (Arizona cypress) in December.

127

An old *Cupressus sempervirens* (Mediterranean cypress)
by a Wairarapa road.

suitable conditions. It is very hardy, will thrive in any reasonable soil, dislikes salt winds and in Mexico inhabits upland country. It is wide-branching in habit and makes a good shade tree. The foliage is usually an attractive light green.

Some re-evaluation of this species is now being undertaken by the Forest Service as it has advantages over *C.macrocarpa* — in particular, canker has only a minor effect. It has paler timber (can be stained) which is moderately durable. It is generally lighter branching and has superior stem form in the absence of the fluting common to *C.macrocarpa*.

C.macrocarpa (Monterey cypress, or macrocarpa) is one of the most important timber trees introduced to New Zealand where it was first planted (at Mt Peel Station) in 1864. Its common name comes from its natural habitat of Monterey Bay on the coast of California, where it occupies a narrow strip just 5km long — the smallest natural habitat of any American conifer. (It is of interest to note that the mainstay of New Zealand exotic forestry, *Pinus radiata*, originates from the same area, where it is known as Monterey pine.) The species has grown remarkably well as a timber and shelter tree in many localities. It has shown an ability to thrive in most climatic conditions where soils are reasonably good and free. It has also shown high resistance to salt winds and has been widely employed in coastal planting. Canker disease is a problem in some districts. Grown individually, it branches very strongly and develops a wide-spreading crown, but has nevertheless produced some excellent timber when spaced at proper intervals in managed plantations where the trees make straight, clean boles.

Round and sawn timber from farm woodlots and shelter trees is widely used for posts and rails. The reddish heartwood forms early and a good percentage is present in logs from older trees. Natural round branchwood from old trees has proved durable in the ground, a service life of 20-25 years being usual. Logs are easily sawn and timber is moderately light, hard, strong and fissile, with a close-grained, even texture. It seasons well and the heartwood is stable. A good all-round building timber, it is used for framing, flooring and weather-boarding, for joinery, and more recently as a substitute for kauri in the boat-building industry and for decorative panelling.

The tree has great potential but only latterly has there been extensive appreciation of its timber qualities. Growers should however pay careful attention to the seed source as seed is very variable; good strains without fluted boles are essential for establishment of woodlots or shelterbelts which will yield highest quality timber. Eating of the foliage has long been held responsible for abortions in cows, though many foresters feel there is inadequate evidence for this belief.

C. sempervirens (Mediterranean cypress) is a hardy tree which will grow to well over 30 m, assuming a spreading habit in the process. It will thrive in most soils and withstand dry conditions. Its timber is brownish, fragrant and regarded as durable and suitable for milling. There is a cultivar 'Stricta'(Italian cypress) which we frequently see in this country as a formal ornamental tree for street and avenue planting. This variety is tall-growing and of columnar habit, its erect branches clinging closely to the bole of the tree. In Israel and parts of Europe it is used extensively as a shelter tree to counter hot, drying winds. It could be used in many areas in New Zealand with good effect for cutting off cold westerlies. When employed for this purpose it should be spaced at about one metre intervals. The virtue of upright branch growth is that a single line of these trees would not normally exceed 1-1.5m in width, so that no fencing adjustment subsequent to

planting is necessary. The tree is subject to canker and can be increased true to type only through vegetative propagation; seedlings may revert to wild types. The timber is fragrant and fine-textured and was used in the gates of Constantinople and the massive doors of St Peter's Cathedral in Rome.

C. torulosa (Bhutan cypress) is a large, hardy and dependable tree which comes from limestone country in the Himalayas. It is usually of tall (20 m) pyramidal outline with short horizontal or drooping branchlets and makes a handsome ornamental specimen, usually of symmetrical form. Its timber is hard and close-grained, reputed to be worth milling and durable in the ground. In spite of its native environment it will grow in a variety of conditions including peat.

Propagation of *Cupressus* species is by seed, but it is emphasised that seedlings are very variable and often of poor type, bearing little resemblance to the form of the parent.

A well-tended *Cupressus macrocarpa* woodlot near Bulls, aged 19.

Cupressus torulosa (Bhutan cypress) makes a shapely golf-course tree.

Erythrina

Fine roadside specimens of *Erythrina crista-galli* (coral tree) in January.

A genus of about 30, the majority of which are inappropriate for farm planting, mostly from tropical areas with some hardier species from South Africa.

E.caffra (coral tree) is a native of South Africa. It grows to more than 20m in its own country but in New Zealand it is more likely to be about 7-10m. It is a deciduous species which becomes a round-headed spreading tree, with big clusters of scarlet cockscomb flowers in spring giving a whiskery appearance. These are produced on angular bare branches with wicked thorns which disappear as the wood matures. The species has a spread half as wide again as its height and so makes a magnificent shade tree. Like the rest of the genus a sunny hot site is best in areas where temperatures are above -5°C in winter.

Erythrina variegata var. *orientalis* (syn. *E. indica*) makes a farm shade tree in Northland.

E. crista-galli (coral tree) only marginally qualifies for inclusion in this book as it is only an exceptionally large specimen that would reach 6 m. It is a deciduous tree from Brazil and is often seen in New Zealand. Until it develops into a tree it sends up many new branches each season. Where frosts do not exceed -10°C a branch will usually stay green and eventually develop into a gnarled trunk, which is the source of the next year's growth. Flowering is variable, ranging from early to late summer. They are bright red and pea-shaped, arranged in stiff columns 20-60 cm long, and make a bright splash of colour when situated in an open full-sun position. These specimens have rather unpleasant thorns and will thrive in most soils which are well drained. *E. crista-galli* is the hardiest of the genus.

E. variegata var. orientalis is often known as *E. indica*, a familiar sight in warmer areas of the North Island but it is not seen where temperatures fall below -5°C. It grows into a large spreading tree with an attractive rounded head and will reach about 9 m. Large bright green leaves follow the heads of scarlet flowers which appear during the spring. Unlike many other *Erythrinas* this tree has no prickles. It is a good deciduous shade tree, sometimes seen as a single specimen in paddocks or yards where it is particularly suitable for such use.

The timbers of this genus are of poor quality, being very light and brittle. The species can be reproduced from seed or from spring cuttings taken with a heel.

The silhouette of *Erythrina crista-galli* (coral tree) in winter.

Eucalyptus

This is by far the most important genus of the Australian forest, its members covering 95 percent of the forest area. Since the genus was named in 1788 more than 500 species have been identified and there are numerous hybrids, both natural and artificial. Ranging from semi-arid sand plains to the snowline, the evergreen eucalypts have evolved to handle Australian conditions. They range in size from dwarf mallees only a metre high to the giant members of the mountain ash group and provide timber for all purposes with a great range of characteristics. The very durable properties of some of these hardwoods are well recognised in New Zealand which has imported large volumes for use as bridge timbers, railway sleepers, wharf piles and telephone poles. Trees of the genus have other virtues — oils are extracted from the leaves, tannin from the bark and nectar from the flowers. The wood is pulped for paper and some species are now being grown in New Zealand especially for that purpose. They provide shade and shelter and offer a handsome addition to the beauty of the landscape.

The genus is now grown extensively throughout the world with over a hundred different species in New Zealand alone. Insufficient care has been given in the past to suitable site selection with the result that there have been many disappointments when trees have been planted on unsuitable soils or in climatic conditions where they have had no hope of growing successfully. Native and introduced insects have also severely attacked particular species so that their future planting would be unwise. It therefore behoves the planter to make some effort to ensure that the chosen eucalypt will find the site an acceptable one. However, because of their versatility and the large number of species available the planter can be assured that there will without doubt be at least one eucalypt which will thrive in the selected conditions.

A number of eucalypts are potentially suitable for production of timber for special purposes and can thus serve as long-term replacements for the dwindling resource of indigenous hardwoods. The Forest Research Institute has carried out a study resulting in recommendations set out in the Forest Service policy statement Exotic Special Purpose Species (see Appendix 1).

Most eucalypts have several conspicuously different types of foliage. Soft, variously shaped juvenile leaves are found on seedlings, saplings and coppice growth, and these are sometimes opposite. There is occasionally an intermediate form of leaf, but in the tougher adult form leaves are usually alternate.

Identification of eucalypts should be attempted only with caution, a single characteristic being usually insufficient for the purpose. Features normally required are the general size and form of the tree, the nature of the bark on the trunk and branches, adult and juvenile leaf forms, and structure of flowers, buds and fruit. Having acquired all those details together with some good reference works the amateur tree grower (and many professionals too) can still find accurate identification a formidable task.

The choice of which species to include in this book has not been easy and was finally a subjective one. However all important species recommended in the Forest Service policy statement have been included and these are marked with an asterisk. In addition, samples of eucalypts suitable for shade, landscaping, shelter, flowers and other useful purposes covering a wide range of site conditions have been included.

Propagation of all eucalypts is from seed, but with such a large number of species it is unwise to generalise on the particular methods of handling the seeds and seedlings.

(Note: In Australia the multiplicity of common names for *Eucalyptus* species has caused much confusion. This can be avoided if only botanical names are used. We do not wish to add to the confusion so no common names are given. The timber of the eucalypts also attracts a variety of trade names, eg timber from *E. regnans* and *E. delegatensis* are both sold as Tasmanian oak and Australian oak. We know of one wood-turner in New Zealand who will have nothing to do with 'gum' but is happily buying Tasmanian oak!)

*E. botryoides comes from a narrow coastal belt of southern New South Wales and East Gippsland in Victoria. It was first planted in New Zealand in 1890, but plantings of significance were commenced in the 1920s. On a favourable site the tree will grow to 30-40 m with a diameter of over one metre and a good straight trunk. Its ability to withstand strong saline winds on open coastal locations is one of its main attributes, but in such situations it is likely to have more branches with a poorly defined main stem. It will grow in a wide range of soil types including raw peat, wet swamps and drier sites, and even in sand provided rainfall is adequate. It can withstand temperature of -8° C.

Left: A thinned and self pruned stand of *E. delegatensis.*

The furrowed bark is a feature of mature *E. botryoides*.

E. cinerea provides quick screening for a farm shed.

The timber is reddish brown and coarse- to medium-textured. It is hard, strong and durable and can be used in the round or sawn for general construction work; although of attractive appearance it is rather heavy for furniture. The sapwood rots quickly but the heartwood is useful for posts.

The seedlings handle easily and this species will coppice from stumps.

E.cinerea comes mainly from the tablelands of New South Wales where summers are not extreme and frosts are common. Its principal value is as an ornamental tree and known as the silver dollar gum it has been widely planted in this country. The stem-clasping glaucous-blue leaves are quite distinctively different from most eucalypts and the young grey-blue shoots at the ends of branchlets are very beautiful.

Reaching only a moderate size in its native areas, it seems well suited to New Zealand conditions, growing very rapidly to 15m. This ability has made it a mixed blessing to new home owners wanting to overcome the starkness of a bare section and suddenly realising that they have a tree which is far taller than the house, drops leaves into the gutters and interferes with overhead wires and neighbours' views.

It is essentially a tree requiring room to grow and expand which it will do on most soils, and is well worth growing amongst dark-green-leaved trees where it provides an interesting contrast. If the tree is cut back close to ground level in the spring it will produce new growths bearing the distinctive juvenile foliage. The timber is of negligible value.

E.cladocalyx is a South Australian species with palatable foliage readily eaten by stock. It is a eucalypt which has great versatility both in its usefulness and its tolerance of sites. It does well in most conditions and can cope with limestone country. It has grown to large dimensions (30m high) in Poverty Bay, Hawkes Bay, Manawatu and Wairarapa. It will however remain a rather small tree on a dry site. It usually has a trunk of straight form with the crown open because foliage is concentrated at the ends of branches. It is a good farm tree which can be used for shelter and ornamental planting and will produce poles when grown in plantations. The wood is pale yellow-brown with fine uniform texture. It is hard, moderately strong and moderately durable and is a good all-purpose timber. Young seedlings cannot tolerate temperatures below -4°C but are out of danger after the first year.

Cattle grazing under *E. botryoides* aged 3½ years.

E.delegatensis, previously known as *E.gigantea*, is often found in farm woodlots. It is the most commonly planted eucalypt in State Forests in New Zealand. In its native Victoria, south New South Wales and Tasmania it grows right up to the snowline where it attains a height of 50-60m, developing a straight branchless bole with brown fibrous bark retained on the lower half or more of the trunk. It has a well-foliaged crown with grey-green leaves. In New Zealand it has grown well in colder areas of both islands, preferring good soils and damp locations and a rainfall of 1500-1600mm providing there is good drainage. It is not damaged by snow and is very frost tolerant (temperatures to -12°C). It appears to dislike humidity and hot summers, succumbing to various fungal diseases. Correct siting is most important as it will not do well in unsuitable climatic conditions. The very pale brown or pinkish timber is open-textured, straight-grained, moderately hard, strong and tough, but not durable. Its lightness and ease of working make it most suitable for joinery, furniture and house construction. It is similar to *E.regnans* but since it is a slower growing tree it should be planted only where it is too cold for the former species. Seedlings are easy to handle, hardy and grow rapidly.

E.fastigata comes mainly from the southern highlands of New South Wales and was first planted in New Zealand when about 50 hectares were established in Whakarewarewa forest in 1899. It grows to 50m with a long straight bole and relatively large well-branched crown. It needs to be planted in tighter spacing than most eucalypts, as given the chance the branching will become very heavy and coarse, resulting in a tree of poor form. The bark persists on the trunk and large branches as a grey-brown finely fibrous covering, but is shed from the branches to leave a smooth white surface.

It is an inferior tree to *E.regnans* but can withstand more severe conditions, so should not be planted if the site is suitable for *E.regnans*. The timber is very pale brown and straight-grained with moderate strength and durability. It is suitable for turnery, furniture, handles and veneers.

E.ficifolia is the species well known as the scarlet flowering gum which is extensively used in parks and gardens. It has a very limited natural occurrence in Australia, coming from a narrow coastal belt only 80km long on the south-western tip of the continent. There it grows in dense thickets on low sandy rises. It has demonstrated its versatility by showing it can do well in many parts of the world; from a straggly shrubby plant it has been developed into a shapely round-headed tree on a short squat bole, not normally growing above 10m. Since it originates in an area where it thrives on free-draining sandy soils with wet winters and dry summers it will do best in New Zealand in similar conditions. During mid- to late summer it provides a blaze of colour with clusters of 5cm wide flowers all over the crown. Since most plants are raised from seed the colour cannot be accurately forecast, but it is usually light to dark red or crimson. True colour can be guaranteed only from grafted plants.

Young plants are frost tender for the first two years, but will grow in less than ideal circumstances. The timber is of no economic value.

E. fraxinoides comes from a very small area of the eastern highlands and coastal areas of New South Wales where it grows to 40m with a one metre diameter on cool moist sites. In New Zealand it has shown its ability to withstand quite hard winters (-10°C) and has grown well in Wairarapa and Manawatu. It prefers generous rainfall and well drained soils and will tolerate clays. It is a very attractive tree especially when young, with cream-coloured bark and slightly glaucous leaf twigs. The timber is pale, straight-grained and non-durable and can be used wherever *E. regnans* or *E. delegatensis* is suitable.

E. globoidea has formerly been known as *E. scabra* and *E. eugenioides* as well as its common name of white stringy bark. It is one of the smaller (25-30m) eucalypts and comes from eastern New South Wales. It grows with a straight trunk which may be up to two-thirds of the tree height. It has been widely planted in New Zealand and has done best in Waikato, Bay of Plenty, Taranaki and other areas with moderate climates and temperatures not lower than -9°C. It prefers moist, well-drained soils and will not thrive on dry sites or tight clay. Needs rainfall of 1000 -1500mm.

The timber is one of the best hardwoods as it is hard, strong, tough and durable, generally straight-grained and mills well. It is a good general-purpose

E. ficifolia is very colourful in summer.

Wide spaced *E. fraxinoides* on a sheep farm near Te Kuiti.

Winter flowering is the main attraction of *E. leucoxylon.*

farm timber and for this reason the species can be recommended for farm woodlots where the climate is too severe for either *E.muelleriana* or *E.pilularis*.

E.leucoxylon is one of the iron-bark group and in Australia is of value for its timber which is especially hard, tough and very durable. It comes mainly from central Victoria where it enjoys a Mediterranean-type climate, growing to 20-25m. The variety found in New Zealand called 'Rosea' grown only for its ornamental value. It reaches 15m with wide-spreading crown and in winter there is a profusion of flowers which vary considerably in colour ranging from light pinks to crimson red. These blooms are generally laden with nectar and pollen which are eagerly sought by native birds and bees at a time when other food is scarce.

It grows on a variety of soils from fairly heavy and slightly acidic to sandy loams. The young plants are relatively hardy and will stand temperatures down to -9°C, particularly in dry areas.

This species should be widely planted in colder areas where the summer-flowering *E.ficifolia* would not survive.

E.macarthurii has a restricted natural occurrence in the southern highlands of New South Wales and was established in the Waikato in 1874. It proved to be a hardy and easily grown shelter tree and in the 1920s was widely planted from Northland to Canterbury. It

This mature clump of *E. macarthurii* is typical of many earlier plantings.

E. maculata planted by Mr Fred McWhannell shows its interesting bark.

E. maidenii has an attractive grey bark.

prefers relatively moist soils and will withstand exposure to wind and temperatures to -12°C. It is a very vigorous grower and acquires noble proportions with a height of up to 40m. At the peak of its planting popularity it was believed to be capable of producing valuable timber. It has however proved to be variable and unreliable in this respect; often the timber warps, twists and dishes as well as being difficult to handle on the sawbench and to season. Natural durability is also variable. It is included in this list because it was one of the most widely planted eucalypt species on farms and there are still many mature trees to be seen. It can now be recommended for planting only as a shade or amenity tree.

E. maculata is widely distributed in New South Wales and Southern Queensland where it grows on a wide range of soils, but it prefers those which are slightly moist, well drained and of moderately heavy texture. It grows up to 50m on best sites and is a shapely tree with a straight clean bole with seasonal variations in colour including a most attractive mottling. It produces timber which has a variety of uses, principally construction, but is only moderately durable. Its main role in New Zealand is as a landscape tree in climates

with a mild winter, as seedlings are extremely frost tender.

E. maidenii (very closely related to *E. globulus*) is one of the southern blue gums coming from coastal escarpments of New South Wales which has grown well in many parts of New Zealand. It can be found from the far north to the far south and is as happy in coastal areas exposed to saline winds as in elevated areas. It is soil tolerant, growing equally well in clays, loams and peat. On optimum sites in Australia it grows to 60m and up to 2m in diameter. The timber is hard, strong and moderately durable with interlocking grain. Its ability to withstand wind and cope with a variety of climatic and soil conditions gives it many desirable attributes, and it is a very easy species to handle. Unfortunately the crown can be severely defoliated by the eucalyptus tortoise beetle.

E. microcorys (tallow wood) is widely distributed in New South Wales and Queensland where it has great commercial value; in New South Wales it is considered the best of the native hardwoods. It has not been widely planted in New Zealand, but it has done very well in Poverty Bay, Bay of Plenty and Waikato.

It is one of the handsomest of all eucalypts, growing to 30-50m with a densely packed crown of bronze green foliage. Good free-draining loams and friable clays seem to be the most suitable. Seedlings are frost tender for the first year, but once established the trees can withstand moderate frosts. Good growth and form can be obtained when grown in small clearings in existing vegetation, when open-grown lower branches of the crown are not shed. The timber is yellowish-brown; it is hard, strong and very durable. Its greasy texture makes it very suitable for dance floors and it is one of the timbers used for electric fence standards.

E. muelleriana is found in a small coastal strip of southern New South Wales and Victoria and was planted in New Zealand only after the turn of the century, mostly in small woodlots. It is unlikely to survive temperatures lower than -6°C and so survival has in some areas been confined to hilltops. Under forest conditions it will grow to 30-40m where it is a tree of good form with a straight bole half or more of tree height. It appears to be fairly tolerant as to soil and can do well in heavy clays, but should not be planted in frost hollows. It will stand limited exposure to wind and requires rainfall of about 1 200-1 500mm. It grows rapidly in youth and quickly forms a pole stand responding readily to thinning. As an open-grown tree it can become a very handsome addition to the landscape. The wood is pale yellow-brown, heavy, hard, strong and from mature trees very durable. Younger trees will produce moderately durable wood. Its capacity to produce durable timbers for farm use make it the principal tree for consideration as a woodlot planting in the milder North Island areas.

E. nicholii is in its natural state a rather inconspicuous poorly shaped tree, but as an ornamental it is one of the most attractive rough-barked trees. It grows to about

E. nicholii softens the visual impact of a loading race.

Three-year-old *E. obliqua.*

10m and is much admired for its fine light green foliage and rounded compact crown. The new leaves have a delicate pink to plum tint and are valued for floral work. It will grow in a wide range of soils and is frost hardy. It is not a timber tree so is more suited to the homestead garden than out on the farm.

E. obliqua, an ash group tree, is often referred to as a stringy bark because it has persistent bark to the small branches. It is widely distributed in the cooler southern parts of Australia, being of considerable commercial importance. Plantings in New Zealand go back over 100 years and it appears to be best suited to southern parts of the North Island and to Marlborough and Canterbury. Its performance has been very variable as it has a tendency to a high incidence of branch defects, the development of epicormic growths and extreme variation in form and vigour. It is known that some of these faults are provenance related and until these are remedied widespread planting cannot be recommended. Nevertheless the tree could be useful for farm timber as it does better than *E. regnans* on dry clay soils, and it yields a pale brown timber of moderate hardness, strength and durability. Its milling qualities depend on tree form. Good quality

E. ovata growing well in a wet patch in the Wairarapa.

timber is suitable for flooring, turnery, handles and veneer.

E. ovata is a small to moderate sized tree coming from South Australia and Tasmania. Its justification for inclusion in this list of eucalypts is its ability to grow in extremely wet conditions which can include inundation for several months of the year. There has been some confusion over identification of this species which has some very close relatives, and there are certainly plantings in New Zealand which masquerade under the name of *E. ovata*. It is an easy tree to handle and will grow vigorously in waterlogged areas and peat swamps where it can also withstand wind. The timber is of doubtful worth and the tree should never be grown for its wood value, its most suitable use being as a shelter tree for wet areas. It was subject to severe defoliation by eucalyptus tortoise beetle with many trees killed in the epidemic of the early 1960s.

E. pauciflora comes from the colder parts of eastern Australia where in its native state it usually has a short crooked bole growing to 10-15m. It is often found above the summer snowline where it can withstand heavy winter falls. Its timber is not of any commercial value and because of its poor form it is seldom worth milling, although it is durable and could be used for rough farm posts. Like many of the inferior timber eucalypts, *E. pauciflora* is very often a strikingly handsome tree and certainly has a place as a shade tree and landscape specimen. It grows best in free soils in high rainfall areas, and in such conditions will reach 20m

E. pauciflora open-grown in the Waikato.

140

Cattle under five-year-old *E. regnans* in Hawkes Bay.

E. viminalis near Taihape.

with a wide open-branched crown bearing scarlet pendulous branchlets and very shiny dark green leaves. The bark is shed in irregular patches to leave a smooth mottled surface of dark and light grey, green, white and bronze which gives a most attractive appearance when wet.

E. pilularis comes from southern Queensland and coastal New South Wales. It has been in New Zealand for over 100 years with plantings for the most part confined to the north, where it has done best. It has shown its ability to tolerate poor soils, growing well on poor gumland clays as well as on clay and sandy loams. Good drainage is essential. This species will reach 30m and has outgrown pines and other exotics on poor clay soils. It is one of the most important hardwood species in Australia where the timber is used extensively for general construction work. The wood is hard, strong, tough and has moderate to good durability especially from mature trees. Many of the hardwood railway sleepers imported from Australia were of *E. pilularis*. This species has good potential as a farm woodlot tree for its timber has many uses; it is the eucalypt most suited to the poorer North Auckland

clays besides doing well in other warmer sites. Seedlings will stand only very light frosts.

E. regnans is one of the tallest forest species in the world, exceeded only by Californian redwoods. These trees grow to typical heights of 60-80m with straight trunks of good form going up to two-thirds of this height with open fairly small crowns. They are native to southern Victoria and Tasmania and have been grown in New Zealand since 1860, being now planted over many areas of the country. The stand at Newstead near Hamilton includes the tallest exotic tree in New Zealand. *E. regnans* prefers cool climates and rolling country with good air drainage. Temperatures lower than -9°C will kill young trees. Rainfall needs to exceed 800mm and reasonable fertility suits the species best. It is not tolerant to salt winds.

The timber is pale brown, open-textured, straight-grained and somewhat resembling oak (it is marketed in Australia as Australian or Tasmanian oak). It is not ground durable. The wood is easy to work, dresses well, and is suitable for a wide range of uses where durability is not needed, including cabinet work, veneers, joinery, general construction and pulpwood.

E. saligna is well known in Australia as Sydney blue gum, the species being mostly found within 160 km of the northern coast of New South Wales. It was first planted in New Zealand about 1870 in North Auckland and Waikato, later spreading to other areas, but it has not done well in cooler parts of the country. A mature specimen will be up to 50 m in height with a straight trunk of good form for half or two-thirds of the total. The bark is shed in long flakes leaving a white to blue-grey surface. A good stand of *E. saligna* is very impressive. Climate is the main restriction as to choice of site as the species is tolerant of most soil types. Seedlings will be killed at temperatures below -6°C and although older trees will survive, growth will be slow. It will tolerate some exposure, but breakage will occur if there are strong winds. A minimum rainfall of 760 mm is necessary. The timber is red or pink, hard, strong, and tough, sometimes having an attractive wavy grain. It is moderately durable and easy to work. Because of its non-greasy nature it can be used for flooring and steps, but its future in New Zealand is likely to be mainly for use in special purposes such as furniture, cabinet work, turnery and veneers.

E. viminalis is widely distributed in south-eastern Australia and along with *E. macarthurii* is one of the most widely planted eucalypts in New Zealand. It thrives in most parts of both islands, and in good conditions grows into a large handsome tree with a smooth whitish surface on the upper part of the trunk and a wide open crown. It will grow to 30 m and is widely tolerant of soil and climatic conditions. The seedlings are very easy to handle. The timber is not durable and for milling purposes is entirely unpredictable often warping and twising badly; since much of the timber is available on farms this is most unfortunate. Should a mill be handy it may be worth putting some timber through it for general farm use as was done with trees from the stand on page 141.

A well tended stand of *E. saligna* in an agroforestry situation.

Fagus

There are approximately 16 *Fagus* species and these come from the northern hemisphere. They are hardy, deciduous trees, usually of shapely form growing easily in most soils. They should not be confused with the dozen or so southern beeches *(Nothofagus)* which come from the southern hemisphere and are mainly evergreens, several being native to New Zealand. Beech timbers are valued for their hardness and texture so they are widely used in some countries for furniture-making, flooring and many other woodenware purposes.

F. grandifolia (American beech) is sometimes seen in New Zealand. It is smaller in size than *F. sylvatica* and usually develops a massive, low-branching crown on a distinctive, smooth, blue-grey bole. The tree is rather shallow-rooting, with a tendency to produce root sprouts which can cause annoyance. The European species is the better one for farm purposes.

F. sylvatica (common or European beech) is the species most often seen on New Zealand farms. There are some fine specimens in public parks, and older-established estates often possess beech groves and single trees of imposing beauty. The tree will grow in most soils, usually to 25-30m. In good, moist but well-drained soils, especially those containing lime, it will grow to even larger size. Beech is notably foliaceous

and valued for the density of the shade it casts as well as for its golden-brown autumn colouring. It is fairly wind resistant in inland areas, and it will also endure

Above: A young *Fagus sylvatica* (common beech) begins to turn colour in Autumn. This one grows in the central North Island. *Below: Fagus sylvatica* 'Purpurea' (copper beech) on a Te Awamutu farm.

sea winds provided they are not unduly salt-laden. In winter, the shapely outlines of a well-grown beech are beautiful, but it is in the spring when the bare limbs are clothed with a mass of glossy green leaves that the true magnificence of this tree is realised. *F.sylvatica* has many cultivars most of them suitable for larger homestead gardens. The best known of these are 'Pur-purea' (copper beech), 'Pendula' (weeping beech) and 'Riversii' (purple beech).

The trees are propagated from seed which should be sown in a rich and somewhat moist seed-bed in spring. Horticultural varieties are grafted on European beech stock.

Ficus

Ficus is a very large genus of chiefly tropical trees, many of which are cultivated for their fruits. Several species are used in Australia and America for shade or avenue purposes, but these are frost tender and can be grown in New Zealand only in selected areas.

The best known American species, grown for farm shade or landscape improvement, is *F.elastica*, (india-rubber tree). This can be grown only in warm and frost-free areas. Of the Australian shade species, the two best known in this country are *F.rubiginosa* (rusty fig) which is a very shapely small tree but difficult to grow except in favoured coastal regions, and *F. macro-phylla* (Moreton Bay fig) which has been successfully established in some parts of the North Island, particularly in Auckland and northwards.

F.macrophylla comes from north-western Australia and is a magnificent evergreen shade or avenue tree for those who possess the soil and climatic conditions necessary for its cultivation. It has a wide, umbrella-like spread and abundant, shiny green leaves. The young seedlings are frost tender and unlikely to endure more than -3°C, but they become hardier with age. The tree grows to variable heights, dependent upon the conditions in which it is cultivated. In deep, free loams or sandy soils with some moisture it can reach a height of up to 25m with a spread of branches equalling its height. Reasonably salt-laden winds are not injurious. The strong, wide-spreading, water-seeking roots are liable to cause damage if the tree is planted too close to buildings, pathways or underground drains. No information on its timber qualities has been tracked down by the authors.

Most of the trees are easily propagated from cuttings which should be struck in a cool, moist situation.

The wide-spreading branches of *Ficus macrophylla* (Moreton Bay fig) make it a good park tree.

Fraxinus

A fine *Fraxinus excelsior* (common ash).

The *Fraxinus* genus, known commonly as ash, is a group of hardy deciduous northern hemisphere trees. Although there are some 65 species, only two of them are likely to be useful for landscape planting in New Zealand. These are the English (or common) ash and the American ash, both of which grow to fairly large size and yield valuable timbers famed for their toughness and elasticity. These timbers are sought particularly for the manufacture of oars and skis, tool handles, sporting gear such as baseball bats and tennis racquet frames, furniture and aeroplane parts. The trees are hungry feeders, growing best in heavy fertile country with regular and plentiful rainfall, but wet clays are not suitable. They are noted for their ability to retain their shapeliness in windy situations. Some of the smaller species are elegant little trees which can be used effectively in homestead gardens, and most nursery catalogues contain particulars.

F. americana (white ash) is a handsome, quick-growing tree which, with its long straight bole, can attain a height exceeding 30 m. It grows best in the conditions described for European ash but will succeed in most soils provided they are not shallow. Its wood has the characteristic ash qualities.

F. excelsior (European ash) is a tree which can, in good fertile conditions, reach a height of well over 30 m. It is a native of Europe and is regarded as one of that continent's most valuable timber trees. It grows best in deep, moist loams and has done well on peaty soils. It is a tree of graceful growth habit, usually with stout

Autumn foliage of *Fraxinus oxycarpa* 'Raywoodii' (claret ash) near Hunterville.

up-curving branches well clothed with characteristic pinnate leaves, and is often used for shade or avenue planting. The wood is used for purposes stated above.

Propagation is from seed which should be collected in February and sown in a sandy seed bed, after first removing the wings. Ornamental cultivar varieties are grafted on *F. excelsior* stock.

Fruiting Trees

Citrus (grapefruit) will survive browsing of the lower branches by stock.

These brief notes are included in the hope of stimulating the reader into realising that fruit trees around the farm can be of benefit. For high-quality produce a fairly demanding maintenance programme must be followed. This is well known to most home orchardists and there are plenty of manuals on the subject. What is suggested here is that worthwhile results can be obtained without too much effort, and both people and animals will be the beneficiaries. Readers will often have noticed old deserted home orchards with venerable but healthy and sometimes peculiar shaped trees continuing to yield fruit, with animals grazing underneath. The authors suggest an 'easy care' programme with a few trees scattered around in odd corners of the farm and perhaps used to screen an ugly shed. Farmers spend many hours working away from the house, yet few know the pleasure of picking a ripe peach, plum or nectarine from the tree as they go past a corner in the back paddock. Apples will probably be riddled with codlin moth, but the cattle won't mind. They have been known to listen for the fruit dropping, and compete for possession of it. Besides, a vegetable knife can do wonders for something with a bit of codlin or brown rot, and when bottled or in jam nobody will ever know what the original fruit looked like. The shelter of farm sheds can be profitably used, with perhaps the milker taking home fresh grapefruit for breakfast. Certainly the fruit will have blemishes, but it will be fresh, free and available.

Citrus trees (orange, tangelo, grapefruit, lemon) are half-hardy evergreens. The main requirement of citrus is a well-drained site sheltered from winds and heavy frosts. A north-facing slope is best to take advantage of maximum sunlight and to allow air drainage in times of frost. Both common and lesser known citrus species are best bought as grafted trees, as seedlings take many years to fruit and might then be of poor quality.

Most citrus trees flower in spring and summer and fruit in winter and spring, providing fresh ripe fruit when there is a shortage. They respond well to mulch, and to twice-yearly feeding applied to the soil under and around the tree. Some citrus grow easily from cuttings, so this method could be tried if money is short.

Cydonia oblonga (quince) is very hardy and deciduous. This attractive tree may be grown easily from hardwood winter cuttings in good soil which does not become dry. In spring it is covered with pale pink flowers followed in autumn by aromatic, golden, downy, pear-shaped fruits which are useful for jams, preserves and desserts. Very popular with our grandparents, it is seldom seen now except as a remnant orchard tree.

Corrective pruning prevents the quince from developing its naturally low-branching habit.

Diospyros kaki (persimmon) is hardy and deciduous. This most decorative tree should be seen more often. Occasionally it is found near old homes still fruiting well in spite of considerable age and neglect. Difficult

Fruit and foliage of *Diospyros kaki* in autumn.

to raise from seed, it is best to buy named grafted varieties, preferably the non-astringent ones recommended by the New Zealand Tree Crops Association. These have delicious fruit ripening in autumn, at which time the large (15 cm) leaves turn brilliant colours of yellow, orange and red before falling. The persimmon requires a good average soil sheltered from wind. The shape of the tree depends on the variety, but most are spreading with rounded tops.

Diospyros kaki (persimmon) used to shade a Waikato yard.

A young Waikato *Cydonia oblonga* (quince) in spring.

Eriobotrya japonica (loquat) making a fine shade tree near Mangakino.

Birds are liable to eat the fruit before it ripens, so pick the most mature fruit and allow it to ripen indoors, not eating it until the fruit appears semi-transparent and over-ripe.

The wood is heavy and is nearly all sapwood which is very strong, hard and tough. Before the advent of laminating processes, plastics, and now steel, it was always used for the heads of golf clubs.

Eriobotrya japonica (loquat) is a hardy evergreen. This large-leaved species with its luscious juicy fruit is seldom seen yet it is easy to grow in most soils and forms a dense well-shaped shade tree wider than it is high, the foliage and young bark being very palatable to animals. The juicy yellow fruits are borne in clusters and ripen in early summer, being popular with birds as well as people.

Usually grown from seed which germinates readily, the loquat takes about 12 years to fruit, but is well worth waiting for. If grafted plants can be obtained the wait is not so long, but the trees are more expensive.

For a large-leaved tree the loquat stands wind surprisingly well.

Feijoa sellowiana is a hardy evergreen. The easy-to-grow feijoa is propagated from seed, fruiting in about five years. Cuttings are difficult, but a skilled person can be successful. An average soil is needed, and planted about 2.5 m apart they form an effective and beautiful windbreak, the red flowers in December somewhat like a pohutukawa being followed by delicious green fruit in winter when other fruit is scarce. Stock will readily eat the foliage if the tree is not

Feijoas are real survivors. These bear fruit in spite of grazing by sheep and cattle.

protected. Umbrella-shaped unprotected trees have been seen laden with fruit with sheep lying in the shade beneath.

Malus domestica (apple) is a very hardy deciduous. Any seedling which germinates in the garden or compost heap can be moved to a fenced-off portion of the farm in average soil, where it will grow into a medium-sized tree bearing pink and white spring blossom followed by autumn fruit. These will be readily eaten by animals who listen for the apples to drop, disregarding codlin and bird-peck.

Prune when young to make a spreading tree, which will bear fruit of unknown quality in about six years. The variety 'Splendour' grows readily from cuttings. Timber is heavy with fine even texture. The heartwood is hard reddish-brown and mainly used for turning.

Prunus armeniaca (apricot) and *P. cerasus* (cherry). The apricot is suitable for special areas only, where there are severe winters and hot dry summers. If apricots do well in your part of the country you might try growing these. Commercially they are grown only in the south of the South Island and in parts of Hawkes Bay, but occasional trees are known to bear crops elsewhere.

The same applies to the cherry, although groves of cherry trees fruiting well were known many years ago in the Waikato both at Ohaupo and near Ngaruawahia. Both could be tried from seed, but best results would be from grafted trees bought from a local nurseryman.

Prunus salicina (Japanese plum), *P. domestica* (European plum). Very hardy deciduous plum seedlings appear in odd places, usually where a picnic or smoko has occurred a year or two before. Allow these to grow, or move them to an area fenced off from stock in a situation not too exposed to wind. Trees are covered in small white flowers in early spring, and the fruit ripens in summer.

Prune off low branches to the trunk while the tree is young, or allow much branching if easy-to-reach fruit

This untended straggling *Prunus domestica* (plum), grown from seed, produced a large crop of fruit.

is wanted. More than one tree in blossom at the same time is needed for pollination. The plum will bear at about six years from seed.

Prunus persica (peach), *P. persica* var. *nectarina* (nectarine), *P. dulcis* (almond). Hardy deciduous. Peach leaves, like poplars are a good source of zinc and farmers in areas prone to facial eczema might like to grow these where leaves will drop into their pad-

View from the road. Cattle appreciate the shade of a *Malus* (apple) in a Northland drought.

149

A *Prunus serrulata* (flowering cherry) in spring, undamaged by bulls grazing in the paddock.

A nectarine tree fruiting well — no pruning, no spraying.

A magnificent old *Pyrus communis* (pear) on a Waikato dairy farm.

docks. Pink almond and nectarine blossom and white or pink peach blossom appear in spring, the fruit ripening in late summer and autumn. An average soil, not too dry, suits the *Prunus* species, with protection from wind. All may be propagated from seed provided the seed tree is not a hybrid, the trees bearing fruits at three or four years. Prune when young to required shape. Peach and nectarine are fairly short-lived and should be replaced every 10 years or so, as fruit production drops, but almonds last much longer.

Prunus species generally have fairly heavy wood and smaller pieces are easily worked with hand tools. Larger pieces are suitable for cabinet-making and veneering. The wild cherries (*P. avium* from Europe and *P. serotina* from North America) produce timber which is valued for furniture in the high quality mahogany class.

Pyrus communis (pear) is a very hardy deciduous. A site similar to that needed for the quince will suit the pear, which thrives on ample moisture. Early pruning for a good shape, if necessary, results in an attractive tall tree flowering in spring with fruit ripening in autumn. Pollination can be difficult, so it is best to buy grafted trees recommended for your district, a pollinator being needed for fruiting in most cases.

The pear slug can be very damaging to young trees, so watch out in summer for the black shiny creature that can defoliate a tree very rapidly, and spray with a pesticide. This pest also attacks quinces and some plums, especially young trees.

The moderately hard timber is pinkish brown with straight close grain and fine even texture. It has excellent turning and veneering properties and is used for reproducing flesh colours.

Ginkgo

Ginkgo biloba (maidenhair tree), related to the conifers, is a native of China. It is the sole survivor of a family stated by some authorities to have existed no less than 200 000 000 years ago and to have been virtually wiped out by the last great ice age. Whether or not this is so, at least we know that it is the one and only species of the genus. It has been regarded, until recently challenged by the dawn redwood (*Metasequoia glyptostroboides*), as having the oldest ancestry of any known tree. It has been cultivated from time immemorial in temple gardens in China and Japan, where some living trees are claimed to be up to 1 000 years old, but it is unknown in a wild state.

As we know it in this country, *G. biloba* is a graceful, deciduous, erect tree, slender and sparsely branched when young, assuming a broad conical crown with age. It grows slowly and as a rule up to 15-25 m but it can reach in some conditions 30 m. It is hardy, usually pest-free and will grow in most soils, preferring those that are free and slightly moist. It will withstand but is not happy in wind. *Ginkgo* transplants easily and will grow within the influence of the sea. Its odd-shaped, fan-like leaves turn a beautiful clear yellow before falling. It is one of the most graceful of trees and is suitable for specimen, group or avenue planting. The timber is soft, easily worked, and used by the Japanese for chess sets and other carving.

Male and female flowers are borne on separate trees but it is not possible to tell the one from the other until the flowers have appeared. The female plum-like fruits are covered with a fleshy substance which emits an offensive smell in the process of decomposing. Cleansed of the pulp, washed and roasted, the nuts are a favourite food in China.

The seed retains viability for only a limited period. It should be stratified in damp sand, kept in a cool place over winter and sown in early spring. It is possible, though difficult, to grow the tree from cuttings taken in late autumn.

A brilliant gold *Ginkgo biloba* (maidenhair tree) near Feilding, about to drop its autumn leaves.

Gleditsia

Gleditsia triacanthos (honey locust) covered in pods in autumn.

There are about a dozen *Gleditsia* species, coming from North and South America, Asia and Africa. Most of them are small trees or shrubs. The one most likely to be of interest to New Zealand planters is *G.triacanthos* (honey locust), a native of the U.S.A. This is a handsome, deciduous tree which in late autumn bears long pods that are readily eaten by cattle, sheep and pigs. These pods, which can be as long as 40cm, contain seeds packed in a sweet, sticky substance with a strong and rather sickly honey smell. There is considerable variation in yields but some trees in New Zealand are bearing in excess of 110 kg per tree. With wide-spread planting (10m) grass will grow right up to the base, making this an ideal tree for three-tier farming (pasture, fodder and timber). At this spacing yields from well-selected trees should exceed 10000 kg of beans per hectare. The highly nutritious fruits are liked by all stock, probably because of their high sugar content.

The tree, which grows to 25m, has slender, spreading, somewhat pendulous branches forming an open flat-topped crown. The leaves are finely divided compound or doubly compound and turn pale clear yellow in the autumn. The pollen-bearing blossoms are eagerly sought by bees for their nectar. Trees are either male or female; approximately 10 per cent should be male to ensure successful cropping. Honey locust grows readily in most parts of New Zealand and thrives in deep rich soils. It is capable of growing wherever it can get its roots down, whether the site be a rocky slip face or on drained swamp. It can withstand severe drought conditions and could be useful for soil stabilisation. The timber is hard, strong and coarse-grained. The heartwood is bright brown or reddish, takes a high polish and can be used for furniture, panelling and turnery. Because it is ground durable it is widely used in U.S.A. for posts and railway sleepers, but should be well dried before use. *G.triacanthos* has the fault of developing very strong, three-pronged thorns which, in some circumstances, may be a danger. A form *(G.triacanthos* f.*inermis)* is thornless, but trial plantings of seed of this variety have resulted in a fair percentage of thorny plants. For those who wish to grow thornless trees, the best and safest way is to graft on *f.inermis* which at present has the disadvantage of generally being a lower yielder of beans than *G.triacanthos.*

Whether or not honey locust will live up to its American reputation as a stock-food tree in New Zealand remains to be determined. Odd trees in various districts are bearing pods of varying quality and a number of farmers are carrying out experimental work with the species in areas as far apart as Southland and Bay of Plenty. Those who wish to undertake trial plantings are warned that there is a very wide variation in pod-bearing capacity within the species and only those strains known to be prolific should be the subject of experiment.

Propagation is by seed, the outer shell of which is very hard. They should be covered in very hot water and allowed to soak for 12 hours before planting out in spring. Seedlings are easily transplanted. Since bean yields are so variable the only way to ensure a heavy crop is to graft on good scion wood and this is being successfully done in early spring using whip and tongue method or an acute cleft.

Glyptostrobus

There is only one species of this tree, which is a native of the province of Canton in southern China. It is one of the very few deciduous conifers.

G.lineatus (Chinese cypress) has lateral branches of very fine foliage resembling *Taxodium distichum.* It grows into an attractive conical shaped tree but as it is uncommon in this country information on its final height is vague. It is similar to *Taxodium* in its site requirements, in its native state usually being found in damp situations and on banks of streams. It is reasonably hardy and in the Waikato has withstood temperatures of -9°C, thriving on peat soils and growing to 11 m in 10 years.

Not readily available in New Zealand, it is nevertheless a tree which is worthy of greater attention to the range of species which enjoy damp situations. Its foliage ranges from rich dark green, sometimes with a bluish tinge, and turns russet brown in autumn. It is easily propagated from softwood cuttings in summer.

The rare *Glyptostrobus lineatus* in summer.

Grevillea

There are well over 200 *Grevillea* species, most of them being native to Australia. The majority are small shrubs, many of them very beautiful flowering plants well known to farm homestead gardeners. *Grevillea robusta* is the largest and most important species of the genus and two others reach useful tree status. These three evergreen trees grow equally well in dry inland areas and in high rainfall coastal localities, but are only moderately frost resistant. Their timbers are light, strong, tough and classed as cabinet woods of high quality.

G.hilliana (red silky oak) comes from the same localities as *G.robusta,* but is slightly smaller in size. Its timber is red-coloured, very hard and exceptionally handsome. It is in great demand, when available, for veneer work. The tree requires soil and climatic conditions similar to those necessary for *G.robusta.*

G.robusta (Australian silky oak) can grow to 25-35 m in deep, moist loams but would be somewhat smaller in drier or poorer conditions. It is a straight-boled tree with graceful, fern-like foliage, and where reasonably hot summers are experienced the whole of the sunny side becomes a blaze of rich golden-orange flowers. Its branches are brittle and prone to break under wind stress, and it can often lose its leader, so for these reasons the tree should be given whatever shelter is available. Silky oak comes from the northern rivers district of New South Wales and from Queensland. It grows naturally near the coast but it does not object to inland situations provided winter frosts are not too severe. It is cultivated in New Zealand mostly as an ornamental tree so it is a common feature in parks and on farmlands in warmer areas. No serious attempt to grow it as a commercial tree is known. The wood is pale greyish-brown or

brownish-grey, straight-grained, strong and tough, with a silver ray, and much esteemed as a furniture timber. It has a silky sheen which comes out under polish and gives it the name of silky oak. It is not ground durable.

G. striata (beefwood) has dark red timber which resembles freshly cut beef in colour. It grows to medium size, rarely exceeding 15-20m. It has a very wide range over most of the Australian mainland states, growing in both coastal and inland areas. The timber is hard, tough, strong and durable. The species is slightly more frost tender than the other two, but once established, will tolerate very dry conditions.

For those who possess suitable sites and wish to add variety to their surroundings, any of the silky oaks would be both useful and ornamental.

The trees are easily propagated from seed which is borne in pods and ripens in late summer. The seed is shed within a few days of ripening and so the pods need careful watching for signs of maturity. Viability is high for a limited time only; seed kept for more than a year usually fails to germinate.

A Tauranga *Grevillea robusta* (silky oak) in summer.

Grevillea robusta (silky oak) flowers in January.

Idesia

A deciduous monotypic genus originating from China and Japan. The species grown in New Zealand is *Idesia polycarpa*, a large specimen existing at Ruakura Agricultural Research Station. There the visitors' book records that the Japanese Secretary of Agriculture called in 1915 and on his return to Japan sent some seed of both male and female to Ruakura. Many older specimens in New Zealand have come from this initial planting.

Fruit of *Idesia polycarpa* in November.

I. polycarpa grows to 15m with a broad crown and strongly horizontal branch structure. The leaves are thick and heart-shaped, 15-20cm long and nearly as wide. The flowers are inconspicuous, the species' particular attraction being the enormous crop of berries which are borne only on female trees. These first appear crimson-scarlet, turning later in autumn to deep red, in a formation similar to bunches of grapes. They continue to hang in position during winter after the leaves have fallen, giving a most impressive display which is of no interest to birds.

The tree is best suited to a sheltered position, disliking temperatures lower than -9°C, and late frosts will damage new season's shoots. It likes a hot summer and dry autumn and prefers neutral or slightly acid soils.

Idesias are well worth planting in suitable situations as they are handsome trees at all times and there are no berry trees superior to them. It is however preferable to plant both male and female trees to ensure that berrying takes place.

Propagation can be from seed which is easily germinated, but grafted forms are available from nurseries.

A fine *Idesia polycarpa* on a Te Awamutu dairy farm.

Jacaranda

A Northland *Jacaranda* in January, in a country school garden.

Fifty species of trees and shrubs belonging to this genus are native to Central and South America and the West Indies, but only one is cultivated in New Zealand.

J.mimosaefolia syn. *J.acutifolia*) deciduous to semi-evergreen, is from Brazil and is one of the most beautiful of flowering trees. It has an open irregular head with finely divided fern-like pinnate foliage. During the hottest part of the year it bears great branched 20cm clusters of narrow, trumpet-shaped, mauve-blue flowers. Its ability to establish in New Zealand is very much dependent on the climate as success demands a hot, sunny and preferably sheltered position. Jacarandas are susceptible to frosts when young, but often come back after a freeze to become multi-stemmed shrubby plants. However if protected for the first few years they become quite frost resistant and develop into good-sized trees growing to 15m, with a spreading top.

They can grow in a wide variety of soils, but do best in sandy soils and those which are not heavy and wet during winter — north of Auckland and in some East Coast areas — although some fine specimens are grown as far south as Waikato and Hawkes Bay. It is preferable to look down on the tree to see the flowers to advantage, so in all respects the site should be carefully chosen.

Increase is by seed, which forms in large flattened pods often used for floral arrangements.

Jacaranda flowers against the sky in January.

157

Juglans

Dairy cows enjoying the shade of *Juglans ailantifolia*
(Japanese walnut) near Te Awamutu.

The *Juglans* genus was much larger in the past than it is today; only about twenty-one species remain, the most important and widely cultivated of these being *J. regia*. In America a native species, *J. nigra*, has the distinction of yielding that country's most valuable timber. All are deciduous and except for *J. regia* have attractive yellow autumn colouring. Because its kernel is readily accessible usually only *J. regia* is planted for its edible fruits. Access to the meat of other species is through a hard shell and the fruit of these are usually harvested when green and used for pickling.

J. ailantifolia (Japanese walnut) is a quick-growing species which will reach 15 m and is often used as a shade tree. It is shapely and hardy and will grow in most soils. Its ripened nuts are not usually eaten but if gathered while still green and with the outer shell not yet hardened they are useful for pickling and marmalade. *J. ailantifolia* var. *cordiformis* (heartnut) is a form differing only in the shape of its nuts which are flattened and distinctly heart-shaped.

A twelve-year-old *Juglans cinerea* (butternut) beginning
to turn colour in autumn.

158

A nine-year-old *Juglans nigra* (black walnut) on the authors' farm in the Waikato.

J. cinerea (butternut) is less handsome than black walnut, being a short-trunked spreading tree seldom more than 10-18 m high, with timber lighter than black walnut and generally inferior. It bears elongated nuts but is often not a good specimen tree because its large spreading limbs are broken off by wind.

J. nigra (black walnut) is the producer of the most expensive timber not only in U.S.A. but also in New Zealand. It is one of the trees which has been evaluated by the Forest Service for its potential to replace indigenous hardwoods. Surveys have been made on about 300 mature black walnuts in New Zealand but very few have been milled. The results obtained so far indicate that this tree when well grown on selected sites and tended carefully is capable of producing timber and veneer of a quality equivalent to American standards and suitable for the same purposes — high-quality furniture. Because of its good machining properties, attractive grain and shock-resisting ability it has always been in great demand for gun stocks.

The heartwood is resistant to decay.

Black walnut is a handsome tree for amenity planting, with pinnate leaves up to 60 cm long which have from 15 to 23 lance-shaped leaflets attached to the stem. It will grow to more than 35 m high and can have clear butt logs of 4-5 m. In autumn the leaves turn a beautiful butter-gold and in spring new leaves are a lovely soft green. The nut kernels retain their distinctive flavour and texture after cooking and are sometimes used in confectionery and ice creams.

Even if grown for amenity purposes it is worthwhile obtaining seed from a reliable source. Black walnut grows best on deep, well-drained fertile soils; since most of these sites are in private hands it is an admirable tree for even the smallest farm holding. Early spring growth is subject to wind damage so it will do much better if shelter is provided.

Farmers considering planting on any scale should contact the Forest Service for the latest information, since the results of continuing research are always coming to hand.

J. regia (English or common walnut) is not a native of Britain. The tree came originally from India and Asia Minor and is now extensively grown in many countries. It is a rather slow grower but will, with age, reach a height of 15m or a little more, and develop a shapely crown of spreading branches with ash-like leaves. It grows best in deep, well-drained loams, and dislikes heavy clays, but is otherwise tolerant. Walnut timber is valuable and is used in the better class of cabinet-making. Surprisingly few farmers grow the walnut despite the fact that as a shade tree for paddock or stockyard it has few equals. Being deciduous, it is a particularly good subject for sheep or cattle yards, affording shade in summer without interfering with the sun's beneficent influence during winter months. Apart from its value as a shade provider, it is well worth growing for its edible nuts which find a ready market at worthwhile prices. Grafted varieties should be used for best-quality fruits. In warmer areas of high humidity there can be serious loss of fruit due to walnut blight and preventive spraying is then necessary.

Walnuts are propagated from nuts which will germinate readily if stratified in damp sand over winter and sown in spring. The special fruiting varieties are usually grafted on to common walnut stock.

Juglans regia (common walnut).

Juniperus

There are about 60 junipers which come from many countries, all north of the equator. One occasionally sees, in older settled districts, a hedge or low shelter-belt of common juniper, but the genus is best known in New Zealand for its garden forms, of which there are well over 50. In other lands juniper timbers are held in high regard. These timbers are, for the most part, soft, straight-grained and easily worked. Some possess ground durability to a notable degree. They are characteristically fragrant and from them, and from the foliage of the trees, oils are distilled and used in medicine and for the manufacture of perfumes. The trees are soil tolerant and some of them are frost hardy. Juniper foliage has diuretic (water-making) properties so it would not be wise to allow stock free access to it. They are all evergreen conifers, the larger specimens tending to develop fluted trunks.

J.chinensis (Chinese juniper) grows to about 15 m and is of variable form, but it is usually an attractive pyramidal shape with dense foliage of two different types on the same tree. It grows best in fairly good soils containing lime, and is one of the shapeliest of the junipers. There are several ornamental forms, often seen near Japanese temples. It is a hardy species whose timber is durable.

J.communis (common juniper) has a wider natural distribution than any other tree in the world and is, at its best, a shrubby tree which grows to 7-10 m. It is usually low-branching and can be used for windbreak purposes. Unless it is occasionally trimmed, however, it is likely to grow untidily. *J.communis* is a very hardy species which appears to be able to grow in any soil, but does particularly well when lime is present. Its blue-black berries are used in the manufacture of gin. Many ornamental varieties are derived from it.

J.procera (East African juniper) is probably the largest of the junipers. It comes from Kenya where growing at high altitudes it attains a height beyond 30 m with dense neat foliage of pyramidal form. It is only moderately hardy and could not be grown in districts where temperatures go below -6°C. Its timber is valuable for milling and for ground use, also for pencil casings and in furniture manufacture. Any reasonably friable soils are suitable for its cultivation.

J.recurva var. *coxii* (Chinese coffin pine) owes its common name to the use of its long-lasting scented boards for coffins. It is a graceful pyramidal tree with

Juniperus virginiana (pencil cedar).

glaucous weeping branches. Specimens of over 30 m are recorded but it is a slow starter. (It was formerly known as *J.coxii*.)

J.virginiana (pencil cedar) is not a large tree, usually growing to a maximum of 15-25 m and developing a narrow, pyramidal or columnar form with a densely foliaged system of branches and branchlets. It will grow on dry gravelly slopes and in most soils, but prefers open loams with some lime. It is a good subject for poor soils, provided they are free, and it is hardy, withstanding reasonably severe frosts. The timber is reddish, soft, straight-grained, easily worked and ground durable. It is used in America, whence the tree comes, as fence posts and railway sleepers. It is said to be one of the best timbers in the world for pencil casings. Because of its fragrance the wood is used in the manufacture of chests and it is a first-class flooring timber. Wood shavings and foliage are distilled for the oils they contain.

Junipers are propagated from seed or from cuttings. Seed should be stratified for at least six months in damp sand before sowing in spring. Most species grow readily from cuttings.

Lagunaria

Only one species is known as belonging to this genus; it is a native of Queensland.

L.patersonii (Norfolk Island hibiscus) has slightly larger leaves which are whiter than those from Queensland but it is not sufficiently different to have a separate name. It grows to about 10m in the best conditions but is on the whole very tolerant of a wide variety of soils, the exception being impoverished or heavy clay. It will survive light frosts and one of its chief attributes is its ability to withstand wind, including salt sprays and ocean-borne winds. It prefers plenty of sun and light and resists droughts. It grows naturally into an erect, pyramidal and handsome tree, densely foliaged with olive-green leaves, and producing all summer till late autumn solitary light-to-deep-pink 6cm open bell-shaped flowers. These somewhat resemble single hibiscus blooms, hence the common name. Lagunaria is an under-utilised tree in New Zealand; apart from its willingness to grow on most sites, its ability to withstand desiccating winds and droughts, its long flowering season and attractive form, it can also be pruned and trimmed to make a hedge, and does not seem to suffer from diseases or insect pests. Nothing is known of its timber qualities.

It is usually raised from seed but can be propagated from cuttings. The brown seed pods contain numerous fine stiff hairs with a needle-like ability to penetrate the skin and cause irritation, so care must be used when handling them.

Flowers of *Lagunaria patersonii* (Norfolk Island hibiscus) in summer.

A twelve-year-old *Lagunaria patersonii* (Norfolk Island hibiscus) in summer on an exposed Waikato hillside.

Larix

Larix decidua (European larch) thrives in a cold climate.

The larches are among the few deciduous conifers. There are about a dozen of them and they come from the colder areas of North America, Asia and Europe. They will grow in a wide variety of soils, including those containing lime, but they demand good drainage. They dislike wet situations and they are inclined to sulk if exposed to strong and persistent winds. They are unsuitable for cultivation in warm or humid localities, their preference being for short summers and long, cold winters. Their timbers, which are hard, strong and moderately ground durable, have sharply defined heartwood and narrow sapwood. They are some of the heavier softwood timbers. Those most suitable for cultivation in New Zealand conditions are the European larch (South Island) and the Japanese larch (North Island). Other species mentioned below may have a limited use for special purposes.

The larches are frequently planted as specimen or ornamental trees. As individuals they are usually of pyramidal form with gracefully curving branches.

The soft emerald-green buds of the European larch appear in early spring, long before those of most other deciduous trees. The russet hues in autumn are a pleasant addition to the landscape, especially when used to break the monotony of evergreen conifer forests.

L. decidua (European larch), comes from the mountainous country of central and southern Europe. It thrives in cold situations, yielding a timber of considerable value. This is of a brownish colour, rather coarse, hard and of moderate durability. The tree grows in any free soils but does especially well in good deep loams. It does not dislike limestone, but its growth in that class of country would possibly be slower than normal, and it requires reasonable shelter from high winds. It dislikes plains, coastal sites and wet soils. It has done best in inland sites from Rotorua southwards and in many parts of the South Island. Growth is fairly rapid, the tree eventually attaining a height beyond 30 m with a long, slender bole. For long-term timber production, advice from the Forest Service should be sought so that the most suitable planting and tending techniques will be used.

L. kaempferi (Japanese larch) has timber which is very similar to that of European larch. It is a somewhat smaller tree (30 m) than the other, but it usually makes more rapid growth as a sapling. Free, well-drained soils with some moisture are best. It is hardy and withstands extremes of temperature — young trees have survived 1 000 m altitude in Canterbury. It also withstands exposure, but for good stem form, shelter from wind is necessary. Not a great deal is known about the quality of New Zealand-grown timber, but in the United Kingdom where both species have been grown, trees of comparable age produce similar timber.

L. x eurolepis (Dunkeld larch) originated at Dunkeld in Scotland and is a hybrid between the European and the Japanese larches. Under cultivation it grows with much vigour. It is a bigger tree than either of its parents and more resistant to insect and fungus attacks. In the U.K. it is widely grown for its considerable commercial value. Free, drained soils of some fertility are best.

L. laricina (Tamarack), is very hardy, coming from eastern and central Canada and U.S.A. It grows to about 20-25 m, straight and slender, and yields a useful durable timber. The tree grows in Alaska where the ground is often frozen for long periods. It is more likely to grow in wet conditions than any of the other larches.

L. occidentalis (western larch) is from the U.S.A. and British Columbia. It is the largest of the genus and is capable of growing to 50-55 m with a 4 m girth in suitable conditions. It yields a hard, fine-grained timber of good quality which is used in America for building construction, flooring and railway sleepers and is similar in appearance to *Pseudotsuga menziesii* (Douglas fir). The tree is very hardy and although it will grow in drier loams, it likes best a deep, moist, porous soil. It is less prone to wind damage than other larches. It is extremely difficult to grow in New Zealand (a statement which may inspire some readers to try and prove the experts wrong).

Propagation is from seed which is often difficult to extract from the cones, not germinating freely unless stratified for a few months beforehand.

Foliage and fruits of *Larix decidua* (European larch).

Liquidambar

Liquidambar styraciflua in May in very wet ground.
Various colours resulted from the one seed source.

There are four species of *Liquidambar,* all deciduous.
The one known best in New Zealand, *L. styraciflua,*
comes from eastern U.S.A. where, under the common name of sweetgum, it grows to large size — up to
40 m — with a long, straight bole and shapely crown.
The timber is commercially valuable and is one of the
important hardwoods of America. The hard, straight,
close-grained wood is bright brown tinged with red,
the heartwood having a satiny lustre and varying
figure. Its beautiful natural grain makes it popular for
furniture but it has many other general uses. The tree
grows naturally in a great variety of soils (which
include adequately drained clays) but it does best in
fertile loams inclined to moistness. The name sweetgum probably has reference to the gummy substance
which is exuded and used in the manufacture of drugs
and perfumes. Apart from the value of its wood,
L. styraciflua is extensively planted in many countries
as an ornamental subject.

In New Zealand the tree varies in size according to
the conditions in which it is grown. It can be no more
than 15 m or so in some localities and as high as 30 m
in others; wherever it grows it retains its shapely
outline and is prized for the superb beauty of its
autumn-tinted foliage which ranges in colour from
orange, bronze or purple to deep or scarlet red. These
foliage tints are more vivid in cold than in mild areas,
and benefit from being in a sheltered position.

The species is noted for its soil adaptability, but
good, moist soils are most suitable. It dislikes alkaline
sites. It is resistant to cold and allergic to droughts; it
can cope with very wet conditions and will grow
within the influence of the sea.

Seed sown in spring will usually germinate freely
and quickly. The seedlings handle without trouble.

Liquidambar styraciflua foliage in autumn.

Cuttings taken in late autumn can be rooted if placed
in a moist but well-drained and shady spot. As the
colour is so variable and unpredictable seedlings are
best left in the nursery for the first year and the finest
coloured ones marked in the autumn before planting
out.

Liriodendron

This is a deciduous genus of only two species, one from North America and one from China, the latter being rare and seldom seen in New Zealand.

L.tulipifera (tulip tree) is a native of eastern U.S.A. where it is regarded as a desirable forest tree. In congenial conditions it can grow, with a tall massive bole, to heights approaching 50 m. Its timber, known as yellow poplar or whitewood, is soft and easily worked and is widely used in America for the manufacture of furniture and many other general purposes. The bark produces hydrochlorate of tulipiferine — a heart stimulant. In New Zealand the tulip tree is regarded as one of the most distinctive and beautiful of the autumn-tinted foliage trees when its curiously saddle-shaped three-or four-lobed leaves turn butter-yellow. The shape is pyramidal, sometimes broadly spreading. The 5-7cm wide cup-shaped, greenish-yellow flowers are usually unobtrusive, hiding as they do among the leaves; but they are very beautiful and eagerly sought for floral decorative work.

The root system is deep and wide-spreading, and the tree is rather exacting in its requirements, preferring somewhat moist, fertile and well-drained soils and some protection from strong winds. It does not like limed or over-dry soils, and is reasonably resistant to cold. Once established it grows rapidly and in average loamy soils it can be expected to attain a height of from 25 - 35m.

Propagation is from seed which should be sown in early spring in a sunny situation and, if possible, in a sandy soil. Viability is usually very low. The young seedlings should be handled carefully because of a tendency of the fleshy roots to resent exposure to the air. Seedlings do not flower until 10 - 20 years old, so it may be preferable to plant grafted specimens.

Liriodendron tulipifera (tulip tree) in summer.

Autumn foliage of *Liriodendron tulipifera* (tulip tree).

Lithocarpus

A genus of about 100 trees and shrubs all except one (which is indigenous to western U.S.A.) being natives of eastern and south-western Asia. They are evergreen trees botanically intermediate between oaks (fruit resemblance) and chestnuts (flower resemblance).

L.densiflorus (tanbark oak) the American species, attains its greatest size of up to 25 m along the west coast, getting smaller as altitude increases. In New Zealand it has generally been a slower grower and prefers rich moist soil, but will stand drought once established. Open grown, the trunk is short and thick, and often disappears in a mass of large horizontally spreading limbs which form a broad, dense, symmetrical, rounded crown. The leaves are light green, smooth and shiny and in late summer become thick and leathery, losing the downiness which is apparent on the underside when the leaves are young. The bark is a source of tannin which gives the tree some commercial importance in its native area. The timber is difficult to season, very hard and strong, and of high quality.

L.edulis is similar in form and foliage to *L.densiflorus* but is smaller (15 m) with glabrous leathery leaves resembling *Quercus acuta*. Its edible acorns have a sharp tapered point and it is widely planted in Japan as an ornamental. It needs a sheltered position to do well.

Propagation is by acorns which are in burr-like cups.

A group of *Lithocarpus edulis* on a Waikato golf course.

Maclura

A monotypic genus which has a very limited natural range centred on Oklahoma and Arkansas, deriving its common name from Osage Indians.

M.pomifera (Osage orange) is a medium-sized thorny tree with a crown of irregular ragged contour. It can

Young *Maclura pomifera* (Osage orange).

grow to 15 m, and often has a divided trunk which is usually short and seldom exceeding 750 mm. The tree is very hardy, drought-resistant, and will grow on any well-drained soil. Its durability for hedges and windbreaks and the usefulness of its timber encouraged its planting throughout the U.S.A., but it is still fairly uncommon in New Zealand.

Osage orange is a deciduous tree developing in late summer yellow-green balls which become 75-125 mm in diameter before maturity in autumn and which remain on the tree after leaf fall. These fruits are unpalatable to humans and animals, but are quite acceptable to birds. They are borne only on female trees. The leaves turn bright yellow in the autumn.

The tree is probably of more novelty value now since stockproof hedges are no longer necessary. The bark is still however used for dyes of yellow and khaki shades; the timber is particularly useful and reputed to be the most durable of all North American woods. It was used for pulley blocks, insulators and farm wagon wheels in the horse-and-buggy days, and is still prized for the construction of bows used in archery.

Osage orange is easily grown from seed.

Magnolia

The magnificent *Magnolia grandiflora* (evergreen magnolia).

The Magnolia family is quite a large one, with a variety of species most of which are more suitable for garden planting rather than use on the farm. Present-day Magnolias are only a remnant of a group of north temperate forests growing before the Glacial Period. They are believed to be almost as ancient as the Ginkgo and were probably as widely distributed. Native to most parts of the northern hemisphere they are very adaptable, needing a reasonable depth of good soil and responding to rich living, good drainage and plenty of moisture. They are tolerant of heavy clay soils and atmospheric pollution. Being large-leaved they appreciate a sheltered situation.

M. campbellii (pink tulip tree) attains its greatest dimensions in warmer areas and can exceed 30 m in its wild state (it comes from the Himalayan part of Asia), but is considerably smaller in cultivation. It is a deciduous tree which bears very large flowers, goblet-shaped at first, later spreading wide like water lilies' petals, usually pink within, deep rose-pink without. A large tree carrying hundreds of flowers is an unforgettable sight. Flowers are not usually produced until 20-30 years old, but some of the forms now available in New Zealand will flower at 6-8 years.

M. grandiflora (laurel magnolia) is from the south-eastern U.S.A. and is one of the most magnificent evergreens. Forest-grown trees are commonly 20-25 m high but open-grown they will be shorter, developing with age a massive round head. The leaves which are bright green on top, usually coated beneath with rust-coloured brown, are 75 mm wide and up to 200 mm long. The large, conspicuous, fragrant, creamy-white flowers contrasting with lustrous green leaves appear in early summer and are the crowning glory of the tree. It continues to flower until autumn, each flower lasting two to four days when the petals fall and egg-shaped fruit appear.

The timber was widely in demand for venetian blind slats until the advent of plastic and is now used for furniture. It has a fine uniform texture and has the ability to stay flat without warping, but is not durable.

There are many other forms and varieties of Magnolia but most of those available in New Zealand are smaller and more suited to the home garden.

Plants are raised from layering or summer cuttings. In cold wet conditions losses can easily occur during transplanting and young plants must be handled carefully.

Foliage of *Magnolia grandiflora* 'Ferrugineus'.

Melia

A small genus of deciduous trees originating from Asia, only one of which is generally cultivated.

M.azedarach (bead tree) is a medium-sized tree which, in New Zealand, will grow in most soils and reach a height of 10-12 m. It is hardy, although young trees will succumb to temperatures lower than -8°C, and naturally of shapely form, with a spreading, hemispherical crown of deep-green, ash-like leaves. Its greyish-blue or lilac-coloured flowers are fragrant and borne in open clusters in spring. The beauty of its foliage, its limited height, its shapeliness and panicles of lilac flowers make the tree a popular one for avenue or ornamental planting.

The flowers are succeeded by yellowish, bead-like berries which contain the seed. These berries are oily and inflammable. They ripen in autumn and seed should be sown in spring. The pale brown wood is light in weight, soft and woolly-fibred and of little value. In India it is sometimes used for the manufacture of cigar boxes. *Melias* can be heavily cut back or pruned if desired.

Propagation is from seed or from mature shoot cuttings. The latter should be struck in a cool, moist situation.

A well-protected *Melia azedarach* on a Waikato farm.

169

Metasequoia

M.glyptostroboides (dawn redwood) is the single species of a genus long thought to be extinct, for like the Ginkgo it is a living fossil. The tree was rediscovered in central China near Chungking by a Chinese botanist in 1941 and has since been propagated in many countries. Despite its colloquial name it has no close affinity to the Californian redwoods. The natural home of the tree is confined to an area of about 800 sq km where the tallest trees are about 30 m high and considered to be approximately 300 years old. The wood from these trees is brittle and only the future will tell of its timber qualities and potential as a commercial producing tree.

It is a deciduous conifer closely related to the taxodiums which it somewhat resembles. The beautiful larch-green foliage and erect conical growth habit make it a fine specimen, with the added advantage of attractive golden-brown colouring in the autumn. The bark is shaggy cinnamon-brown. Earlier planted specimens indicate that in New Zealand the tree does well in moist fertile soil. One of the first to be planted is the one at 'Tupare' in New Plymouth and this, after approximately 35 years, is over 30 m tall and has a diameter of nearly one metre. It can tolerate fairly acid soils and temperatures of -8°C but is subject to disfigurement by severe winds.

Propagation is usually from cuttings, which can be taken from either softwood or hardwood.

Metasequoia (dawn redwood) in summer.

Morus

Morus nigra (black mulberry) in the grounds of a Northland school.

There are 15 species of *Morus* or mulberry. The deciduous trees are best known for their 7 cm x 9 cm leaves, upon which silkworms live, and for their edible fruits; but they are also fine ornamental trees which can be used effectively for shade or specimen planting. They are hardy and accommodating and will grow in most soils. Growth habit is spreading, with a short trunk and a heavy canopy of glabrous or slightly hairy leaves. Height rarely exceeds 15 m.

M. alba (white mulberry) is a native of China where it has from time immemorial been the backbone of the silkworm industry. Its fruits are white, changing to reddish-pink, sweet and edible. It is similar to the black mulberry, but tends to have a narrower habit with smooth leaves, whereas the black mulberry has rough hairy foliage.

M. nigra (black mulberry) probably comes from Persia. This tree is long-lived and has a widespreading head, becoming gnarled and picturesque with age. It is the best of the mulberries to grow for the fruit, these being dark red and juicy and larger than those of white mulberry. The berries are favourites of birds but the resulting droppings stain patios and clothes on the drying lines so it is therefore advisable to plant mulberry trees some distance from the house. The timber is excellent for chair work.

The best method of propagation is from cuttings 30-60 cm long with side twigs trimmed which should be taken after the leaves have fallen. These should be inserted in the ground for at least one third their length.

Nothofagus

This is a small genus of very ornamental, fast growing, evergreen and deciduous trees originating in South America and Australasia, and commonly known as southern beech. Some are native to New Zealand so reference to these is made in the native section of this book. Related to *Fagus,* they are reasonably hardy, but are generally not wind resistant. Four of the South American species were planted by the Forest Service in the mid 1930s, but otherwise they have not been widely established in New Zealand. Nothofagus is common in the United Kingdom where it grows faster than many other species; however a cloud hangs over its usefulness because of its timber handling qualities.

N.alpina (syn. *N.procera)* (rauli) is a deciduous species from Chile where it grows to 40 m. It is similar to and grows at about the same rate as *N.obliqua* in New Zealand. Its timber is widely used in Chile for cabinet work, furniture and window frames, and is superior to that of *N.obliqua.* The heartwood is durable.

N.obliqua (roblé) is a large elegant deciduous tree growing to more than 40m. It comes from Chile and does not seem to have very demanding growing conditions; although in Southland the NZ Forest Service found they were not doing very well in badly drained heavy clay. In Masterton they have reached 11 m in 11 years. The trees could be planted more often as they are very attractive in summer, and in the early winter the foliage turns magnificent red and orange. They are some of the last trees to lose their leaves, which last until mid-August. Timber of mature trees is very hard, heavy and durable and is similar to oak.

A companion species of the roblé is the evergreen *N.dombeyi* which in its native habitat grows to 40 m. It has been reported as doing well in the South Island.

Propagation is by seed which is not easy to obtain as some trees appear to be very shy bearers.

A young *Nothofagus alpina* (rauli) turning autumn colours near Taihape.

An attractive young *Nothofagus obliqua* (roblé).

Nyssa

The summer foliage of *Nyssa aquatica* growing in a Waikato swamp.

There are eight *Nyssa* species, most of them coming from the U.S.A. Two are useful deciduous trees which could find limited employment in New Zealand. Their woods are cross-grained, moderately heavy, hard and tough, but are not ground durable. They are used in America for the manufacture of plywood and where timber is subject to heavy wear. One species is a good ornamental tree and the other could be used in very wet areas.

N.sylvatica (black tupelo) is a 15-25 m tree with a pyramidal but irregular crown. It comes from a large area of eastern U.S.A. but is also found in Canada and Mexico. It grows naturally on moist sites and under cultivation makes a good specimen or ornamental tree. Its oval-shaped, leathery leaves turn scarlet in autumn. Not a common tree in New Zealand it is sometimes seen in parks and on farmlands. In suitable conditions it is outstanding for the autumn colouring of its foliage.

N.aquatica (water tupelo) is a slightly larger tree than *N.sylvatica.* It grows to 25-30 m along the Atlantic and Gulf coasts in southern U.S.A. and also in the valley of the Mississippi. It is a swamp species, found on sites that are often under water for long periods, and frequently growing in association with *Taxodium distichum* (swamp cypress). The tree has a clean bole, usually with a slightly buttressed base. Under cultivation it makes rapid growth in moist but drained soils, and slower growth in permanently boggy areas. The ability to grow in wet sites is its main virtue, for its autumn colouring is nothing compared with *N.sylvatica.*

The trees are propagated from seed, which should be sown in spring. The young seedlings require careful wrenching before moving.

Olea

Magnificent old *Olea europaea* (olive) in Cornwall Park, Auckland.

Olives have been cultivated since time immemorial — some trees are reputed to be over 1 000 years old and there is archaeological evidence that they grew in Crete in 3500 BC. Grown only in warm temperature climates they are at their best in full sun growing in deep rich soil, but will also grow in shallow alkaline or stony soil. They thrive in areas with hot dry summers and also perform adequately in coastal areas. The only one known in New Zealand, and it is not at all common, is the European olive. It is a pity it is not seen more often. It can tolerate quite severe frosts (down to -8°C) and can be found from Kaitaia to Canterbury.

O. europaea is an evergreen tree with willow-like foliage, a soft grey-green that blends in well with other colours. The smooth grey trunks and branches become gnarled and picturesque in maturity. It is slow growing but will eventually reach a respectable size — in Hamilton there is a specimen 17 m high with an 18 m spread. The olives themselves blacken and drop from the tree in winter and must be leached and processed to become edible. The wood is yellowish brown streaked with dark pigment, is hard, heavy and close-grained with occasional burls and swirls making the veneer very valuable.

It can be propagated from seed and cuttings but cultivated varieties may give better fruiting qualities.

Paulownia

A well-protected *Paulownia tomentosa* near Paterangi.

A small deciduous genus originating in China, also known as the princess tree, presumably because it was named after Anna Pavlovna, a daughter of Tsar Paul I. It was introduced into U.S.A. about 1830 and escaped from cultivation. It now grows prolifically in all areas where winters are not too severe with seeds freely germinating on vacant lots, mine tailings and other inhospitable sites. The timber was introduced into Japan centuries ago where it is extensively used for furniture, wooden chests, gift boxes and small items of turnery. It weighs only 330 kg per cubic metre and can be sliced into veneer of only 0.125 mm which is sometimes used for visiting cards. Supplies for the Japanese market have been drawn from China, Taiwan and some South American countries where the tree is grown on a strict silvicultural regime with rotations of anything from five to twelve years. A substantial export trade of logs from U.S.A. has recently developed. No work on its possibilities as a New Zealand crop tree has been done although it is known to grow particularly well. It should be seen more often as an amenity tree, suitable as it is for large open spaces.

Paulownias are quick-growing wide-spreading trees with short thick trunks which will often divide when open grown, although in the first year the tree usually has a single stem which can grow 3 m. At this stage or after cutting back to the ground the tree bears enormous leaves 30 cm long and up to 20 cm wide. To get the best form it may be advisable to cut it back to the ground each winter for the first three years of its life.

The foxglove-shaped purple flowers are carried in large erect panicles (15 - 30 cm), but though buds are formed in autumn they do not open until spring when they make an impressive display about the same time as the leaves appear. There is always a risk in marginal areas of a late frost clipping this growth but the gamble is well worthwhile. Because of the colour of the flowers *Paulownias* are better planted where they can be viewed from above. They prefer deep rich moist soils but on the whole are very tolerant of most soil conditions.

There are two main species grown in New Zealand. The one known as *P. fargesii* is a magnificent tree growing to 18 m which may be more suitable for colder areas than the more common *P. tomentosa* and has the advantage of flowering at an earlier age. The flowers are fragrant, heliotrope with freely-speckled dark purple in the throat. Botanists now think that this species may not be *P. fargesii* but rather *P. lilacina*, a cultivar.

P. tomentosa is a well-known species forming a round-topped tree with a wide spread often equalling the height of up to 15 m. The flowers are heliotrope and slightly darker than *P. fargesii*. It is usually 10 years old before flowering.

Propagation is by seed which is borne in top-shaped capsules, or by root cuttings. Fruits hang on to the tree so that both capsules and flower buds are present at the same time. This gives the tree an interesting winter appearance. Seeds are very light (10000 to a gram) and are easily germinated. Smaller specimens are easily transplanted.

Seed pods of *Paulownia*.

Flowers of *Paulownia* in spring.

Phebalium

Phebalium squameum grown as a windbreak at Pirongia.

A genus of about 35 species mostly native to Australia. Only one is likely to be of use in farm situations, its particular value being its suitability for windbreaks.

P. squameum (syn. *P. billardieri*) is an evergreen tree which has a strictly erect habit of growth requiring a minimum of side trimming. The foliage is pale green, similar to that of the olive, and small white flowers are produced but these are rather inconspicuous. Correct soil conditions are important if the tree is to grow to its maximum of eight-10 m. It will not stand wet feet or alkaline soils, needing free draining conditions, and if these are not present deep preparation is essential. Roots are not invasive.

Little information on wood quality is available although it is known to be very hard, suitable for rails and other above-ground use where long straight lengths are required.

Propagation is easily achieved by using indoor or open ground cuttings.

Picea

There are about 40 *Picea* species. They come from the colder parts of the northern hemisphere, being evergreen conifers of pyramidal form with tall, tapering trunks and needle-like foliage. They are commonly called spruces. Some of them grow to large size; most are shallow-rooted and if not given at least partial shelter are liable to wind damage. The genus is a somewhat confusing one because of the great number of varieties and natural hybrids and the wide variation among individual trees within the species. Spruces have many insect enemies, frequently causing serious damage; this potential danger can be lessened if sites are carefully chosen. Summer heat does not worry them but they do best in areas with very long cold winters. Some flush early and are subject to damage from late frosts. They have pendulous cones which helps to distinguish *Picea* from *Abies* — the latter have erect cones.

Spruce timbers are generally soft and resinous and although they are valued in other countries for milling and pulping and for special purposes such as instrument making, it is unlikely the trees will be grown to any great extent for timber production in New Zealand except in the very cold areas. However they are handsome trees and very hardy and they will, no doubt, continue to be grown for their ornamental appeal in warmer areas. Sitka spruce could be considered a quite useful timber tree for good, moist sites in very cold and exposed areas in the far south.

P.abies, formerly called *P.excelsa* (common spruce or Norway spruce) is the most important of the European species. This tree is familiar to all as the conventional Christmas tree. When grown alone it branches almost to the ground. It is very hardy and prefers soils that are deep and moist. Growth is quite satisfactory where these soils are combined with high rainfall and long cold winters. The tree is shallow-rooting and should be given shelter from high winds. It can attain a height of up to 40 m; its timber is white and soft and in parts of Europe constitutes one of the main building timbers. There are more than 30 varieties, most of them garden dwarfs.

P.omorika (Serbian spruce) comes from a small area in Yugoslavia and can be recommended as it is of excellent form and stays healthy in warm areas. It has a very narrow crown of downward sweeping branches that turn up at the tip. It can reach 30 m but seldom has a spread of more than three to four metres so is therefore very suitable if space is at a premium. A most adaptable tree which grows naturally in limestone country.

Young *Picea omorika* (Serbian spruce) shows its distinctive columnar form at an early age.

P. orientalis (Oriental spruce) is from the Caucasus. It is a large, densely branched tree of broadly conical habit, branching to the ground. It has the shortest (6 mm) needles of any spruce and when young resembles a Norfolk Island pine. With its bright green healthy appearance it is one of the best and most adaptable species in cultivation. It will grow to more than 20 m and can stand slightly warmer climates than most spruces, having been successfully planted in the Waikato.

P. polita (tiger-tail spruce) is a Japanese species which can attain a height in excess of 30 m, but is usually considerably smaller. Its stout, sickle-shaped leaves have very prickly points. It is considered to be one of the most ornamental of the spruces and will grow in most free soils.

P. pungens (blue spruce or Colorado spruce) comes from a harsh climate (the Rocky Mountain slopes of the U.S.A.) and is not happy in New Zealand, being very liable to defoliation. It is the parent species of the well known 'Koster's Blue' spruce. It produces many glorious forms, the small blue trees looking most attractive. Unfortunately by 20 years they are usually very unsightly.

P. sitchensis (Sitka spruce) is from a forestry point of view the best spruce; it is the fastest grower and reaches the largest size. An important pulp and timber tree in north-west U.S.A. and British Columbia, it is hardy enough to grow in Alaska. It inhabits the coastal areas where it can reach a height of 60 m or even more. The timber is regarded as the best of all spruce timbers and is widely used for all building purposes, being light, strong and easily worked. The tree is growing satisfactorily in several cold South Island areas. Deep, moist, well-drained loams are most suitable for its cultivation. In warmer climates defoliation can make it go through an unsightly period each year.

A young *Picea orientalis* (Oriental spruce) growing well at a high altitude near Taihape.

Above: Picea sitchensis (Sitka spruce) growing in the rough of a golf course. *Right: Picea abies* (Norway spruce) at home in a cold climate.

P. smithiana (Morinda spruce) has a weeping habit and bears the largest cones of any spruce. While growing they are light green, in contrast to the dark leaves; as they ripen they turn a dark brown. A tall tree in its native Himalayas it does not seem to exceed 30 m in New Zealand. It is a good spruce for many areas as it will withstand warmer climates, but as it flushes early late frosts can damage it. Not suitable for severe climates. (Known also as West Himalayan spruce.)

All spruces are propagated from seed which germinates freely if sown in the spring following collection. Growth of seedlings is extremely slow. Ornamental forms are usually grafted on Norway spruce stock.

Picea smithiana (Morinda spruce) providing shade on a King Country farm.

Pinus

There are between 80 and 90 species of the *Pinus* genus which come from widely scattered areas of the world, both temperate and tropical. Many of them yield valuable softwood timbers, the durability of which can be considerably lengthened by chemical preservative treatment and so used for purposes which bring them in contact with the ground. Turpentine, wood tars and resin are obtained from pine woods, and oils used in medicine are extracted from pine foliage. In addition, pines are among the best of the pulping woods. The trees grow naturally in various conditions and in most types of soils, each species having its own preferences. Some are able to withstand severe salt-wind exposure and are favoured for coastal planting.

There is so much variation of type within most *Pinus* species and so many poor forms that it is very necessary for planters to exercise care in plant or seed selection. The Forest Service collects seed from trees only of good form and approved type, so prospective growers are urged to ensure that their supplies of either seed or plants come from this source.
P. radiata is firmly established as the dominant member of its species so the others listed below will be of limited interest. It may not generally be known that the Forest Service carried out extensive plantings of many pine species during the earlier part of this century. Anyone wishing to obtain further information on this species could refer to *Exotic Forest Trees in New Zealand* by G.C. Weston, published by the New Zealand Forest Service in 1957. Mr Weston gives very full details of some 40 species of pine, and what has been learned from those early plantings.

One species of pine which was not recorded as being tried is *P. aristata*, the bristlecone pine. There is no reason why it should have been planted in New Zealand since its natural habitat is in the high mountainous regions of central North America. In the White Mountains of California in heights in excess of 3000 metres the species has struggled on for centuries, growing incredibly slowly and concentrating what little nourishment it gets into the few live branches which remain on older trees. Archaeologists working on early Indian habitats counted rings on recently felled trees, establishing that these pines are the oldest living things on earth — certainly over 4000 years old and thus joining the elect company of the redwoods and other trees of great significance.

Harvesting *Pinus nigra* (Corsican pine) for posts.

Needle Blight Disease in Pines

Dothistroma pini is a fungus disease which causes needle cast of conifers. Its symptoms are as follows:

— brick-red bands appear on green needles and persist long after these have withered and become dull brown or grey

— the red zone is distinctly marked off from the rest of the needle

— small black spots (fruiting bodies) erupt in the red infected band.

The first symptoms are often found in branches near the ground. Some of the pines and other trees which are grown in New Zealand are susceptible to this disease and are listed below. Should your woodlots show signs of the disease you should contact the nearest office of the Forest Service.

Susceptibility of Conifer species to Dothistroma

highly susceptible (at all ages): *P.nigra* subsp. *laricio*, *P.ponderosa* in the central North Island, *P.jeffreyi*

highly susceptible (but exhibit a high degree of resistance with age): *P.radiata* — variable resistance after 10 years of age, depending on hazard

moderately susceptible: *P.pinaster*, *P.canariensis*, *P.lambertiana*, *P.muricata* (blue strain) variable, but usually more resistant than *P.radiata;* exhibits resistance with age, probably earlier than *P.radiata*

slightly susceptible: *P.contorta*, *P.elliottii*, *P.monticola*, *P.nigra* subsp. *nigra*
slightly susceptible (usually infected only when growing near other highly infected species): *Larix decidua*, *Picea sitchensis*, *Pseudotsuga menziesii*

very slightly susceptible: *P.coulteri*, *P.patula*, *P.strobus*, *P.sylvestris*

Leaves

Pine trees have their needles in groups, varying between two and five, and this grouping is of help in identification. The following applies to species in this book:

Groups of two needles:
P.contorta
P.elliottii (sometimes three)
P.muricata
P.nigra subsp. *laricio*
P.nigra subsp. *nigra*
P.pinaster
P.pinea
P.sylvestris

The blue form of *Pinus muricata* (bishop pine) near Taihape.

Groups of three needles:
P.coulteri
P.palustris
P.patula (sometimes four or five)
P.ponderosa
P.radiata (sometimes two or four, rarely more)

Groups of five needles:
P.monticola
P.strobus

P.contorta (lodgepole pine) comes from the American Pacific coast between Alaska and California and also from inland areas east of the Rockies. There is wide variation of type within the species, as it appears that coast and inland types are different in their characteristics and behaviour. The coastal type is able to withstand considerable salt-wind exposure, but it is liable to be a stunted and often distorted and twisted tree. The inland type is usually a tree of far better form, developing a long, cylindrical bole with a narrow,

Bark of *Pinus nigra* subsp. *laricio* (Corsican pine).

open crown. It is able to stand considerable exposure and is probably the best of the pines for high-altitude planting in New Zealand. Plantations have been established at 1 200 m in the North Island. Although it prefers good loamy soils it will grow well in poor or badly drained soils. Its timber is slightly harder than that of *P. radiata*, but not so useful. Its role is more in protection rather than production forestry. In the central North Island it has adapted to the harsh conditions so successfully that it is now regarded as a pest in the Waiouru area.

P. coulteri (Coulter pine) from California and Mexico is mainly of interest because of its huge cones. These are reputed to be the heaviest of any pine and weigh, when green, more than 2 kg. They measure from 25 cm to 35 cm in length and are egg-shaped. The tree is a slow grower, hardy and will withstand frosts and exposure to wind.

P. elliottii (slash pine) is from the south-eastern United States and is suitable only for warmer climates. It prefers moist situations and has been established in Northland, Bay of Plenty and Westland where it seemed to be performing quite well on podzol soils. Most stands are of poor form, but improvements can possibly be made by correct siting and use of appropriate provenances. Prone to damage from opossums.

P. monticola (western white pine) yields a timber very similar to that of *P. strobus*. The tree comes from coastal and inland areas of western U.S.A. and Canada where it grows in deep, well-drained loams in high rainfall areas. In New Zealand it has been satisfactorily established on pumice land, in some sour clays and on poorly drained sites.

P. muricata (bishop or muricata pine) comes from coastal ranges in California. There it is a stoutly-branched tree of about 25 m, often with a flat-topped head and showing a preference for swampy sites, but growing also in drier soils. It is notable for the fact that its prickly cones remain on the branches for many years. There are two distinct strains in New Zealand — 'green', a relatively slow-growing tree of poor form with short needles and 'blue', a tree of generally better form with longer bluish-green foliage, widely distributed as a shelter and plantation tree. The poor green form predominates. It grows in a wide range of soils including sand dunes and very poor, dry gravels. It tolerates wet and other difficult sites better than radiata pine. Blue strains produce timber similar in quality to *P. radiata*, but as the tree is slower growing, it is likely to be useful only on sites where *P. radiata* is unhappy.

P. nigra subsp. *nigra* (Austrian pine), a native of Europe, is usually a heavily branched, densely foliaged tree, useful for wind shelter purposes. It is very hardy, surviving in bleak exposed areas, and is salt-wind resistant. It will grow in poor soils, especially those containing lime. The timber can be used for most purposes for which pine is suitable. In the U.S.A. it is widely planted as an ornamental because of its symmetrical form until mature at 60-70 years, when it becomes flat-topped. Although widely grown in New Zealand until about 1930 planting has been discontinued in favour of Corsican pine and other species.

P. nigra subsp. *laricio* (Corsican pine) from Southern Italy and Corsica is a tree commonly confused with Austrian pine. It is, however, a much more useful species over a wide range of soil and altitudes. It grows best in climates with 1 000-1 500 mm rainfall and fairly low winter temperatures. Although hardy,

Pinus patula (Mexican pine) on a Northland hillside.

severe spring frosts will limit growth. It is windfirm and resistant to moderate exposure. Best sites are at lower altitudes on deep, well-drained soils south of latitude 38°. The timber is slightly denser and harder than *P.radiata* and is popular for posts and poles. Because of its tolerance of all but extremely difficult sites it may have some future in forestry.

P.palustris (longleaf pine), sometimes called pitch pine, is another of the south-eastern coastal species from the U.S.A. Its timber is hard and tough and esteemed in its native home for strength and moderate durability. It has been planted on a wide range of soils, has remained healthy and will produce a stand even on strongly podzolised fine sands. As with most *Pinus* species, there is a good deal of variation in type and careful seed selection is necessary. The tree is slow-growing and is remarkable for its long needles which often exceed 30 cm.

P.patula (Mexican or patula pine) is a native of Mexico, a tree of graceful habit with drooping foliage and reddish bark. It will grow to 20 m or so in well-drained, fertile soils. It dislikes wet soils, heavy clays and dry summers and will not tolerate salt-laden winds. It is only moderately hardy so cannot be planted in very cold situations although the tree is growing well in some localities of the Rotorua district. An attractive tree, it is frequently used for ornamental planting, although prevailing winds cause disfigurement.

P.pinaster (maritime pine) comes from the Mediterranean regions of Europe and the mountains of Alge-

Pinus patula (Mexican pine) as a golf course tree.

ria. Probably the first exotic conifer introduced into New Zealand, it was firmly established in Northland before 1840; so much so that it was once considered indigenous and seeds sent back to Europe were for a time identified as being from *P.nova-zelandica*. Now widespread over coastal zones of the North Island it is usually of very poor form with twisted stems and heavy branching. The Forest Service has carried out extensive trials and it appears that wood produced from hard gumland clays and dune sites is capable of matching *P.radiata* grown in the same area. For pockets where soil or climate are unsuitable for *P.radiata*, maritime pine of good provenance (Portuguese strain is the most vigorous) if well tended has considerable potential.

Right: Foliage of *Pinus pinaster* (maritime pine) in spring.

184

Pinus pinea (umbrella or stone pine) makes a good golf course tree.

P. pinea (umbrella or stone pine) is a smaller tree of Mediterranean origin with a very distinct, dense flat-topped umbrella-shaped head of spreading branches, familiar to travellers through Italy. Suitable for sandy soils and coastal areas, it has large edible seeds.

P. ponderosa (ponderosa pine) is the largest of the American pines and possibly the most variable. It comes from western North America and extends from British Columbia to Mexico. Its timber is hard and close-grained and is used for flooring and in general carpentry. The tree will grow in most soils and in varying conditions of climate. It does best in light, moist soils in high rainfall areas, but will also grow in dry, arid country with rainfall as low as 500 mm. Planting of ponderosa pine for production forestry cannot be justified as timber quality is disappointing, and the tree is susceptible to insect, fungus and animal damage, although it has done quite well on cold dry mountain slopes of Otago. Choice of right provenance seed may be the answer.

P. radiata (Monterey pine) is a native of California where it grows naturally in a small area near the sea in Monterey County and on some offshore islands. (See also *Cupressus macrocarpa.*) It was first introduced to New Zealand in the late 1850s and planted on Mt Peel Station. It is a tree of little worth in its native country but has shown remarkable adaptability to better conditions in New Zealand where it has in the last half century become the most important commercial tree. Its planting, harvesting and utilisation

Pinus ponderosa (Ponderosa pine) struggling in a very stony riverbed in the South Island.

186

Cattle under *Pinus radiata* (Monterey pine).

A magnificent *Pinus ponderosa* (Ponderosa pine) in the Cheviot Domain.

have been instrumental in making forestry and downstream industry a major part of the country's economy. The tree will grow in most soils from sands to clays, but does best on deep, freely drained sandy loams. It is drought resistant, and provides good shelterbelts except when there is a hard clay pan when it is subject to windthrow. Safe altitude range is up to 800 m in the North Island and 450 m in the South Island (although there are many instances of successful plantings above these heights). In suitable conditions it will make very rapid growth reaching millable size in under 25 years.

Forestry encouragement incentives have done much to stimulate planting of private woodlots which are a rewarding form of farm diversification. It is anticipated that there will be a strong world demand for high-quality clear softwoods for many years to come. *P. radiata* is a remarkable species which grows much faster in New Zealand than do other softwoods in most major wood-producing countries: farmers should take advantage of this situation. Excellent and up-to-date advice on all procedures for establishing, tending, harvesting and marketing of *P. radiata* woodlots is available from the advisory officers of the New Zealand Forest Service.

P. strobus (Weymouth pine) is known as such in England, no doubt because Lord Weymouth introduced the tree into that country in the early 1700s. In America it goes under the name of eastern white pine. It grows naturally in mid-western and eastern areas of the U.S.A. and Canada, where its timber is used for flooring and joinery work. In New Zealand the tree appears to be growing satisfactorily in the Rotorua area.

Best growth has been obtained in fairly fertile soils, but poorer sites are not uncongenial. Not suitable for exposed situations.

Pinus strobus (Weymouth pine).

12 year old open ground *Pinus sylvestris* (Scots pine).

P. sylvestris (Scots pine) is the one pine native to the British Isles and has been planted only experimentally in New Zealand, but it does tolerate very dry and difficult sites. It has grown vigorously at 1 100 m in the North Island and survived at 1 000 m at Arthur's Pass. Generally poor at lower altitudes, it could be used in high altitude protection forestry.

In the time of Samuel Pepys, Scots pine was imported only in one size — 3 inches by 9 inches by 12 feet. These lengths were termed 'deals' in England. The word 'deal' came to be used to describe any kind of coniferous wood regardless of size, and is still common in much of the English-speaking world.

Propagation is from seed, but it must be emphasised that seed within species is very variable. It is important to ensure that seed, or seedlings if they are being purchased, originate from trees of known good form and vigour. Vegetative propagation is likely to be available for some species in the future.

A well sited *Pinus sylvestris* (Scots pine).

Platanus

Platanus (planes) growing in the Waikato provide shade and interest.

The Plane trees are a small genus of magnificent large deciduous trees from Europe and North America and are well known in New Zealand. They are frequently seen, cruelly lopped, in city streets, and more happily in their natural form, on farmlands. Their main role is in the provision of shade on farms, or in parks and avenues. They are accommodating trees which grow on most soil types though not reaching their full potential on limestone country. Given plenty of room, their squat boles carrying the wide spreading branches and magnificent canopy of broad five-lobed maple-like leaves will add beauty to any landscape. The mottled bark is a distinguishing feature of the plane, thin plates peeling off the trunk exposing conspicuous areas of whitish, yellowish or greener inner bark.

The timber is not often used in New Zealand, but in Europe it is valued for its distinctive and highly decorative figure, especially when cut on the quarter when it is known as lacewood.

P. x *hybrida* (syn. *acerifolia*, x *hispanica*) (London plane) is a large noble park tree with tolerance of atmospheric pollution and severe pruning. It grows to more than 30 m and bears rounded, burr-like fruit clusters in strings of two to six hanging like baubles on the branches from early summer to the following spring.

P. occidentalis grows to massive proportions in its native North America where it is of considerable commercial importance because of its tough timber. It has a wide buttressed trunk and variegated bark, and can grow to over 40 m. This tree has single smooth seedballs while those of the others hang in pairs or even fours and are somewhat bristly.

P. orientalis (Oriental plane) is shorter and thicker than the London plane. The bark is rougher and more knobbly. It comes from south-east Europe and is in most respects similar to the London plane.

Propagation is from seed in the round fruitballs about 2.5 cm across which turn brown in the autumn and break up in late winter. More reliable is to take hardwood winter cuttings about 20-25 cm long, inserted in the ground to half their length.

Populus

Poplars have probably had as much impact on the New Zealand landscape as any other tree. The various species can be seen throughout the country, not only adding to its beauty, but also used for soil conservation and for shelter. A great deal of experimental work has been carried out in the field of hybridisation to breed strains which will resist the ravages of disease and improve growth rate. The arrival in the early 1970s of two rust diseases *(Melampsora larici-populina* and *Melampsora medusae)* brought an almost complete halt to the planting of poplars and necessitated a reassessment of those varieties which could be used by soil conservation authorities for erosion control. Rust-resistant varieties have been imported, and after testing is completed at the National Plant Materials Centre (Ministry of Works and Development) at Aokautere these are released for field use. An extensive breeding programme is also in progress to develop new cultivars specifically adapted to New Zealand growing conditions. Poplars are a large and useful genus which includes some of the fastest-growing of all trees. They are mainly deciduous, native to many parts of the northern hemisphere, and one of particular importance comes from China. For the most part they are wind tolerant but may suffer damage if strong winds persist during spring.

They are essentially trees of the fertile and moist alluvial riverflats. Sandy loams or silts are preferred and on these soils they make very rapid growth. However, provided adequate moisture is available during the growing season they will grow readily on a wider range of soils. Sheltered gully bottoms and lower slopes are also suitable planting sites. They dislike heavy, stiff clay soils which do not allow a free root run, or soils with a very high stagnant water table. Undrained swamps, dry soils and acid peat soils are not the best sites, but poplars will grow under such conditions.

Although the trees have been in New Zealand since 1840 they have never played the part that they have in Europe, where poplars are planted on a massive scale as an adjunct to agriculture. Their ability to grow successfully outside a forest environment, and to do well when planted either singly or in small groups,

Italian hybrid poplars stabilising a hillside in Hawkes Bay.

Italian hybrid poplars pruned for cattle fodder.

means that very small areas can be planted and grown for production of timber in conjunction with animal grazing. In Europe and the U.S.A. the wood is pulped for paper, veneered for plywood and also used for firewood. The Lombardy poplar is one of the best known in New Zealand but because it produces inferior wood it has led to a lack of appreciation of the fine quality timber which other poplars produce. Poplar timber has many special uses because of its white colour, lack of smell and resins, workability, softness, light weight, relatively high strength in proportion to weight and its resistance to splintering. It can be veneered but for best quality trees must be carefully

pruned to produce clear wood. On the farm it can be used for gates, yards, battens, truck and tray bottoms, bridge decking etc, but only after treatment as poplar is not ground durable. Because of its lightness and strength it is periodically in demand (at the whim of the fashion designers) for women's high heeled shoes.

The foliage is readily eaten by cattle and can be useful as a supplementary food during drought situations (see also page 47). The correct time for pruning poplars is late January and February. Good farm management will ensure that stock are available to make use of the prunings.

The poplar is a tree of tremendous potential, well

A King Country hillside stabilised with Italian hybrid poplars.

The silver undersides of *Populus alba* (white poplar) leaves on a windy day.

A row of *Populus nigra* 'Italica' (Lombardy) used to stabilise a river bank.

proven overseas, but yet to be developed in New Zealand where it can grow extremely well. With rust-resistant clones now available, poplar should be planted much more extensively. Only a few of the species already planted will be mentioned by name because it is hybrids that are likely to play the future dominant role. The scale and speed of research on these is such that anything written here will soon be obsolete. Anyone wishing to plant poplars should first discuss with the Catchment Board authorities the most suitable species for his or her locality.

P. alba (white or silver poplar) is from Europe and Asia. This species is a large suckering tree of wide spreading habit, lively and conspicuous on account of the white woolly undersurfaces of the leaves which are particularly noticeable when ruffled by the wind and which turn a magnificent yellow-gold in autumn. It is an excellent tree for stabilising soils (it is said that many of Poverty Bay's roads hang on roots of silver poplars) but can spread rapidly due to its aggressive suckering habit. It will withstand salt winds and drought conditions and is resistant to rust disease. There is an upright variety *P. alba* var. *pyramidalis* of similar height to the Lombardy poplar. Large speci-

View from the road. *Populus alba* (white poplar) in the Wairarapa.

mens are found in Otago, Nelson and Hawkes Bay. A Greek legend explains why the leaves are white below: during a fight with Cerberus — the three-headed watchdog of the Underworld — Heracles wore a garland of black poplar foliage around his head and perspired so freely that the lower side was bleached.

P. deltoides (eastern cottonwood) is a native of eastern North America. In December it releases large quantities of seeds with dense silky hairs resembling cottonwool. In the open it grows to massive proportions: diameters of up to two metres and heights of 40 m. It develops a narrow conical crown which with maturity becomes broad and open and it grows very rapidly during the first 40 years. It has a widespread root system making it windfirm; like most poplars its roots seek out moist spots and can give trouble by blocking drains. These trees were used extensively for farm shelter and many plantings over 100 years old can be found throughout both islands. The largest deciduous tree in New Zealand is a *P. deltoides* 'Virginiana' at Frimley Park in Hastings.

P. nigra 'Italica' (Lombardy) is a poplar which has dominated certain landscapes in New Zealand because of extensive planting and its distinct habit of growth. Reaching 30 m, with a small diameter emphasising its spire-like form, it is generally considered to be a sport, originating from cuttings from a tree in North Italy. It can be propagated only from cuttings and the timber is of little value. The tree was extensively planted as shelter as well as single specimens (the exclamation mark of landscape architecture) and it is a pity that the rust disease means that its survival cannot be guaranteed although it continues to grow well in the drier eastern districts of the South Island.

Trees weakened by old age have been most affected by rust and the bulk of the very susceptible 'semi-evergreen' Lombardy have died. In recent years rust has been less prevalent due to the loss of the semi-evergreen host, together with several dry seasons. Planting of the Lombardy poplar for shelter cannot however be recommended, except in the colder and drier parts of the country.

Above: Populus deltoides (eastern cottonwood) casts a long shadow on a Waikato dairy farm. *Right: Populus nigra* 'Italica' (Lombardy) thriving in Mangles Valley.

194

P. tremula and *P. tremuloides* (European and American trembling aspen) owe their names to the flattened leafstalks of the leaves, causing them to quake in the wind; the species are also known as quaking aspens. Both sucker freely and grow to 15 m-25 m; they can be seen over a remarkably wide range of conditions from sea level to high-altitude mountainlands in Europe, Asia and North America. Splints of *P. tremuloides* from Canada were imported into New Zealand to supply the match industry but these are now made from *P. deltoides* grown in Australia. Their white stems and bright golden autumn leaves make them fine ornamental trees.

P. trichocarpa (black cottonwood) is a native to western North America and attains the greatest size of any American poplar; in the Puget Sounds specimens exceeding 70 m have been measured. This tree is also known as the western balsam poplar because the buds and young leaves give off a strong balsam fragrance. It should not be confused with *Populus candicans* which is the true balsam from which the drug 'Balm of Gilead' is taken and used as a constituent of cough medicine.

P. yunnanensis (Chinese or Yunnan poplar) originates in China and until very recently all stock has come from cuttings of a male clone exported from that country in early 1900. New seedlots have recently been introduced and clonal material is being tested. In its juvenile form the tree has large shining glabrous and quite distinctive leaves which make it a striking and handsome specimen. It grows semi-erect, retaining its pyramidal form for many years and eventually acquiring a rounded crown. It is a vigorous, healthy-looking tree which is resistant to rust disease and is unpalatable to opossums. It will withstand most winds except salt-laden ones. The yellowish-bronze spring growth is very attractive but the autumn colouring is a dull brown, although on the volcanic plateau and in the South Island it is bright yellow. Its timber is of doubtful value. With some justification this species is finding increasing favour as an amenity tree.

Propagation of practically all species is by rooting winter cuttings which transplant readily. Cuttings should be about 1.5 cm x 30 cm and planted to nearly their full length. Alternatively, wands of about 1 m can be directly planted in situ if stock do not have access. Where open planting in stocked paddocks is to be carried out, three metres poles should be used, usually obtainable from Catchment Board nurseries. Presoaking of poles in water encourages establishment but silver poplar poles should not be left in stagnant water longer than one week or rooting will be inhibited.

Twelve-year-old *Populus yunnanensis* (Chinese or Yunnan poplar) in the Waikato.

Pseudotsuga

This is a genus of five evergreen species. Two come from America and three from Asia. One species is widely cultivated for its valuable timber: *Pseudotsuga menziesii* (Douglas fir or Oregon pine) is among the most important timber trees of the North American Pacific coast, furnishing more than one fifth of the total annual timber cut of the United States. The tree covers immense areas in British Columbia and the U.S.A. where it grows in the coastal regions to heights approaching 100 m, rivalling in size the giant *Sequoias*. It is found naturally in a variety of soils, but it makes best growth in deep, rich, well-drained loams with plenty of soil and atmospheric moisture. The timber is highly prized for its strength and suitability for building and constructional works of all kinds, and it is exported from American and Canadian Pacific ports to all parts of the world. In New Zealand it is used for laminated beams and scaffold planks, and when sandblasted it becomes a fascinating interior panelling.

The value which other countries place upon Douglas fir as a forest tree is demonstrated by the fact that in a 10-year period following the 1914-18 war, the British Forestry Commission planted 32 000 000 seedlings of the species. In New Zealand the tree has been grown extensively by both State and private interests; there are something like 50 000 hectares under cultivation. Sawn timber from 65-70-year-old trees, and from thinnings, is meeting with strong demand. The timber is not naturally ground durable. heartwood having a life of five to 10 years, and it is not amenable to pressure treatment.

Douglas fir is regarded with favour in New Zealand because of its adaptability to a variety of conditions, its satisfactory growth rates and its comparative freedom from disease (although the effect of defoliation through needle blight disease has increased considerably during the last 10 years). It grows in a wide range of soils but, as in its native home, the most suitable are deep, well-drained and reasonably good soils in areas of 1 000-1 500 mm rainfall. Growth in poor soils, in sandy soils or in drier situations is not so satisfactory. The tree dislikes wet or alkaline soils. It is very hardy and it will stand severe frost exposure except when very young. Warm climates are not favourable and present strains are unlikely to do well further north than Rotorua. Altitude limits are about 1 000 m in the North Island and 550 m in the South Island.

As with any woodlot planted for timber utilisation, establishment and tending techniques are most important if yield and quality are to be maximised.

Advice on these should be sought from the Forest Service. Since its rotation is more than twice as long as *Pinus radiata*, the economical return should be closely considered before planting woodlots on sites suitable for shorter rotation species. Its main advantage appears to be that it will grow at altitudes where *P.radiata* suffers from snow damage. Many people find it aesthetically pleasing — it has been successfully used as a visual barrier between the highway and *P.radiata* plantations. The wildings around Queenstown are a good example of natural landscaping.

Douglas fir makes a specimen or ornamental tree of noble aspect with a tapering bole, pyramidal crown and large feathery branches. Some of the South Island trees are among the finest and largest of New Zealand's exotics. Owing to the immense size it is likely to reach, the tree should always be given ample room to develop. It should not be planted in clay when grown alone because of a tendency to blow over in high winds in such conditions. Sites selected for specimen trees should be those where the roots can go down freely and thus provide the stability necessary for secure anchorage.

Propagation is from seed and only that from Forest Service sources should be used.

A fine *Pseudotsuga menziesii* (Douglas fir, Oregon pine).

Quercus

A young *Quercus cerris* (Turkey oak) near Tauranga.

Oaks are probably the most important hard wood yielders in the northern hemisphere. They range from the cool temperate regions to the tropical mountains, the southern limit being in northern South America. The northern species are all deciduous while most of the southern species are evergreen. There are now about 450 recognised species which, with natural varieties and forms, plus hybrids and cultivars, bring the total number to about 800. In general they are hardy, long-lived and deep-rooting. Most of them are attractively shaped and their silhouettes in the winter are a fine addition to landscapes. Autumn colouring is a very attractive feature of some of those mentioned below.

The timber is so highly regarded that other timbers which resemble oaks are marketed under that name (eg *Eucalyptus regnans* is sold as Tasmanian oak). Oak timber is extremely variable largely due to the influence of growth conditions on the structure of the wood. When growth is rapid as in vigorous young trees the rings are wide with a large proportion of dense summer wood. The timber is consequently hard and heavy and well adapted for constructional purposes (it is often used for exterior joinery in old English houses). By contrast when wood is grown slowly as in old age, or when trees are closely spaced, the rings are narrow and the timber is comparatively soft, light in weight and more suitable for conversion to veneer, or for manufacture of furniture and high class joinery. Oak is usually straight grained and its strength properties are such that it is the standard to which other timbers are compared. The heartwood has long been accepted as synonymous with durability, but the sapwood will take treatment. These general remarks on timber quality apply to both the North American and the European trees.

The timber of the locally grown trees compares favourably with tawa and with the British-grown oak but there has been insufficient time for testing the qualities and durability of faster grown timber.

Oaks have a long association with New Zealand, records showing that the first plantings were made in the Bay of Islands in 1824. English immigrants planted them throughout the country, possibly because of the ease of transportation of acorns. Widely established as amenity trees, they are also useful for shade. The acorns are readily eaten by pigs, ducks and other livestock. Oaks thrive in deep rich soils, but are generally fairly tolerant as to site conditions.

Q. alba (white oak) is the best known of the North American white oak group. It is deciduous, very similar to *Q. rubra* in form, and has an average growth rate. In its native state it can reach 40 m but more commonly is about 25 m. The acorns mature during the early autumn and are carried through the winter. The leaves turn bright yellow then brown and cling to the tree all winter. The timber is highly valued for its uniform strength and suitability for a wide variety of uses; it is one of the heaviest, strongest and hardiest of all the oaks. Often used for liquor barrels, it is also very popular for panelling and fine quality woodwork.

Q.canariensis (Algerian oak) is from Spain, Portugal and north-west Africa but not from the Canary Islands as the name might suggest. A vigorous deciduous oak, it grows fast and is happy on heavy clay or other soils. Its leaves have some autumn colour and are carried through well into the winter. The acorns are large and dark, in short stalked cups. The majority of the single specimens in New Zealand are hybrids, mainly with *Q.robur*. Where a group is to be found the trees are probably from grafted stock.

Q.cerris (Turkey oak) comes from south and east Europe. The leaves are very variable in shape, ranging from a few marginal lobes to very deeply cut lobes. The tree bears fairly large acorns, is a good deciduous species for dry inland areas, and is fast growing with an ultimate height of up to 35 m. Its form is good, but the timber is of poor quality, rather brittle and with poor seasoning properties.

Q.coccinea (scarlet oak) is from eastern North America. It is a species for soils inclined to be dry and sandy, is hardy and will grow up to 25 m if conditions are good. It has a round spreading head and makes a fine deciduous shade tree. It is the most reliable species for a good, long-lasting red leaf colour in the autumn, this particularly applying to the cultivated variety 'Splendens'. The timber is usable, but is generally inferior to other North American oaks.

Q.ilex (Holm oak) is from the Mediterranean region

A symmetrical *Quercus ilex* (Holm oak) photographed from the road.

and is the most widely planted of the evergreen oaks in New Zealand. It is usually grown as an open-planted tree of particular value because of its resistance to salt winds. It can attain a height of 15-20 m and is often as wide as it is high. It has a preference for light sandy soil or dry loams, but is not happy in clay. It is hardy and makes a good shade and ornamental tree. The timber is denser than other oaks and is very close textured, hard and compact. It is difficult to season.

The magnificent *Quercus canariensis* (Algerian oak) in Cornwall Park, Auckland. Note the person under the tree.

199

Many of the oaks have magnificent autumn foliage. This is a young Wairarapa tree.

Q. palustris (pin oak) is one of the American deciduous oaks, with bright green smooth leaves which turn red or yellow-brown in the autumn. Young trees are of pyramidal shape with a central stem and downward sloping lower branches which tend to curve upwards slightly towards the tips. It grows to a height of 25 m, but with maturity the crown loses its pyramidal form and becomes broad and open. It grows naturally in poorly drained flats, edges of swamps and other moist sites. Acorns are broader than long, are very small and take two years to mature. The timber is generally inferior, having excessive knots and being difficult to season.

Q. robur (English oak) is a deciduous tree which to the Englishman is a symbol of strength and endurance. It grows best in moderately good loamy soils inclined to dampness in localities that are not too humid. For paddock planting as a shade or specimen tree English oak with its short sturdy bole and its wide spreading crown of massive branches has a rugged but symmetrical beauty that is equalled by few other trees. It can grow to about 20 m. This tree dominated the ancient forests of England where the timber was used extensively for building, furniture and ships: the Royal Navy relied on it until the advent of steel and from the 16th to 19th centuries entire forests were ravaged in the interests of naval supremacy.

Q. robur 'Fastigiata' (Cypress oak) is of narrow columnar form with upright branches tending to

Quercus palustris (pin oak) in autumn with *Acer platanoides* (Norway maple) in the left background, near Kimbolton.

spread with age. It is now being seen more frequently in New Zealand.

Q. rubra (red oak) is from eastern North America and is deciduous. It has a short trunk on which develops a good spreading crown. It grows faster than most oaks, usually reaching 20 m or more and is reasonably soil tolerant but likes good moist loams best. It will resist cold, but not drought. The leaves turn a good red in

View from the road. A stunning sight on rounding a corner near Pirongia.
Quercus robur (English oak) in autumn.

Bark of *Quercus suber* (cork oak).

the autumn but it is less reliable in this respect than *Q. coccinea*. It produces a generally useful timber, but this is considered inferior to other white oaks.

Q. suber (cork oak) is another evergreen and is similar to the more widely grown *Q. ilex*. It is a short-stemmed wide-spreading tree of medium size growing up to 20 m. It is very cold resistant and is extensively grown in Spain and Portugal. The cork is the outer bark which is about 75 mm thick, and is stripped without injury to the tree about every nine years. In spite of this seemingly drastic action cork trees can live to 500 years. The tree is not common in New Zealand, but it grows quite well and there are some fine specimens in Albert Park in Auckland and the Christchurch Botanical Gardens.

Propagation is normally from acorns as oaks grow best on their own roots. However unless seed is collected from a natural stand or from a tree which has been cross-pollinated by another provenance of the same species a high proportion of hybrids may result, providing of course that another compatible species is growing nearby. This is very likely to happen in parks or private sections where a number of species grow in close proximity. Isolated oaks are usually shy seeders. Seed should be collected in the autumn and sown fresh, but if this is not done then it should be stratified until sown in the spring.

Robinia

Robinia pseudoacacia is often found in clumps.

Robinia pseudoacacia (thorny acacia, black locust or robinia) is one of the many useful North American trees that have found favour in other countries. It is the only tree of timber importance among the 20 or so *Robinias* and comes from the eastern U.S.A. where it grows to 20 m or more in good loamy soils and to somewhat smaller size in poorer soils. It dislikes heavy clays and wet conditions. It has a wide-spreading suckering root system so is used extensively in erosion control work. More than 65 million of this species were planted in the afforestation of the Tennessee Valley. One of the first trees to be brought from North America to Europe, in 1601, there are now more than 1 million hectares of man-made *Robinia* forests, the largest plantings having taken place in Korea and in the Balkans, U.S.S.R. and China. On the basis of area occupied, *Robinia* takes second place in the world after eucalypts amongst fast-growing broadleafed species. As a farm tree it has many satisfactory attributes in that it is easy to plant, it regenerates, it has no serious diseases, and the wood is hard, has great strength and durability and is easily workable. It has a particularly high calorific value and its ability to burn even when wet makes it popular as firewood. Overseas it is extensively used in architectural work, laminated beams, panelling, parquetry etc; it is on record that in the U.S.A. in one year 25 million insulators were made from it for use on telegraph poles. The tree is an important source of bee food and can also be used for enriching mine tailings because it is leguminous and capable of developing nitrogen-fixing nodules in its root system.

It seems extraordinary that with its many virtues this tree has been so little utilised in New Zealand. Its ground durability has generally been recognised: in 1977 a Queenstown farmer wrote in the *New Zealand Farm Forestry Journal*, 'when I bought the farm property 31 years ago many of the old fences had been patched up with *Robinia* posts which were only limb pieces, bark and all, about 4 inches (10 cm) in diameter. Some of these then appeared to have been there some time. Today the fences have been replaced but the *Robinias* have been left where they were and are quite sound.'

R. pseudoacacia is a graceful deciduous tree with long heavily foliaged branches and bunches of white flowers that hang downwards in the manner of *Laburnum*. It is open-crowned, requires plenty of light and should not be planted in situations where it is shaded. The tree is hardy and frost resistant. Its main faults are that it grows thorns, and has a propensity to sucker. Its branches tend to brittleness.

Probably the main reason for its lack of use in New Zealand is because nearly all local forms have a distinctly twisted bole which detracts from its use as a post or for milling. Overseas literature makes little mention of this characteristic and photos of the trees both in U.S.A and Europe when growing in forest situations show that it is quite capable of growing straight and true: the name 'shipmast' locust indicates that this ability was appreciated by shipbuilders. Root cuttings of shipmast locust were imported in 1945 but reputed superior characteristics of the variety were not reproduced here. An improvement in form could surely be achieved by propagating from trees with the straightness required for good timber production.

Propagation, apart from the use of root cuttings, is by gathering seeds as soon as they ripen — usually in the early summer — and sowing in the autumn or the following spring, first soaking in near-boiling water so that the outer case is soft. Seed retains its high viability for several years.

Right: Robinia pseudoacacia (thorny acacia, black locust) in the Waikato.

Salix

View from the road. Autumn colours of *Salix babylonica*
(weeping willow) near Pirongia.

The willows are hardy deciduous trees. There are something like 300 species, most of them coming from the cooler parts of the northern hemisphere. Though of limited use as timber yielders, some of them possess a charm that has a strong appeal for those whose aim is landscape improvement. They are moisture-loving trees which are at their best on the banks of streams or watercourses and on moist flats, but they will tolerate most soil types. Some can be grown in drier soils provided these are not too shallow. All varieties can withstand heavy pruning.

The first importations recorded were those of *S.babylonica*, planted in Akaroa in 1840. These are said to have originated from cuttings taken from near Napoleon's grave on St Helena where sailing ships often called for fresh supplies. From there they spread to many of the earlier settlements throughout the country. Although there are now many species in New Zealand, probably only about 30 can be found outside special collections. Most are represented by one sex as they were propagated by cuttings.

Some species are frequently employed on farms as shade trees and in suitable conditions they are excellent subjects for that purpose. In times of grass shortage they can be used as stock fodder trees. Dry matter yields from leaves and soft shoots in excess of 15 tonnes per hectare per annum are obtainable from osier types and research into the best methods of utilising this as a stock food is being carried out at the Aokautere Soil Conservation Centre.

The interlocking root systems of many willows make them useful in some localities for the prevention of soil erosion, and considerable research has gone into the selection of the best varieties. The need for shelter in an expanding horticultural industry has increased the demand for species suitable for shelter, resulting in extensive planting of *S.matsudana* and its hybrids in particular.

Since these willows are propagated as single clones there is always a risk of disease which could wipe out all plantings. Breeding is carried out and new importations are being made with a view to lessening this risk, and generally to provide fast-growing non-brittle trees of good form and foliage unpalatable to opossums. For land stabilisation, river control and windbreaks, shrub and osier-type willows are required and some of these are also suitable for stock fodder and basket making. Willows are important trees for bees for they provide early spring supplies of pollen and nectar at a time when other food is in short supply.

Willow timbers although soft and woolly are straight-grained with fine even texture and are very tough. They will stand up to prolonged wearing conditions (truck deckings for instance) better than harder woods. They are not durable in the ground; sapwood can be treated but heartwood is resistant.

Trunk and branches of *Salix alba* 'Vitellina' (golden willow) in winter.

S. alba (white willow) is a large elegant tree of conical habit with slender branches drooping at the tips. It will grow to 25 m. The leaves have thick white down beneath giving the tree a whitish-grey appearance particularly attractive when conditions are windy. In autumn they turn a beautiful golden yellow. *Salix x sepulcralis* is a hybrid between *S. alba* and *S. babylonica* with branches less weeping than the latter.

S. alba 'Chrysocoma' (golden weeping willow) is a *S. alba* hybrid which is one of the most beautiful weeping trees available in New Zealand. It is a medium-sized wide-spreading tree producing vigorous arching branches which terminate in golden-yellow weeping branchlets. These are particularly attractive in winter.

S. alba 'Coerulea' (cricket bat willow) is a cultivar of *S. alba* that will grow with upright habit to about 25-30 m. It is from this tree that cricket bats are made, but it is not often seen in New Zealand. Grown in good moist conditions it can be milled for bats in only 15 years.

S. alba 'Vitellina' (golden willow) is a 15 m tree with bright yellow branchlets made more conspicuous by regular pruning. These branchlets are very attractive in winter and early spring before the leaves come out. The lower branches droop at the tip and give the tree a semi-weeping habit. A most handsome variety of *S. alba* is a golden weeping willow, *S. alba* var. *tristis*, derived from a cross with *S. babylonica*. It has a wide crown with long pendulous branches.

S. babylonica (weeping willow) is a native of China. This well loved, graceful and often stately tree can grow to 20 m with an attractive wide-spreading and pendulous habit. It grows best in soils where drainage is reasonably good. In drier soils it frequently attracts disease and dies while young. It makes a fine shade tree and in farm situations is often seen with its branches trimmed back to a regular height by cattle or sheep. For landscaping it is at its best when associated with water. One version of the origin of the name is that it was given by Linnaeus who was under the false impression that it was the tree referred to by the Psalmist when he told of the Israelite captives in Babylon 'hanging their harps on the willows'. This gave rise to the legend that the previously erect branches were thereby weighed down and have been pendulous ever since. It is now considered that the tree referred to by the Psalmist was not a willow at all but the narrow-leaved poplar, *Populus euphratica*.

S. babylonica is one of the first of all trees to show its new season's leaves — a sure sign that spring is close.

S. caprea, the true goat or pussy willow, is seldom found in New Zealand; the common garden pussy willow grown for its catkins and for shelter is a hybrid of *S. caprea*. It is a male clone which will not seed and is now called *S.* x *reichardtii*.

S. cinerea is the willow which has infested most swamps throughout the country and is commonly called pussy willow. Both sexes of this species were imported from Europe about 100 years ago and this has made it very easy for seedlings to spread. Although it prefers moist conditions it is not at all demanding and can grow well in drier soils reaching a height of 9 m, usually with a many-stemmed trunk.

S. fragilis (crack willow) is New Zealand's most common and wide-spread willow which has naturalised along many of the larger rivers. It becomes a large tree up to 20 m high with wide-spreading branches and a broad crown. The twigs are very brittle, snapping at the base with a cracking sound.

Salix matsudana (Pekin willow) grown as shelter for a horticultural crop.

S. humboldtiana 'Pyramidalis', a native to Central and South America, is tall and narrow with slender erect tapering form growing to 10 m. The leaves are long and very narrow. It is more site selective than other willows and must have a good free-draining location. It is almost evergreen in milder climates, but tends to have a weak root system resulting in windthrow.

S. matsudana (Pekin willow), originating in China, is a medium-sized tree of conical habit with slender stems and long, narrow leaves. Its hybrids are extensively used for shelterbelts where space is at a premium. It is extremely vigorous and will withstand any amount of above- and below-ground pruning.

S. matsudana 'Tortuosa' (corkscrew or twisty willow), is an oddity whose branches and twigs are conspicuously twisted and contorted. These are seen to advantage after the foliage has dropped. It will grow to 15 m on a straight bole and will develop a rounded form.

S. viminalis is the most common of the osier types which are the source of basket-making material. Like the pussy willow, both sexes were imported and it has been widely planted for river protection work. Seedling development has caused problems with the blocking of some waterways. It is really only a medium-sized shrub but may develop a useful role as summer animal fodder.

Propagation is by cuttings which will grow very easily, regardless of size. Anyone using willows for soil conservation work or for shelter should obtain the latest information and advice available. Continuing research at the Soil Conservation Centre (Ministry of Works and Development), Aokautere, near Palmerston North, is improving the range of willows available for specific purposes.

A fine *Salix matsudana* 'Tortuosa' in the Waikato.

Schinus

Trunks and foliage of *Schinus molle* (pepper tree).

A genus of about 15 species of evergreen trees, mostly from South America.

S.molle (pepper tree) from Peru is a quick-growing tree often used for street planting in warmer districts, where its vigorous rooting system can upset paving. Trunks of older trees are heavy and interestingly gnarled, with many knots and burls. It has heavy limbs and light branchlets which droop with bright green leaves divided into 50-70mm long leaflets. It grows in any soil, tolerates drought when established and even survives poor drainage. Will reach 10-15m height with a broad spread and rounded head — not unlike a weeping willow. Most females bear pea-sized pinkish red berries which make a most attractive display. It is a fine specimen and shade tree suitable for farms or large homestead gardens and is worth planting.

Since no information on its timber has been found it must be left to readers to find out its qualities.

It can be grown easily from berries but seedlings are not readily transplanted so should be container-grown. The tree is damaged by frosts for the first year or two so should be protected if temperatures go below -8° C.

Sequoia

The *Sequoia* is among the oldest living trees known to man. The common name of this conifer is derived from the colour of the timber and bark, the botanical name commemorating a Cherokee chief, Sequoiah, who invented the Cherokee alphabet. The natural occurrence of the tree is confined to a narrow strip extending 800 km along the Pacific coast of the United States. Millions of years ago Asia and North America were covered with a forest of trees of the *Sequoia* family, but during the Ice Age huge fields of ice moved down from the north, obliterating the land bridge at Bering Strait and erasing all *Sequoias* except those in California.

S. sempervirens (coast redwood) is most useful for general farm planting, and those farmers who have suitable conditions for its growth will find it an extremely satisfactory tree to cultivate. Few, if any,

exotics can equal its claims for general usefulness. Grown in ordered plantations in good, moist soils, the clean-barrelled boles of these trees, even in young New Zealand stands, present an impressive and imposing spectacle. Shelterbelts of the species growing on high, dry country, although usually lacking in vigour owing to the dry conditions, nevertheless stand windfirm and effectively break the force of damaging winds.

The tree is a native of California where it grows in what is called the 'fog belt', a narrow coastal strip extending from southern Oregon to the vicinity of Los Angeles. There it is a most impressive tree, combining tremendous height with diameters approaching 7 m. It has the distinction of being the world's tallest living tree (110 m). It is also long-living (500-700 years) with specimens over 2000 years old recorded. The thick bark (up to 0.3 metres) protects

Fourteen-year-old *Sequoia sempervirens* (coast redwood) in the Bay of Plenty area. These trees have been pruned to 8m and are putting on an average of 4cm per annum diameter at breast height.

the tree from fire. The durable timber is easy to work, resists decay and insects and is used for many jobs where timber has to be in ground contact, eg railway sleepers and bridge timbers, and also for shingles and decking. *S. sempervirens* appears to have been first introduced to New Zealand about 120 years ago and at one time an estimated 4000 hectares had been planted, but only about one per cent of this was successful. There is little doubt that where the tree has failed to come up to expectations, the fault has been in choice of sites.

There is still a place for limited plantings of redwood. The climate of California is not too dissimilar from that of parts of New Zealand, and other conifers from that state which have grown well in this country are *Pinus radiata* and *Cupressus macrocarpa.* Strength of locally grown redwood is inferior to that of the Californian, due to the faster growth rate (wide growth bands) and resulting lower density. The heartwood is usually a uniform deep reddish-brown, non-resinous and free of odour. Where strength is unimportant there are many ways to utilise the light, durable, stable heartwood produced by local specimens, including shingles, interior panelling, weatherboards, food storage containers (no resin taint), joinery etc. Greater structural strength can be obtained by lamination.

One of the finest stands of the species in the country is 6 ha in Whakarewarewa Forest, Rotorua. Planted in 1901 the stand is informally dedicated to the men of the Forest Service who gave their lives in the two World Wars. The best growth among these redwoods is at the foot of slopes, where the soil has greater depth and mists and fog prevail. Here the height of the tallest tree was 55 m in 1979, with a diameter of 1.64 m.

More research is required to determine guidelines for favourable establishment techniques, expected growth rates, enrichment plantings and general details pertaining to the species. The tree has promise in the field of erosion control utilising its deep-rooting ability and coppicing potential (resprouting from stumps, root suckers). A change of tree shape in the environment and the advantageous factors of fire and insect resistance are added benefits.

At present a 50 to 80 year rotation is expected, with good sylvicultural practice to ensure maximum heartwood development. Initial growth rates can be expected to compare with pine, but rotation time is longer due to volume of heartwood required.

Propagation is from seed, but softwood summer cuttings are not difficult to strike.

A six-year-old *Sequoia sempervirens* (coast redwood) growing with *Pinus radiata.*

Sequoiadendron

This tree along with the *Sequoia* (*q.v.*) is a survivor of the northern hemisphere Ice Age. It is a monotypic genus until recently included under *Sequoia*. It too has a thick deeply furrowed reddish-brown bark, but has denser, more bushy foliage.

S.giganteum (Wellingtonia or Sierra redwood) also comes from California at about the same latitude as its relative (*Sequoia*) but further inland, usually growing on mountain slopes where it thrives in shallow grassy basins. The tree grows to 100 m and it can be 30-70 m before the first branch, while diameters of 10 m are recorded at three metres above the ground. One stump showed 3 400 annual growth rings and another was thought to contain 4 000. The 'General Sherman'

tree with a trunk volume of 1 400 cubic metres is generally acknowledged to be the world's largest living thing. The timber, which is a dull purplish red-brown, is difficult to handle and is no longer milled commercially although it can be used for much the same purposes as *Sequoia sempervirens*.

Not planted extensively in New Zealand, it occurs in isolated small groups or as a specimen tree. It is not as quick growing as the *Sequoia*; nevertheless in the South Island a tree has reached 36 m in 100 years. In free, well-drained positions it has developed into massive dense windfirm shelterbelts on very exposed sites. In warmer climates it is susceptible to a form of canker.

Propagation is from seed.

Sorbus

Fruit of *Sorbus aucuparia* (rowan, mountain ash) in autumn.

The *Sorbus* genus of about 80 species concerns only those treegrowers who dwell in the colder parts of the country, and then only to a limited extent, for these deciduous trees are of interest solely as ornamentals. Those species which reach small tree size are attractive both for their scarlet berries and for the brilliance of their autumn foliage which are best in areas with dry autumns and cold winters. Their timbers have no commercial value. They are very hardy trees, some of which have special soil preferences.

S.aucuparia (rowan tree, mountain ash) from the cooler parts of Europe and Western Asia is probably the best known and most popular. It is an erect and graceful little tree with upward-pointing branches and can grow in sheltered situations to about 15 m. In

spring it has masses of white flowers: in suitably cold districts it bears bunches of red berries and its pinnate ash-like leaves are conspicuous for their autumn colour. The tree grows well in poor soils (but not alkaline) and it will withstand very cold temperatures. It is the parent of numerous hybrids.

S.aria (whitebeam) is a small, bushy tree with pinnate leaves which also bears red berries and is a native of England and southern Europe. It is a lime lover, can live in very cold conditions, and could perhaps find useful employment as low shelter on cold, exposed limestone country. It grows to 10-15 m and in spring is a most attractive tree, bearing bright green leaves with a silvery down underneath.

Left: Sequoiadendron giganteum (Wellingtonia, Sierra redwood).

Both are easily raised from seed and are readily transplanted.

Syncarpia

The *Syncarpias* are a genus of five Australian natives, *S. glomulifera* being the most important species. It is a large, rough-barked timber tree which can, in favourable circumstances, reach a height approaching 65 m. Usually it is considerably smaller. It comes from the coastal areas of the eastern Australian states, growing within the influence of the sea, but in New South Wales it extends inland as far as the Blue Mountains.

The timber varies in colour from reddish-pink to reddish-brown. It is tough, hard, close-grained and ground durable, highly valued for use as railway sleepers and fencing material. The heartwood is not suitable for milling, being liable to warp and twist, but the sapwood is milled for flooring. Because of their resistance to attacks by marine borers, turpentine logs find their main market as wharf piles. These logs are sometimes seen in New Zealand ports and are distinctive because the outer bark is always intact.

S. glomulifera (turpentine tree) is a stately tree carrying a good crown of dark glossy green laurel-like foliage on a clean, slim bole. It can be used with effect in warmer areas for paddock planting where stately height is preferred to spreading shade. If it is grown for timber, the planter could be sure of reaping reliable fencing material. Its preference is for good, well-drained soils, but sandy soils and clays are not uncongenial. The tree is growing well in Waikato, Bay of Plenty and Northland.

Propagation is by seed. The seedlings are frost tender and are able to stand only limited exposure, but they harden with age and can then withstand down to -6° C.

Syncarpia glomulifera (turpentine tree) growing at Mount Maunganui.

Tamarix

Flowers of *Tamarix* in early January.

Most *Tamarix* grown in New Zealand are small shrubs commonly used in garden work, but one species can be regarded as a useful farm tree. This is *T.aphylla*, known as athel tree. It could be used on coastal farms for the establishment of low shelter against persistent salt winds as is done in some Australian localities; when combined with *Casuarina* species a very efficient barrier can be created.

T.aphylla is a native of dry areas in Northern Africa, the Middle East, and India. It grows to about 7-9 m with erect branches, wiry twigs and feathery grey-green foliage. The tiny pink flowers in slender racemes make a colourful splash on the landscape. An evergreen, it has been known to attain a height of 6 m within five years in very dry, sandy conditions. This little tree played an important role in the difficult task of providing defence against wind and shifting sands at Broken Hill in the far west of New South Wales.

Propagation is by open-grown winter cuttings which should be struck in pots as they are very hard to transplant.

Taxodium

T.distichum (swamp or bald cypress) is the best known and most useful of the three *Taxodium* species. It is a deciduous conifer (one of very few) of considerable attractiveness which can be grown in wet, swampy areas where most other trees would perish. It also grows well on dry land where it can attain large size, with a tapering bole and shapely, pyramidal outline. The foliage is very fine and feathery, in the autumn turning a warm rich brown which is very lovely, and in spring new growth is an attractive light lettuce green.

The tree is a native of the southern and south-eastern parts of the U.S.A. where it grows in water, or near water, on low-lying flats, sometimes reaching heights of 30-40 m. Some of these big trees are claimed to exceed 1 000 years of age. It is the dominant tree in the famous Everglades of Florida.

The timber is durable and moderately resistant to treatment. There is a marked contrast between spring and summer rings giving rise to interesting grains, and it is thus valued for panels, veneers and internal use. It can be used for food containers since it imparts no colour or taste. The grain is typically straight and the timber easily worked.

While it will withstand windy conditions the final shape can be disappointing and unsightly. Two neighbouring trees can be quite different; one maintaining an erect pyramidal form, the other being grossly misshapen with three-quarters of the growth on the leeward side. In spite of the fact that it grows naturally in soft, wet country, owing to its peculiar root system the tree is exceptionally stable and wind-firm. In very wet situations its deep penetrating tap root is supported by a secondary system of shallow roots which are often completely submerged in water, developing what are known as 'knees'. It is claimed that their function (they are conical and rise well above ground level) is to enable the water-submerged roots to breathe. Knees are not present in trees grown on well-drained country.

T. ascendens is a beautiful columnar tree with ascending branches, erect at first but drooping later. It enjoys similar sites to *T. distichum*, colours well in autumn and has bright green leaves in spring, but does not grow so tall or wide.

T. distichum is frequently seen in New Zealand as an ornamental tree, often growing on dry land. If planted in waterlogged conditions it is essential that it be 'mound planted' on such a site.

Two other members of the genus are seldom seen in New Zealand but are well worth acquiring.

Taxodium distichum (swamp cypress) in late autumn. At back left is *Liriodendron tulipifera* (tulip tree).

Taxodium distichum (swamp cypress) happy to be near water.

T. mucronatum (Mexican cypress) is similar to *T. distichum* in form, but in warmer areas it is nearly ever-green, casting only some of its leaves. It grows to 30m in its native habitat and one much photographed specimen in Mexico 30m in diameter is claimed to be the world's fattest tree.

Propagation is usually from seed, which is difficult to germinate but if suitable cuttings taken in late autumn can be induced to root this is an inexpensive way to acquire stocks. The young plants will stand considerable frost exposure. The form of the tree when grown from seed is extremely variable.

Taxodium ascendens 'Nutans' in early summer.

"Knees" of *Taxodium distichum* (swamp cypress) on a King Country farm.
These trees completely dried up a swamp area.

215

Thuja

There are six *Thuja* species and dozens of varieties. They are shapely, symmetrical, evergreen conifers coming from China, Japan and North America. They are very hardy and grow best in somewhat moist soils in areas of high rainfall. In drier parts of their habitat they are inclined to be stunted in growth. The two species best known in New Zealand are *T. plicata* and *T. occidentalis* but there are also many horticultural varieties. All *Thujas* make handsome ornamental subjects and are widely used in landscape improvement work.

T. occidentalis (northern white cedar) comes from Canada and north-eastern U.S.A. It is a very hardy, medium-sized tree, usually attaining a height of 15-20 m. It grows naturally in a wide variety of soils: while good and fairly moist loams are best, peat soils are not uncongenial. The tree is subject to scale insect attack if grown in soils that are too dry. The timber is durable and suitable for ground work or for milling. Outside its habitat *T. occidentalis* is usually used for ornamental effect rather than as a timber tree. It is also frequently employed as a hedging plant, its ability to stand constant trimming making it a useful subject for this purpose. Under the name of Arbor-vitae (by which all *Thujas* are known) this tree is believed to have been the first American tree introduced, late in the 16th century, into Europe.

T. plicata (western red cedar) is a much larger tree than *T. occidentalis*. It is, indeed, the largest and most important timber tree of the genus. It comes from North America, and grows to heights of 55m or more in coastal areas from Alaska in the north to California in the south, ascending to altitudes of over 3000 m. The tree is of pleasing pyramidal shape, often with a large buttressed base. The biggest and best trees are found on fairly moist flats and slopes, the banks of streams and in swamps. The timber is light in weight, soft and easily worked, but ground durable and of excellent milling quality. It is used for railway sleepers, telephone poles, boatbuilding, shingles, all carpentry needs and furniture-making. The bark is stringy, and so tough that Indians used it for making

A well-shaped *Thuja plicata* (western red cedar), twelve years old, on peat land.

A young *Thuja occidentalis* (northern white cedar).

ropes and nets.

In New Zealand *T.plicata* is growing well as a timber tree in good moist loams and in damp, clayey soils in areas of 1000mm or more of rainfall. As a shelterbelt tree, where timber production is of secondary importance, it is growing satisfactorily in drier conditions but due to a rather shallow and wide-spreading rooting system, it is not likely to thrive in low rainfall areas. As its lower branches are retained for many years to ground level, the tree is a good shelterbelt subject, being increasingly used as a replacement for disease-stricken *Chamaecyparis lawsoniana*. It is shade tolerant and can be trimmed.

Both *T.occidentalis* and *T.plicata* are very hardy trees which are thriving in localities where temperatures of -10° C are experienced. In New Zealand timber has proved of good quality, light in weight and easily worked. Heartwood content is high, durability is good and round material has been used for posts. Both are most likely to grow more vigorously in cold, rather than in warm areas.

Propagation is from seed which should be sown in spring. Cuttings taken in late autumn will root readily in moist, sandy soils.

Thujopsis

This is what botanists call a monotypic genus; that is, it has but one species, *Thujopsis dolabrata*, a tree very closely allied to the *Thuja* genus and like the latter, commonly known as Arbor-vitae.

It is an evergreen conifer which comes from Japan where it is regarded as an important forest tree. It is very hardy and thrives in most alkaline soils, reaching a height of about 30m, but is a slow grower. An upright tree with wide flattened leaves, dark green above and silvery beneath, it should be planted as a specimen tree so that this foliage can be clearly displayed. Its rather soft wood is fragrant and is said to possess some ground durability. It is unlikely to be grown for timber in New Zealand, but it could receive consideration as an ornamental tree in suitable localities.

A dwarf variety, known as *T.dolabrata* var. *nana*, which does not usually exceed about 3.3 metres, is a very attractive garden subject.

Propagation can be done from cuttings.

Right: The uncommon *Thujopsis dolabrata* (arbor-vitae) near Tauranga.

217

Tilia

The *Tilia* species, known as limes or lindens, come from Europe, North America and Asia. Some yield timbers that are valued in the countries where the trees grow. These timbers are notably even-textured, white, soft and non-odorous. They are used in the toy-making, carving and musical instrument trades and for food storage containers. In Asia the tough inner bark is used for making ropes, mats and shoes.

These deciduous trees are however cultivated more for their ornamental appeal than for timber production. They are mostly tall, stately trees which will, in cool moist soils of all types and in a climate that is not too warm, reach a height of about 30 m. They will tolerate heavy trimming and are commonly used as avenue or specimen trees in European countries; some of the English limes are world-famous as is Berlin's 'Unter den Linden'. The flowers of many species are highly scented and the nectar is enjoyed by bees. The leaves turn yellow before falling and there are many fine specimens in New Zealand, especially in the colder parts of the South Island.

Differences between species are slight and hybrids are common, making correct identification difficult.

T. americana (American basswood) is distributed over much of the eastern half of the United States where the largest and most vigorous trees are found in fertile sites particularly on low lands near streams. Like most limes it readily adapts to difficult conditions such as city streets, and it coppices freely. It grows into a handsome, compact, narrow-crowned tree to 20-25 m high, with 25 mm deeply furrowed bark. It has white flowers and large (20 x 18 cm) leaves.

T. cordata (small-leaved lime) from Europe is a smaller tree in all respects and grows to about 15 m, an attractive vigorous tree with rounded habit. The leaves are bluish-green on the underside and 5-7 cm long.

T. x europaea (common lime) is a hybrid between large- and small-leaved species. Its tendency to produce a profusion of shoots around its base and often

Tilia (lime) trees make a fascinating sight in autumn. These beautify a Waikato farm.

The beehive-shaped *Tilia x europaea* (common lime) is most distinctive.

higher up on larger branches can make it rather untidy. It grows to a large spreading tree up to 30m high, and is the most commonly planted of limes.

T. platyphyllos (large-leaved lime) comes from continental Europe and is a large vigorous tree growing to 30 m with rounded habit and bearing yellow flowers. Its leaves are rather hairy and of variable size, 6-15 cm long.

T. vulgaris is sometimes shown in catalogues but this is another name for the common lime.

Lime seed does not retain viability for long and is best sown as soon as possible after collection. Some species sprout from the root collar and these sprouts will usually root readily.

Tristania

Tristania is a genus of about 25 species of evergreen trees mostly from Australia.

T. conferta (syn. *Lophostemon confertus*) (brush box) is a valuable timber tree but it is also one which is widely used in various parts of Australia for shade and ornamental planting. The timber is hard, close-grained and exceedingly tough, the toughness being exploited for all purposes where excessive wearing qualities are demanded. This timber used to be frequently seen (but seldom recognised) in this country among imported 'mixed hardwood' fenceposts. Those posts branded with the letters BBX indicated that they were split from *T. conferta* logs.

Trees have been successfully established in Auckland areas, parts of Hawkes Bay, the Waikato and the Bay of Plenty. Good heavy soils with a 1000-1500 mm rainfall are most suitable, but sandy loams are tolerated provided the rainfall is adequate. As a timber tree, brush box develops a long, clean bole and will attain, in good conditions, a height of 30-40 m.

Planted as an individual, the height of the tree is considerably curtailed, but its spread is accentuated and, carrying as it does a mass of broad, glossy, dark green leaves, it makes a very handsome shade or ornamental specimen. It will tolerate heavy repeated pruning. For those who have the warmer conditions necessary for its healthy and vigorous growth, it is a tree well worthy of consideration.

Propagation is by seed or from half-ripe autumn cuttings under glass. The young seedlings are frost tender, but once into the sapling stage they are able to endure considerable frost exposure.

A young *Tristania conferta* (brush box) near Tauranga.

219

Tsuga

Tsuga heterophylla (western hemlock) by a farm pond in the King Country.

Foliage of *Tsuga heterophylla* (western hemlock) in spring.

There are about 14 species and numerous varieties of Tsuga, the Japanese name for hemlock. They are evergreen conifers of pyramidal habit which come from North America, the Far East and the Himalayas. Their branches are horizontal, the branchlets numerous and often pendulous at the tips. The trees thrive in regions where atmospheric and soil conditions are inclined to be moist, growing best in free loamy soils. They are hardy, handsome trees, especially in youth. Some of them yield timbers of commercial importance which are used in Japan, China and America for building purposes. The trees are shade tolerant and are best grown in reasonably sheltered situations. In poor soils, or exposed to constant winds, they are not usually successful.

T.canadensis (eastern hemlock) has a flatter crown because of its tendency to fork, and the foliage differs from other hemlocks with a row of leaves upside down along the length of the twig, so that the white-banded underside is uppermost. It grows to 18-24 m. It can be found in the eastern states of the U.S.A., reaching up to Nova Scotia in Canada.

T.caroliniana is again smaller; it grows to about 12-15 m and is found on fairly hard sites in Carolina, U.S.A. at 1 000 m. It is however a valued ornamental.

T.chinensis is widely distributed in central and western China, is very hardy and is lime tolerant. Grows to 30 m.

T.heterophylla (western hemlock). This is a native of the North American west coast where it grows from Alaska, through British Columbia, to Washington and Oregon. It is very hardy and probably the most useful of the hemlocks for timber production in New Zealand. It has been tried locally with varying success, best results having been obtained in cold situations in areas of high rainfall. Growth is very slow when young but it will tolerate extreme shade, remaining green and healthy even when strongly suppressed. It is a tall, stately tree of pyramidal form with a single stem straight to the tip. In its natural conditions it can attain a height of up to 75 m and 6 m in girth. It is considered an important timber tree, its wood being used for building boards, flooring and pulping. The timber is relatively resistant to termites, but is non-durable for ground use. It is soft, non-resinous and straight-grained. The bark contains a high percentage of tannin.

Hemlocks are grown in many countries as ornamentals and fill this role with distinction, for they are handsome trees particularly suitable for farmlands planting but they do not enjoy lime soils. They are very hardy and will stand considerable cold exposure and shade.

Propagation is from seed borne in rather small cones.

Ulmus

Ulmus, known as elm, is a genus of about 35 species which include some of the noblest deciduous hardy northern hemisphere trees. The two most commonly seen in New Zealand are wych elm and common elm. These trees grow in most soils, but they do best in deep loams, disliking heavy clays and shallow soils. They will withstand more adverse and persistent winds than most other deciduous trees, *U.glabra* being suitable for seaside planting. The elm population of Europe has been drastically reduced in recent years by the ravages of Dutch elm disease, which is gradually spreading and for which there is as yet no known cure. The clonal character of the common elm makes it most susceptible to the spread of such a disease.

The timber of elms is highly regarded, being hard, tough, heavy and unusually resistant to splitting. It has been used extensively in the furniture and boat-building trades because of its bending properties. It is not ground durable.

U.americana (white elm) is a vigorous, majestic, branching tree rated as one of North America's most magnificent ornamentals. It is typically vase-shaped with a wide spreading head of branches. It can grow to 40 m but this species too is now affected by Dutch elm disease.

U.glabra (wych elm) is a much safer and more attractive tree than the common elm, and comes from Europe and Asia. It is somewhat smaller in size, rarely exceeding 30 m in height. It is almost always of shapely form and is used extensively in European countries and America for park and farmlands planting. It has larger leaves, a shorter bole and a more wide-spreading crown than *U.procera.* Its branches are inclined to droop and the bare skeleton in winter months is attractive and graceful. The tree is not brittle-branched, nor does it sucker. There are several weeping and golden varieties suitable for large homestead gardens.

U.procera (English or common elm) can attain a height in the vicinity of 40 m but it is usually about 25-30 m. The tree develops a densely foliaged crown which makes it a good subject for shade purposes; but

A splendid *Ulmus* (elm) in the Waikato.

it has the very serious faults of suckering freely and of dropping heavy limbs without warning. In spite of the attraction of its majestic appearance, golden autumn colouring, and the density of its shade, it is a tree which should be regarded with a certain reserve and planted only where it cannot cause damage. The golden-leaved form 'Louis van Houtte' is often seen in paddock plantings and gives a splash of colour when all else is green. This form is suitable for windy conditions.

Seed of common elm is almost invariably sterile, but that of wych elm is fertile and easily germinated in spring. Common elm can be propagated from cuttings or from suckers.

The golden-foliaged *Ulmus procera* 'Louis van Houtte'.

Zelkova

This genus comprises half a dozen deciduous trees from Asia, the Caucasus and the eastern Mediterranean. They resemble small-leaved elms but have a smooth, grey, later-flaking bark.

Z. serrata is a medium-sized occasionally large tree (up to 30 m) from Japan, which branches low to form several arching limbs and a broad, round-topped head. In autumn the foliage turns to yellow, orange and bronze-red. It can withstand heavy pruning, thrives in deep moist loamy soils and is fairly tolerant of shade. The *Zelkova* is a tree of the same considerable quality as the deciduous *Nothofagus*. Anyone seeing the four magnificent specimens at Ruakura, espe-

The magnificent *Zelkova serrata* in autumn. This tree is at the Ruakura Agricultural Research Centre near Hamilton.

cially in autumn, must be inspired to plant this species.

The timber is beautifully grained and greatly valued for furniture and because of its durability is much used for gateways, pillars and posts.

Propagation is by seed or grafting on to wych elm stocks. Specimens can easily be transplanted, as indicated by the successful transplanting of a specimen weighing over two tonnes and with a spread of 10 m from Winchester to London for the 1951 Festival of Britain.

Autumn foliage of *Zelkova serrata*.

The low-branching trunks of *Zelkova serrata*.

10
New Zealand Indigenous Species

In a country which was largely covered with trees 150 years ago, it is regrettable that so little of the native vegetation is being replanted. Many of the shelter, specimen, stock-fodder and timber trees now being grown on farms are exotics. Certainly these are mainly fast growing, tolerant of a wide range of conditions and fulfil their purpose well, some making useful farm timber when the time comes; but the various native species, although slower, evolved for New Zealand's particular climate over thousands of years. They give a magnificent variety of form, foliage, flower and fruit, and of prime importance is the encouragement they give to many New Zealand birds by providing their natural foods. And given the right conditions they are not as slow as most people think.

With only 23 per cent of the original forests remaining in New Zealand and with some of these still being clearfelled, it would be encouraging to know that some farmers are farsighted enough to plant up their own patch of 'native bush' in a sheltered area, realising that eventually they would be providing food and nesting places for endangered birds as well as beautifying their properties. Many native shrubs make excellent low shelter and some will grow under larger trees, preventing the draughts which usually occur as the taller exotic species are pruned up for clear timber, in shelterbelts for instance.

Natives such as mahoe and toetoe are readily eaten by stock, although totara remains untouched. Opossums too can be troublesome, being especially partial to the new growth of kauri. Very few natives are suitable as specimen trees and look unhappy and out of place when planted alone, although in a sheltered situation they may grow well. It is impossible to put too much stress on the importance of good stockproof fencing — finding that animals have broken into a carefully planted area of native bush is most upset-

ting: when many hours of hard work are wasted the owner may not feel like trying again. Only too often does one see dead ring-barked specimen trees standing sadly in a paddock with the remains of their protectors crumbled beside them. If a tree is to last a lifetime, as most will if well protected, then cattle, sheep, goats and especially horses must be kept well away.

For at least the first year, especially in dry weather, trees must be kept weeded, watered and preferably mulched. Hardy fast-growing shrubs or small trees such as *Pittosporums, Coprosmas* and *Aristotelia serrata* will all grow easily and well, soon giving the necessary shelter to more slow-growing select species which will eventually rise above the nurse plants and form their own canopy. It could be suggested at the risk of upsetting farmers that manuka and kanuka make good nurse trees: fence them off from stock and you are well on the way to having your native bush, as

regeneration soon takes place in their filtered light provided adjacent indigenous seed sources are available.

A shallow gully facing east or north, sheltered from cold south and west winds, is best for the native section. Allow plenty of space for planting if a permanent fence is to be erected, as once your nurse trees are established you will often bring home odd plants and the area will soon fill up. Plant the nurse/shelter trees about 3m apart, or closer if the section is exposed, then after a year or two plant among them the less hardy species in small canopy gaps. Most New Zealand trees enjoy company. They naturally grow in close association with each other, which provides shelter from extremes of climate, and this must be borne in mind when the native area is being established.

Much can be learned from careful observation of native plants growing in the vicinity, as natural vege-

tation varies greatly from one district to another according to the climate, the altitude and the proximity to the sea. Many species growing naturally in northern latitudes will do well further south only if protected from cold, or if planted in warmer coastal areas. Purists will insist that only species originally found in the area should be grown, but that would deny tree-lovers the pleasure of planting interesting species which they would otherwise have to travel far to see. No-one objects to nearly every garden plant we grow coming from another country.

In a book such as this it is impossible to include all the New Zealand species, so only the better known trees and shrubs are listed. If you have sufficient shelter and the appropriate conditions, try other lesser-known plants, first checking what their requirements are. The few deciduous trees shed their leaves only in the colder parts of the country, and then for just a short while. These are *Fuchsia excorticata, Plagianthus betulinus,* and *Sophora tetraptera* (and *S. microphylla.*) All others are evergreen.

The satisfaction to be derived from a small patch of 'bush' after only a few years is immeasurable, and increases with each additional planting. The Queen Elizabeth II National Trust has published a *Revegetation Manual* as a guide to those setting about planting a new area in natives, or encouraging an old area to regenerate. It contains all the advice that is needed, including additional sources of information, and is recommended reading.

Agathis

A.australis (kauri) is a magnificent tree, growing to around 30 m with a round bushy top usually rising over the surrounding forest when mature. The trunk is straight with practically no taper, and unless grown in the open is completely branchless up to the crown. The 5-7 cm cones stand out from the thick, dull, narrow 2-4 cm leaves, and contain winged seeds.

The fine quality timber is used for masts, boats, houses, furniture, Maori canoes and many other purposes, including veneers.

Kauri grows naturally only in the north of the North Island, but will grow in colder areas in any good soil not too wet or dry provided it has shelter from frosts and wind. In a favourable situation it will grow up to 50 cm per year, but if unhappily sited or heavily shaded will grow only a few cm in this time.

Propagation is by seed which naturally remains viable for only a short time after seedfall in February-April, although seed can be stored for long periods when moisture content and temperatures are low.

Kauri in Northland, surviving well in spite of the unnatural conditions. How much better the shed would look if a few trees had been planted beside it.

Alectrvon

A. excelsus (titoki) is a handsome 10 m tree with spreading branches, shining pinnate leaves and dark bark; it bears shining jet-black seeds in bright red cups, which never fail to attract attention. The strong, straight-grained, easily-worked timber was used for tool handles, bullock yokes and in coachbuilding. Apart from the country south of Banks Peninsula it is found in coastal and lowland forests throughout New Zealand.

The titoki is frost tender when young and dislikes wind, and prefers a heavy soil which is well-drained.

One authority states that trees of both sexes are needed to produce fruit.

Propagation is by seed.

View from the road. A symmetrical titoki.

Aristotelia

A. serrata (makomako, wineberry) is a small tree up to 7 m, with heart-shaped serrated-edged leaves which have a green upper surface and are purplish underneath. In the wind these leaves are most attractive as they reveal their coloured undersides. The small rose-coloured flowers are borne in great profusion, followed by dark red to black berries provided trees of both sexes are grown. In cold districts this tree is deciduous on open sites. It is susceptible to unusually heavy frosts but makes a fine nurse tree as it stands pruning to encourage it to push up and make effective shelter. A fast-growing tree, makomako is found throughout New Zealand, especially where the bush canopy has been removed in cleared or logged areas or where slips have occurred.

The early settlers used to burn the wood for charcoal to make gunpowder. Present day tree-planters use the makomako as protectors for more tender species, as it will grow almost anywhere.

Easily propagated by seed, or by semi-hardwood cuttings in the first few months of the year. It transplants readily from open sites even at a quite large size.

Beilschmiedia

A fine tawa on the bush edge. Note the straight trunk.

B. tawa (tawa) is an erect tree, growing to 25 m, with light graceful foliage and a smooth dark trunk. The narrow pointed leaves are light green above and usually glaucous beneath, and are most attractive when stirred by the wind. The flowers are insignificant but are followed by 2.5 cm dark purple drupes which are edible.

Tawa is found abundantly in lowland forests of the North Island and less commonly in the northernmost part of the South Island. It likes a fairly rich moist soil and is frost tender while still young. Exposed single specimens in colder upland areas are often windshorn or desiccated by frost. The Maori people used the wood for making bird spears. It is now used for turnery, furniture, panelling, and papermaking.

Tawa seed germinates readily and the tree grows rather slowly. Seedlings need protection from wind but stagnate if shaded.

Carpodetus

C. serratus (putaputaweta, marble-leaf) is a most attractive small tree growing to about 8 m with zigzagging branchlets and serrated-edged green marbled leaves. It has panicles of white flowers about 5 cm across which are sweetly scented, and these are followed by pea-sized capsules which turn from green to black as they ripen in autumn.

Putaputaweta is found throughout New Zealand in forests and by streams. It likes a good deep soil and grows easily. Seedlings are frost hardy. The wood is strong and tough and makes good tool handles. The stem is often riddled with holes of ghost moth larvae and later occupied by wetas, hence the Maori name.

Propagation is by seed or semi-hardwood cuttings.

Coprosma

C. robusta (karamu) is a shrub of about 5 m with opposite, slightly wavy-edged leaves. In autumn the female bush is covered with beautiful orange drupes up to 8 mm in length which are relished by birds. It grows naturally north of North Otago in many situations, and is often found as a seedling coming up in the garden. Fruit is produced about three years after planting.

Although easy to grow it can be made a better shape by an occasional pruning to stop it becoming 'leggy'. If berries are wanted it is necessary to have both male and female plants. It will grow under other trees if required to prevent draughts, but it is hardy and fast-growing so is suitable as a nurse plant also.

It can be propagated by either seed or semi-hardwood cuttings.

Cordyline

C. australis (ti kouka, cabbage tree) grows to about 11 m, with a multi-trunked head of bunches of leaves, and panicles of flowers followed by white berry-like fruit enjoyed by birds. The flowers are beautifully scented, much visited by bees, and can be detected from a considerable distance. The bark is thick, tough and rather cork-like in appearance. The trunks are very fire-resistant, and were used by the early settlers as chimneys for their huts. The leaves made fine kindling. It grows naturally in the North and South Islands in almost every situation from permanently wet swamps to dry exposed hills and is a characteristic feature of the landscape in New Zealand. Take care to plant this tree away from lawns and buildings as its leaves can be a nuisance.

Propagation is by seed which germinates readily, or by cuttings taken from the base of the tree after the top has been cut back. Grass competition can cause mortality, and pukeko will pull out quite large seedlings to eat their roots. Seedlings should grow to about 4 m in 6 years from planting.

Cabbage trees (ti kouka) have a distinctive character all their own.

Corynocarpus

C.laevigatus (karaka) is a handsome tree growing to 12 m, with a rounded head of large shiny leaves. In summer the 3 cm drupes ripen to an orange colour and are held outside the leaves, the tree becoming a most striking sight.

It grows naturally near the coast in the North Island, and in the northern half of the South Island, although groves planted by the early Maori may be found inland in the North Island. Although frost tender when young, it becomes hardier with age. It withstands coastal winds and dry hard conditions, responding well to more favourable situations.

The white wood of the karaka is useful only for firewood. The seeds are extremely poisonous and this should be borne in mind if there are young children in the household, as the karaka fruits when only a few years old.

When ripe the drupes fall to the ground where they germinate and grow rapidly, so this is the best method of propagation.

Karaka in summer. Note the Norfolk Island pines on the right.

Cyathea

C.dealbata (ponga, silverfern) is New Zealand's emblem, easily recognisable by the silvery-white undersides of the fronds of adult plants. The rather stout trunk can grow to 9 m, with the bases of the old frond stalks still covering the upper half.

Ponga is found throughout the North and South Islands in lowland to montane forest and also in shrubland. Its upturned fronds are used today, as they have been for centuries by the Maori, to mark tracks in the forest, particularly those used by night. The ponga is a slow grower and takes several years for the silvery colour to develop. It will withstand dry conditions once established, is fairly hardy and easily grown, but the fronds are damaged by wind so shelter is necessary.

Propagation is by spores.

C.medullaris (mamaku) is New Zealand's tallest tree fern, growing to an imposing 15m or more with a black buttressed trunk and wide-spreading crown up to 10m across. It is found throughout New Zealand except for the eastern part of the South Island, and grows in lowland and hilly forests. Identification is made by the hexagonal scars of the fallen fronds, the tall trunk, and the very thick black bases of the fronds' stalks.

The mamaku is fairly hardy but requires a cool moist root run and protection from strong winds and heavy frosts. If frost damaged it usually recovers.

Propagation is by spores which are found on the backs of the fronds. *C.medullaris* can be transplanted readily provided the fronds are removed and planting is reasonably deep.

Mamaku near Tauranga.

Dacrycarpus
(formerly *Podocarpus dacrydioides*)

D.dacrydioides (kahikatea, white pine) is the tallest of New Zealand's native trees, a magnificent conifer growing to 50 m or more. When young it is cone-shaped with upright branchlets, but with age this changes to a rounded spreading crown. The trunk is usually fluted and buttressed, with greyish bark that flakes off. Kahikatea berries are pleasant to eat raw when they are ripe in autumn, a good tree yielding huge quantities and attracting large numbers of birds. The white pine was originally discovered by Captain Cook in the great forest which once existed between the Thames and Piako rivers.

It is abundant throughout New Zealand in lowland to mountain forests, usually in damp situations where it is often dominant. Stands of conical-crowned trees are a feature of some dairying districts. It grows best in moist ground and will even grow in water, although it may also be found in dry soils. It is hardy past its first year.

The strong, tough, pale, straight-grained timber was earlier used for butter-boxes and packing-cases. It is not durable and is subject to borer attacks, but after chemical treatment can be used for boatbuilding and other purposes. There are now very few pure stands of kahikatea left in New Zealand as it has suffered the same fate as the kauri.

Propagation is by seed which germinates readily.

Kahikatea at the base of a limestone hill. Note remnant native plants in the little valley above.

Dacrydium

A roadside rimu near Rotorua.

D.cupressinum (rimu) is one of New Zealand's best known and most beautiful trees, growing slowly to 40 m. It is recognised by its pendulous branchlets and drooping foliage, and in the forest where the foliage is hard to see, by its peeling flaking bark. Trees are male or female in equal proportions.

Common throughout New Zealand in lowland and upland forests, it is hardy but dislikes wind, and grows best in a good soil with ample moisture although it stands drought when well established.

Rimu timber is hard and strong, and coloured deep red. Because of its high quality and beautiful grain it is much sought for furniture and panelling. Trees hundreds of years old are still being felled in spite of efforts by environmentalists to save them.

Propagation is by seed, which is set in great profusion by the female tree in only one out of perhaps seven years, sometimes with light crops in intervening years. Small seedlings do not thrive with competition from grass. Semi-hardwood cuttings are also used. Growth is slow.

Dicksonia

D. fibrosa (wheki-ponga) is a tree fern which grows to about 6 m, identified by its stout trunk covered with densely matted thick roots and a skirt of dead fronds. Wheki-ponga is found from the Waikato southwards in most forests including planted pines. It is very hardy and easy to grow, but slow to start forming a trunk. It also stands wind better than most tree ferns, and is the hardiest of the larger tree ferns.

Propagation is by spores, or collection (with permission) from under pines due for thinning or felling.

D. squarrosa (wheki) is a slender tree fern growing to about 6 m, with a dark trunk bearing for most of its length the leaf stalk stubs left after the leaves have broken away. The fronds, rough to the touch, make a dense skirt just below the crown for some time before breaking off and falling. Large clumps are formed by underground rhizomes which emerge about a metre from the trunk to start a new plant.

The wheki is abundant in forests throughout New Zealand. In moist sheltered localities many shrubs and ferns can grow on the stem as seed lodges above the dead stubs and roots penetrate the fibre. It is quite hardy and will stand exposure to sun and wind, although it grows better if its roots are shaded. Allow room for it to spread and form a colony.

Offsets can be taken from the base of the trunk, and it can also be propagated by spores.

Wheki-ponga in a swamp near Matamata.

234

Dodonaea

D. viscosa (akeake) is a small attractive tree of 6 m with erect branches and striking reddish-yellow seed capsules with thin broad wings. Plants of both sexes are necessary for seed production. The form *D. viscosa* 'Purpurea' has rich purple leaves and offered by nurseries from about 1930 onwards has become very popular. Dodonaea is found in the North Island near the coast and in similar situations in the northern third of the South Island in areas of scrub. It withstands salt winds and dry conditions, and requires a well-drained soil. Heavy frosts will kill it while young, so it needs protection in cold districts during winter. The heavy, dark dense wood was used by the Maori people for making weapons.

Propagation is by seed, which germinates readily.

Akeake on a dry Waikato bank.

Foliage and fruit of the purple akeake in summer.

Fuchsia

A young kotukutuku on a Matamata farm.

F. excorticata (kotukutuku) is the world's largest fuchsia, growing to 9 m, and one of New Zealand's few deciduous trees. With its peeling, papery, flaking bark revealing a shining yellowish-brown inner bark, it seems out of place in New Zealand's forests. The typically fuchsia flowers are green, red and purple, and are borne on old wood as well as on branchlets. The purple berries, known as konini, are 15 mm long and good to eat when ripe in late summer. They are much favoured by the New Zealand pigeon.

Kotukutuku is found in all types of forest throughout New Zealand. A hardy tree, it grows well in most soils and situations not too dry. The timber, which is dark brown, very strong and durable, is most ornamental and has been used for cabinet work and wood turning, but is usually too irregular. It is also extremely fire-resistant.

Propagation is easy from either seed or cuttings.

Griselinia

G. littoralis (papauma, broadleaf) grows to a medium-sized tree of 12 m or more with rough furrowed bark. Its bold handsome foliage is its main attraction. Apart from the northernmost tip of the North Island it is found all through New Zealand, from sea level to 900 m. In the northern half of the North Island it is commonest in higher altitude forests.

It grows well in most situations, being hardy and able to withstand coastal winds. It can also stand hard pruning, so makes a good hedge. The red timber is dense, strong and very durable and has been used for fenceposts, house piles, sleepers and for boatbuilding. Stem shape can be irregular and it often grows as a many-stemmed shrub.

Propagation is easy from either seed or semi-hardwood cuttings.

A fine papauma (broadleaf) grown as a farm tree.

Hedycarya

H. arborea (porokaiwhiri, pigeonwood) is an attractive tree growing to 12 m with ascending branches bearing shiny serrated leaves. In late spring and early summer the female tree can be almost covered in orange-red ovoid berries 15 mm long, which are relished by pigeons. Trees of both sexes are necessary for the production of fruit.

Pigeonwood is common in lowland New Zealand north of Banks Peninsula and including Westland. A half-hardy tree, it requires protection from frosts while young. Preferring a good moist soil, it dislikes exposure to wind. The wood is soft, white and of little use.

Propagation is by seed or semi-hardwood cuttings.

Right: Porokaiwhiri (pigeonwood) in summer. When fruiting this tree attracts native birds.

236

Hoheria

H.populnea (houhere, lacebark) is a very beautiful small tree of 8 m or more, bearing in late summer and autumn magnificent clusters of white flowers which almost conceal the attractive shining serrated leaves. The northern variety is found naturally only from the Waikato and Bay of Plenty northwards, on stream banks and forest margins. It is very susceptible to attack by ghost moth in some areas and this can shorten its life considerably.

A hardy fast-growing tree suited by most soils, it grows quicker in moist rich ground. The lacebark also makes a good windbreak, and withstands hard pruning. The white timber is strong and tough but not long-lasting. It makes good firewood and was said to be suitable for pulp in the manufacture of paper. In the early days of New Zealand's history the strong bark was used for rope-making and for decorative purposes such as ladies' hats.

Propagation is by seed or semi-hardwood cuttings. In gardens houhere often seeds naturally, providing a good source of supply.

This *Hoheria* was found growing happily in an old stump in the Wairarapa.

Hoheria has magnificent flowers in late autumn.

Knightia

These rewarewa were left when the bush was cleared for farming. Also shown are the slow-growing nikau.

K.excelsa (rewarewa, honeysuckle) is a most striking, narrow tree up to 30 m high, with erect branches and thick, leathery, serrated leaves. In spring and early summer it bears deep red flowers which are usually high in the tree. The natural range extends through the North Island and to the Marlborough Sounds in the South Island, in lowland to lower mountain forests, usually on steep slopes. A slow grower in a dry situation, it responds to a better soil and prefers plenty of light.

Rewarewa timber is extremely attractive and strong, and difficult to burn. Formerly used for fence battens and flooring, its aesthetic value is now appreciated and it is used for interior decorative work, the heartwood being beautifully mottled when quarter sawn.

Propagation is by seed, which must be sown while fresh.

Rewarewa bark is often beautifully marked.

Laurelia

L.novae-zelandiae (pukatea) with its shiny serrated leaves grows to 30 m or more in height. In damp places the pale-coloured trunk forms buttresses which are the tree's most distinctive feature. In autumn the nearby ground is covered with the plumed seeds which are also carried by the wind and these germinate readily. It is found occasionally in Marlborough, Nelson and Westland, but is common all through the North Island in lowland forests. A handsome, slow-growing tree, it requires a damp situation for maximum growth, preferably at the water's edge.

Pukatea wood is strong and tough, and coloured light and dark brown. Moderately ground durable, it has been used successfully for wharf piles, boatbuilding, weatherboards, verandah flooring, framing and furniture. It is difficult to burn, so trees often survive forest fires and are a feature of some recently cleared districts.

Propagation is by seed or semi-hardwood cuttings.

The rounded clumps of pukatea foliage make it easy to identify.

Leptospermum

Kanuka clothing a South Island hillside and providing excellent stock shelter.

L.ericoides (kanuka) is usually an erect tree to 14 m, with loose papery greyish-brown bark that hangs in long strips. The small white flowers cover the ends of the branchlets of the mature tree in summer and are most attractive to bees. Kanuka is distinguished from manuka by its clusters of smaller flowers; manuka bears its flowers singly. It is common throughout New Zealand in forest and scrub, often forming dense groves after fire. A hardy tree, it is not fussy as to soil type, but will not grow in dense shade or waterlogged conditions.

The hard reddish wood was used by the early Maori for making weapons. Early colonists used it for tool handles, wharf piles, wheel spokes and fencing.

Its main use at the present time is for firewood, as it burns well and with great heat.

Propagation is by seed or semi-hardwood cuttings.

L.scoparium (manuka) is another very common small tree to 4m with brownish bark coming off in long strips, and pungent leaves. The small white single flowers bloom in summer. Like the kanuka, manuka is abundant throughout New Zealand. It is very hardy and will grow almost anywhere although in some districts it suffers from a blight which can eventually kill it.

The hard red wood is useful for tool handles and fencing materials, and is a first class firewood, burning well with considerable heat.

Manuka is propagated by seed or semi-hardwood cuttings.

Litsea

L.calicaris (mangeao) reaches 12 to 15m, with a rounded bushy crown if grown in the open. Its small yellow flowers, borne in spring, are sweetly scented, and are followed in autumn by dark reddish drupes 2cm long borne by the female tree.

Mangeao is found naturally only in the northern half of the North Island. It is frost tender when young, so needs the protection of other trees. A soil rich in humus suits it best, with shelter from wind, but it is a slow grower in cold areas.

Mangeao wood is tough and strong, and was used for making casks and wheels. Now its decorative value is realised for such purposes as panelling. Floor 9 of the Beehive is of mangeao.

Propagation is by seed.

Two mangeao trees left when the bush was felled beautify this paddock.

Lophomyrtus

L. bullata (ramarama) is a beautiful shrub or small tree growing to about 5 m. Its oppositely-arranged blistered leaves are green when shaded, but when grown in the open become blotched with red. In late summer and autumn the shrub bears 8 mm long ovoid berries which turn from red-purple to black as they ripen. It is found in coastal and lowland forests of the North Island and in the northern tip of the South Island, usually along margins and on rich alluvial soils.

The wood is red, strong and tough, and often prettily figured. It was used for tool handles and decorative work. Ramarama is reasonably hardy, but requires protection from very hard frosts while young. It grows easily in either sun or shade.

Propagation is easy by semi-hardwood cuttings or by seed.

Macropiper

M. excelsum (kawakawa, pepper tree) is a fast-growing, interesting and handsome small tree to 6 m, with zig zagging branches clothed in large, fleshy heart-shaped, smooth aromatic leaves which are usually disfigured by chewing insects. Male and female trees are needed to produce the edible yellow-orange spikes of berries which are relished by birds.

Macropiper is common in coastal forests and scrub in the North Island and the northern half of the South Island. All parts of the kawakawa have been used for medicinal purposes: treating toothache, bruises, cuts, rheumatic pain, urinary troubles and stomach aches.

It is frost tender when young but becomes hardier, growing well in moist or dry situations, and tolerating dense shade. Propagation is easy from either seed or cuttings.

Melicytus

M. ramiflorus (mahoe, whiteywood) is a spreading tree growing to 6 m or more, usually with many trunks clothed in whitish-grey bark. In autumn the branches bear masses of 5 mm purple berries, but only if trees of each sex are grown. The tiny greenish-yellow flowers are beautifully scented. The mahoe was collected by Banks and Solander when Captain Cook first landed north of Gisborne in 1769. It is very common in lowland and mountain forests throughout New Zealand, usually in open bush or forest margins. A hardy tree in all but the coldest places, it will grow well in most soils but appreciates some shelter. Farm animals eat its foliage readily so plant well back from fences.

In the early days mahoe wood was used for making charcoal for the manufacture of gunpowder.

Propagation is easy by seed or semi-hardwood cuttings.

This small clump of mahoe grows near New Plymouth.

Metrosideros

The well-known pohutukawa flowers at Christmas and New Year. This tree is
one of many in Cornwall Park, Auckland.

M.excelsa (pohutukawa, Christmas tree) is a magnificent tree with a short trunk with large wide-spreading branches. After several hundred years it can grow to 19 m in height, but it is mainly valued for its spectacular dark crimson flowers which adorn the coastlines of the northern half of the North Island in summer. It was first recorded by Banks and Solander during Cook's first voyage in 1769. Pohutukawa thrives near the sea, often with huge roots clinging to rocks and cliff faces, but it will also grow inland if given protection from frosts while young. It withstands salt winds as well as drought, and requires a well-drained soil.

The deep red, heavy wood is strong, tough and durable, the crooked branches being selected for special uses in boatbuilding. It makes good firewood.

Pohutukawa is easily grown from seed or semi-hardwood cuttings. The latter method will result in flowers much sooner, as the tender juvenile stage of the tree will be bypassed.

Myrsine

M.australis (mapou, red matipo) is an attractive shrub or small tree, growing to 6 m, with young branchlets a reddish colour and leaves with wavy margins. In autumn it bears masses of round black drupes about 4 mm in diameter. It is found around margins of lowland to mountain forests, and in scrub in the North Island and in the northern parts of the South Island. Growing in either sun or shade, mapou is not fussy as to soil and is very easy to grow. It can be pruned to make a wind-resistant hedge, and is hardy.

The timber is very strong but not durable, and is used for firewood.

Propagation is by seed or semi-hardwood cuttings.

Nothofagus

N.fusca (tawhairaunui, red beech) is a handsome forest tree of up to 30 m or more, with distinctive coarsely and sharply toothed 2-4 cm leaves. The trunk is often buttressed and is smooth and grey on young trees, and dark brown or black on older trees. During winter the foliage of young plants is often a reddish colour which persists for several years and is most attractive. *N.fusca* was discovered in the North Island by Banks and Solander in 1769.

The tree is found in both islands between the Mamaku plateau and Te Anau, but is absent from Mt Egmont. It grows from sea level to 1 000 m. If given a good soil, red beech will grow quickly and is somewhat open and graceful while young. It is very hardy.

The strong red wood is straight and even, and very durable. Its uses have included fenceposts, railway sleepers, pit props, bridges, wharves and house-building, although its fine qualities are now appreciated more for furniture and similar uses.

Propagation is easy from seed which must be sown while fresh.

A splendid roadside tawhairaunui (red beech) near Apiti. Like most trees, the open-grown form is different from that of the forest.

N.menziesii (tawhai, silver beech) grows to become a tall tree of about 30 m in the forest, with its layers of foliage quite noticeable. The leaves are roughly triangular and are bluntly and doubly toothed, and this distinguishes it from *N.fusca*. Large buttresses often form at the bases of old trees. It grows in lowland to mountain forests between Thames and Foveaux Strait.

In an average soil it grows slower than *N.fusca*, and is very beautiful when clothed in spring with pale green fresh foliage. Silver beech is very hardy. Found naturally in higher rainfall areas, it dislikes drought.

The wood is deep red, straight-grained, hard, dense, tough and strong. Uses for the timber are similar to those of red beech, although it is not quite so attractive. It is only moderately durable in the ground.

Propagation is by fresh seed.

There are three further beech species and all five have differing wood characteristics. Local names vary

Tawhai (silver beech) grown as a lawn specimen.

widely causing much confusion and making timber marketing difficult. In the words of the old bushman: 'You've got three main types of birches (beeches) —red, brown and black. The bark of the red is silver and the wood of the red is pink when its green. The brown quite often has black bark, but the green timber is red. Sometimes the bark of the black is white, but the timber is yellow and sometimes brown when it's green.' *(From New Zealand Forest Service Beech Management.)*

Olearia

O. rani (heketara) forms a 7 m small tree, clothed in spring with rounded clusters of daisy-like white flowers. The leaves have wavy, toothed margins, are shiny on the upper surface and densely hairy beneath. It is found abundantly throughout the North Island, and in Nelson and Marlborough.

O. rani is at all times of the year a handsome plant, withstanding wind and easily grown in most soils in sun or semi-shade. Seed has a short viability and must be sown while fresh, but the better method of propagation is by semi-hardwood cuttings in the first few months of the year, or hardwood cuttings in early winter.

Wind-resistant tree daisies make a fine show in spring. This one is *Olearia rani*, similar to *Olearia arborescens*.

Phyllocladus

Tanekaha growing on a stream bank.

P. trichomanoides (tanekaha, celery pine) has instead of leaves whorls of leaf-like flattened stems which serve the same purpose. There are three species of *Phyllocladus* endemic to New Zealand and which are unlike any other native plant. Growing to a striking erect tree of 20 m or more, the tanekaha is densely foliaged, with its lower trunk bare of branches. In spring it turns a purplish colour as the male and female cones go about the process of producing seed.

Tanekaha grows in lowland and mountain forest north of Wanganui and Waipukurau in the North Island, and in the northernmost parts of the South Island. Tolerating droughts if the roots are shaded, it grows best in a good, fairly moist but well-drained soil. The timber is pale-coloured, moderately durable and strong, and extremely elastic. Its straightness has caused it to be used for fishing rods, bridge building, exterior joinery, boat framing, weatherboards and flooring. The bark yields a reddish dye formerly used by the Maori people.

Propagation is often difficult by seed and semi-hardwood cuttings are not very successful. The best method is to gather duff containing seed or small wildings.

244

Pittosporum

Karo used as a low shelter on the authors' farm.

P.crassifolium (karo) is a most versatile small tree growing to about 8 m, with thick leathery leaves and beautiful red sweetly scented flowers in spring. When the sticky black seeds ripen, the capsules open to show the bright golden glutin within. In the wild it is found in mainly coastal situations of the northern half of the North Island. In spite of its natural habitat, karo is hardy and can be used as a hedge as it withstands trimming, is extremely resistant to wind, and grows quickly. Karo will grow in dry situations such as under large trees, or in areas subject to strong salt winds.

The wood was used for inlaying, and is hard to burn.

Karo seeds germinate freely under the parent trees and transplant easily, while cuttings are difficult.

Flowers of karo in spring.

Twelve-year-old tarata effectively shelter a farm pond.

P.eugenioides (tarata, lemonwood) is an attractive, fast-growing small tree reaching a height of about 12 m. It has shining, pale green wavy-edged leaves that are lemon-scented when crushed, sweet-smelling clusters of pale yellow flowers in spring, and green capsules ripening to black in autumn. The tarata is found throughout New Zealand, mostly in forest margins and clearings or along stream banks.

One of New Zealand's outstandingly beautiful hardy and wind resistant plants, it is attractive at all times of the year and easily grown in a wide variety of situations. It is suitable for planting as a shelter tree in the native section, as the lower storey in two-tier farm shelter, and for horticultural shelter. Being fast growing and bearing its branches right down to the ground when young, it can be trimmed to make an excellent hedge.

The wood is not long-lasting, and is useless as firewood. The Maori used the resin to perfume oil, and bruised leaves and flowers to mix with fat for anointing their bodies.

Propagation is from seed which germinates easily.

P. tenuifolium (kohuhu) is a small tree which can grow to 8 m or more, a variable species with many hybrids and garden cultivars. Its alternate light green leaves are wavy-edged and shiny, the sweetly-scented flowers such a dark reddish-purple they are almost black;

the three-valved seed capsules contain sticky black seeds. Kohuhu is found in coastal to montane forest and shrublands in both the North and South Islands.

Like other *Pittosporum* species it is a beautiful and useful tree. Its branches can be left to form most effective shelter, or pruned off to make a shapely specimen, and it will grow in any situation that is not too wet. It withstands wind, is very hardy, quick-growing, and attracts birds which drop seeds of other species, so increasing the range of vegetation in the vicinity.

Propagation is by seed.

This farm windbreak of kohuhu has been planted only a few years. Note the electric fence.

Plagianthus

Manatu (ribbonwood) growing near a Northland stream.

P. betulinus (manatu, ribbonwood) is the largest deciduous tree native to New Zealand, growing to 15 m with heavy branches. It has adult foliage which is sometimes confused with that of lacebark (*Hoheria*) and similar bark and habit of growth, but it can be distinguished by its deciduous habit and its deeply and coarsely toothed leaves. In spring this remarkably graceful tree bears masses of palest yellow flowers which combine with the new foliage to give it a lime-green appearance. It makes a fine specimen tree.

The manatu is found in lowland forests throughout New Zealand but is not common in the more northern parts where it remains evergreen. It grows on alluvial soils and in forest margins, doing well in good soil, its juvenile stage being particularly wind-resistant.

The wood is of little use. The inner bark yields a tough fibre formerly used by the Maori for making into fishing nets.

Seeds germinate freely, but propagation of the separate sexes (the male tree being the more attractive) is by cuttings.

Podocarpus

P. ferrugineus (miro, brown pine) grows to 25 m in the forest and has a clean trunk and a rounded crown. The bark is very dark grey, hammer marked and coming off in flakes. The curved leaves, about 2.5 cm long and in two rows, are dark green above and paler below. This distinguishes the tree from the matai *(P. spicatus)* which it resembles, as the latter has on the undersides of its shorter, stiffened leaves a bluish-green colour. The beautiful bright red fruits which ripen in winter are relished by wood pigeons, and borne only on female trees. Some trees bear both male and female branches. Miro is found right through New Zealand in all types of forest. A hardy conifer, it grows best in good soil with plenty of moisture and shelter but is slow. A mulched garden tree in Rotorua reached 8 m in 20 years.

The timber is of high quality and used mainly for flooring, housebuilding, and marine piles. It is hard, strong, and sometimes beautifully figured, but not durable in the ground.

Propagation is by seed or cuttings.

P. spicatus (matai, black pine) grows to form a round-headed tree up to 25 m in height, somewhat similar to the miro. The juvenile foliage is straggly and drooping, but the tree gradually develops mature leaves at a height of about 3 m. Small fruits borne by female trees are at first green, ripening to become black with a purplish bloom.

Matai is found throughout New Zealand in lowland forests, especially on river terraces. A slow grower, it will survive on a hard site. The timber is smooth, strong, durable and hard, and has been used for most purposes, chiefly flooring.

Natural propagation is by seed, which takes over a year to mature.

This miro was left when the bush was cleared for farming near Raglan.

P. totara (totara) is one of New Zealand's best known forest trees, reaching 30 m or more, with thick, stringy, furrowed bark. In autumn the female tree bears red, orange and yellow fruits which are most attractive. As a young open-grown tree it will retain its foliage to the ground, but this does not apply in the forest. It is common throughout New Zealand.

Totara is very hardy, will grow in wet or dry situations and will withstand wind. Groves of young totara are a feature of some cleared districts as the seedlings' prickly foliage is not eaten by stock. On good soils totara is relatively fast growing.

The reddish timber is extremely durable but easily worked, and was used by the Maori for canoes, carving and housebuilding. Europeans have used it for bridges, wharf piles, house blocks, fencing and telegraph poles, as well as for housebuilding.

Propagation is by seed and cuttings, which root easily.

Totara gives a park-like appearance to a dry North Auckland farm.

Pseudopanax

Five-finger growing on a Kimbolton farm.

P. arboreus (five-finger) is a small tree growing to 8 m, many-branching with a rounded crown of smooth dark green leaflets grouped digitately, varying from 5 to 7. The scented flowers, and later the ripe fruits of purplish-black, are in umbels at the ends of the branches. These abundant but inconspicuous flowers produce much nectar, relished by bees in early spring.

Five-finger is found abundantly in lowland forests all through New Zealand, especially in second-growth forests. Hardy, wind-resistant and easily grown, it stands most conditions. If grown in a good soil the leaves become large and attractive, so it is suitable for bush margins where it is often found.

It is easily grown from fresh seed or semi-hardwood cuttings, and seedlings can be readily transplanted from open situations.

248

P.crassifolius (horoeka, lancewood) is a striking tree growing to 13m. In its juvenile stage it has long rigid hanging leaves of 15-30 cm, followed after 15-20 years by a gradual change to the mature tree, with slender straight trunk, branching at the top. The leaves then become shorter and upright. It is found throughout New Zealand, especially in second-growth forests.

With its remarkable and striking appearance it should be grown where it can be seen; it thrives in a forest margin situation. It is hardy and wind resistant. The timber is very tough, and has been used for fencing, railway sleepers and jetties.

Lancewood grows easily from fresh seed.

Lancewood changing to its adult foliage. A roadside tree in the Wairarapa.

Sophora

S. tetraptera (kowhai) has 2.5 cm leaflets, grows to 12 m and is one of New Zealand's few deciduous trees. The beautiful yellow to golden flowers borne in early spring by the North Island kowhai are to be seen on many farms as well as in town sections and parks. They are often ruined by tuis who tear them open for their nectar and by pigeons which eat both flowers and leaves in spring.

Formerly found only from East Cape to the Ruahine Mountains in lowland forest margins and beside streams, this kowhai, along with the smaller leaved *S. microphylla*, is now found throughout New Zealand as its popularity has spread. Kowhai grows well in the open and makes a most attractive specimen tree. *S. microphylla* is particularly successful in colder areas. A hardy tree and attractive at all times, it thrives in most soils, but is particularly suited to bush margins where its magnificent flowers can be seen. It seeds prolifically. Very susceptible to hormone sprays it is often damaged or killed on farms. Leaf-eating caterpillars can also kill it in warmer areas. Kowhai timber is hard, tough and durable, and used for cabinet work and ornamental turnery.

It is propagated by fresh seed. If older seed is used, this should first have very hot water poured over it, then left to soak overnight before sowing. Kowhai will also grow from cuttings.

Vitex

V. lucens (puriri) is a handsome, shiny-leaved, round-headed tree growing to 20 m, bearing clusters of pinkish-red flowers for most of the year on the ends of the branchlets. It develops a massive trunk and wide-spreading branches, and lives to a great age. The red drupes are readily eaten by native pigeons and tuis, while the flowers are eagerly sought by tuis and bellbirds. It is common near the coast of the upper half of the North Island.

Found naturally only in the north, puriri is frost tender when young so needs the protection of larger trees, but it becomes hardier with age. It prefers a deep rich soil.

Puriri timber is extremely strong and difficult to work. It is dense, heavy and very hard, and because of its ground durability was found suitable for bridging, house piles, railways sleepers and fenceposts.

Propagation is by seed which germinates easily, and also by cuttings.

Left: A solitary kowhai remains on an old house site near Ngaruawahia.
Above: Puriri makes a fine shade tree.

Weinmannia

W. racemosa (kamahi) is a forest tree, growing to 26m. It takes many years to pass through its juvenile form before reaching the mature stage, but is an attractive tree at any age. After flowering in late spring, racemes of reddish fruits form; as these are produced in great profusion the tree takes on a reddish glow.

Kamahi is found naturally from Thames and the Waikato southwards in all types of forest. It is a hardy tree that will grow in most soils and situations; it is often found as an epiphytic seedling on tree fern fences.

The timber is strong and tough, and has been used for fenceposts, sleepers, house blocks and wharf piles. It is durable in damp situations, otherwise it is perishable.

Propagation is by seed or cuttings.

Kamahi grows in dense stands west of Otorohanga.

11
Table of Wood Properties

This table is to be used as a quick guide to indicate the qualities of some of the wood which could be available from trees mentioned in this book. In most cases the text itself gives a brief description of the wood with the range of end uses. It must be strongly emphasised that the figures in this table should not be used as a reliable base for making decisions which might involve considerable financial outlay. Much of the information has been obtained from overseas publications and may not be applicable to the same trees growing under New Zealand conditions. Evaluations of the wood have been made by different organisations using different criteria, for instance the ability to accept treatment may have been assessed with or without the use of pressure, and the sizes of the pieces treated may have varied from the normal small 50 mm x 50 mm test stakes to 200 mm round posts. Similarly when measuring ground durability this proviso could apply.

Considerable research on timber qualities is however continually taking place in New Zealand so information coming from local sources can be accepted as authentic for New Zealand conditions.

The purpose of including such information in the book is to encourage people to look a little further into possible end uses of surplus timber before condemning it to the firewood heap. If it is not one of the better known natives or *Pinus radiata*, there is a tendency to almost automatically bulldoze unwanted trees over the bank or into a firewood heap for use on 5th November. Our research indicates that almost every tree listed in this book produces worthwhile usable timber which is valued by the people of the country in which it grows, such uses being frequently mentioned elsewhere. Wood is a resource which we discard very carelessly but there is often a good on-farm use for lowly-regarded trees which are no longer required. For instance, *Chamaecyparis lawsoniana* shelterbelts were at one time extensively planted, but due to poor management and deterioration through canker thousands of trees of good straight form have been ripped out and almost all of them have been or are still being burned. In its home states of Oregon and California the timber is highly prized and becoming more so

because the supply is now limited. The timber can be used on the New Zealand farm, for it has a life of at least 11-15 years in the ground, probably much longer, and is suitable for poles for temporary horticulture shelter required during the period that permanent live shelter is growing to effective size.

Many unwanted trees have attributes which make the timber well worth processing, although it is acknowledged that getting such logs sawn up is not always easy. The dominance of pine in the whole industry has resulted in a high degree of disinterest by millers generally in the 'one off' log which a farmer is likely to want processed. But as values of better-known hardwoods go on increasing — their scarcity will inevitably cause this — milling of good quality logs may well be worthwhile even if you feel you are being cheated in the process. The worth of the operation must be measured against prices which are already up to $2 000 a cubic metre: a mobile sawmiller will do a lot of work for a quarter of this amount. A well-grown old plane, chestnut or oak tree could contain 2-3 cubic metres of timber, so do some sums before you too readily condemn it to the scrap heap. You may well find that you or your friends will acquire some attractive and unusual panelling or interesting furniture lengths.

The table is thus to be used with discretion but offers a guide to the enthusiast who often wonders what he or she can do with a tree which has finished its useful life.

Notes

Density: The weight of a piece of wood clearly varies with the amount of water that it contains. When the weight is mentioned as a means of measuring density the moisture content should be stated. Most authorities use 12% as this is an acceptable content for satisfactory woodworking. However in many cases information on average weights of timbers has been taken from sources where moisture content is not stated, but one must assume that it is around the 12% mark. In all species a considerable variation in weight is found to occur, apart from differences arising from moisture content. Exotic trees in New Zealand tend to grow a lot faster than in their native habitats, often producing a wood of lower density, and this should be taken into account when using the figures listed for non-native timbers.

Natural Durability: Assessment is always based on heartwood, and sapwood is classed as perishable. Natural durability is of importance when timber is exposed to dampness, ie above about 20% moisture content, thus is of vital importance when in contact with the ground. Decay resistance of most timbers varies, even in pieces cut from the same tree, so durability has to be assessed in approximate terms. Most authorities use a standard five grading system based on 50 mm x 50 mm pieces. Larger sizes will last longer. For example a piece 100 mm x 100 mm will last about twice as long as the 50 mm x 50 mm. The expected service is measured in ground-contact situations, but if the same timber is used in an above-ground situation then it would be reasonably safe to move its life up to the next classification.

Grade of Durability		Approx. Life in Ground Contact
Perishable	(P)	Less than 5 years
Non-Durable	(ND)	5-10 years
Moderately Durable	(MD)	10-15 years
Durable	(D)	15-25 years
Very Durable	(VD)	More than 25 years

Treatability: The ease with which a non-durable timber can be impregnated with preservatives depends on its permeability. Some timbers are virtually impenetrable, but it is well to remember that round wood is often surrounded by the more perishable sapwood which is easily treatable, thus round wood can often be treated for use as posts where sawn timber from the same tree would not be treatable.

It would be useful if sufficient information were available to expand this table to itemise sapwood treatability of various species as distinct from heartwood. Unfortunately most sources of information do not distinguish between the two. A species with a durable heartwood and treatable sapwood is likely to be ideal for ground contact use, whereas a species with untreatable sapwood should possibly have this removed. This would decrease the strength properties of the roundwood because machine peeling or shaving can reduce total pole strength by about 40%.

There are various methods of pressure treatment using different preservatives, but the resistance of a timber impregnation under pressure will generally be of the same order whatever type of preservative is used.

Simple diffusion treatment is possible with all species when used on freshly cut green wood, thus the tables relate only to the pressure treatment of dry wood.

Permeable (P): Can be penetrated completely under pressure and can usually be heavily impregnated by hot and cold open tank process.

Moderately Resistant (MR): Usually fairly easy to treat, but often there are some problems with specific species.

Resistant (R): Not amenable — difficult to obtain any worthwhile impregnation even after prolonged treatment.

CAUTION: Because of the variability within species, the differences in growing conditions from country to country, and the varying techniques which have been used in assessing the timber qualities, it is unwise to embark on any largescale project without discussing it further with the appropriate experts in the NZ Forest Service, the Timber Preservation Authority and your local timber treatment firm. It won't be any use coming back to the editors as no responsibility will be accepted, but all the information is given in good faith and has been obtained from what are believed to be reliable sources.

Sources of Information:

Overseas Publications:

Building Research Establishment, Princes Risborough Laboratory, *Handbook of Hardwoods.* Her Majesty's Stationery Office.
Handbook of Softwoods, as above.
Collingwood and Brush, *Knowing Your Trees.* The American Forestry Assn.
Albert Constantine Jnr, *Know Your Woods.* Charles Scribner's Sons.
Hall Johnston and Chippendale, *Forest Trees of Australia.* Australian Government Publishing Service.
B.J. Rendle, *World Timbers.* Earnest Benn Ltd.

New Zealand Publications:

Forest Research Institute, *The Natural Durability of Untreated Timbers.* What's New In Forest Research No. 112.
McQuire, Butcher, Hedley and Vinden, *Wood Preservation for the Farmer.* NZ Forest Service reprint 1277 O.D.C. 84.
NZ Institute of Foresters, *Forestry Handbook.*

	density air dried kg/cu m	durability	treatability (pressure treatment of dry wood)
Abies			
alba	480	ND	MR
amabilis	420	ND	
concolor	400	ND	
grandis	450	ND	R
magnifica	470	MD	
procera	420	ND	R
Acacia			
mearnsii	740	ND	MR
melanoxylon	660	ND-D	R
Acer			
macrophyllum	540	ND	
negundo	420		
nigrum	700	ND	MR
pseudoplatanus	610	P	P
rubrum	600	ND	
saccharum	720	ND	MR
Aesculus			
hippocastanum	510	P	P
Ailanthus			
altissima	600		
Albizia			
julibrissin	720		
Alnus			
glutinosa	530	P	P
rubra	600	ND	
Angophora			
costata	960	ND	
Araucaria			
araucana	550	ND	P
bidwillii	470	ND	P
cunninghamii	520	ND	P
heterophylla		P	
Betula			
lutea	690	P	MR
papyrifera	620	ND	MR
pubescens	660	P	P
Brachychiton			
acerifolium	400	ND	
populneum	460	ND	
Callitris			
glauca	650	VD	
Calocedrus			
decurrens	400		

	density air dried kg/cu m	durability	treatability (pressure treatment of dry wood)
Carpinus			
betulus	750	P	P
Carya			
cordiformis	750	ND	MR
glabra	850	ND	MR
illinoiensis	730	ND	MR
laciniosa	760	ND	MR
ovata	1000	ND	MR
tomentosa	800	ND	MR
Castanea			
sativa	540	D	R
Casuarina			
cunninghamiana	900	MD	R
equisetifolia	900	MD	R
glauca	1000	MD	R
torulosa	960	D	R
Catalpa			
bignonioides		ND	
speciosa	400	D	
Cedrus			
atlantica	560	MD	R
deodara	560	MD	R
libani	560	MD	R
Chamaecyparis			
lawsoniana	470	MD	R
nootkatensis	500	D	R
thyoides	360	D	
Cinnamomum			
camphora	640	MD	
Corylus			
avellana	640		
Cryptomeria			
japonica	c.350	D	R
Cupressus			
arizonica		D	
lusitanica		MD	R
macrocarpa	500	MD	R
Diospyros	800		
Eucalyptus			
botryoides	760	D	R
cladocalyx	1000	VD	
delegatensis	640	ND	R
fastigata	620	ND	R
fraxinoides	Light	ND	

	density air dried kg/cu m	durability	treatability (pressure treatment of dry wood)
globoidea		D	
leucoxylon	760-1200	D	
maculata	Heavy	MD	P
maidenii	Heavy	MD	
macarthurii		MD	
microcorys	980	D	R
meulleriana	880	D	R
obliqua	600	MD	R
ovata		MD	
pauciflora	670	MD	
pilularis	720-1000	D	
regnans	620	ND	R
saligna	730	D	R
viminalis	670	MD	
Fagus			
grandifolia	720	ND	
sylvatica	700	P	P
Fraxinus			
americana	660	P	P
excelsior	690	ND	MR
Ginkgo			
biloba	Very light		
Gleditsia			
triacanthos	700	D	
Grevillea			
robusta	610	MD	MR
striata	880	MD	
Juglans			
nigra	640	D	
regia	640	MD	R
Juniperus			
communis	500		
procera	580	D	R
virginiana	530	D	
Larix			
decidua	560	ND-MD	R
x eurolepis	530	MD	R
laricina	560	MD	R
occidentalis	610	MD	R
Liquidambar			
styraciflua	550		
Liriodendron			
tulipifera	480	ND	R
Maclura			
pomifera	760	D	

	density air dried kg/cu m	durability	treatability (pressure treatment of dry wood)
Magnolia			
grandiflora	560	ND	
Malus	750		
Melia			
azedarach	500	D	
Morus			
alba	640		
Nothofagus			
alpina	540		MR
Nyssa			
sylvatica	560	ND	P
aquatica	560		
Paulownia			
fargesii	c300	MD	
tomentosa	c300	MD	
Picea			
abies	470	P	R
omorika		Prob. P	R
orientalis		Prob. P	R
polita		Prob. P	R
pungens		Prob. P	R
sitchensis	430	ND	R
smithiana		P	R
Pinus			
contorta	520	ND	R
elliottii	460		Variable
monticola	420	ND	MR
muricata	490	ND	Variable
nigra subsp.laricio	560	P	Variable
nigra subsp.nigra	560	P	Variable
palustris	640	ND	Variable
patula	460		Variable
pinaster	550		Variable
ponderosa	460	ND	R
radiata	480	ND	Variable
strobus	370	ND	Variable
sylvestris	510	ND	MR
Platanus			
acerifolia (hybrida)	620	ND	
orientalis	640	ND	
Populus			
alba	400-450	ND	P
deltoides	400-450	ND	P
nigra 'Italica'	400-450	ND	MR
tremula	400-450	ND	P
tremuloides	400-450	ND	P

	density air dried gk/cu m	durability	treatability (pressure treatment of dry wood)
trichocarpa	400-450	ND	P
yunnanensis	400-450	ND	P
Pseudotsuga			
menziesii	480	ND	R
Prunus spp.	500-600		
Pyrus spp.	700		
Quercus			
alba	750	D	R
cerris	820	MD	R
coccinea	750		
ilex	800-960		
robur	700	D	R
rubra	770	ND	MR
Robinia			
pseudoacacia	720	VD	R
Salix			
species in text	340-500	P	R
Sequoia			
sempervirens	400	MD	MR
Sequoiadendron			
giganteum	350?		
Syncarpia			
glomulifera	960	D	
Taxodium			
distichum	510	D	MR
Thuja			
occidentalis	340	D	R
plicata	370	D	R
Tilia			
americana	420	ND	P
x europaea	540	P	P
Tristania			
conferta	900	MD	R
Tsuga			
canadensis	470	ND	R
heterophylla	490	ND	R
Ulmus			
americana	560	ND	MR
glabra	670	ND	R
procera	550	ND	MR

New Zealand Indigenous Species

	density air dried kg/cu m	durability	treatability (pressure treatment of dry wood)
Agathis australis kauri	560	ND	MR
Beilschmiedia tawa tawa	720	P	R
Dacrycarpus dacrydioides kahikatea	450	ND	MR
Dacrydium cupressinum rimu	590	MD	MR
Griselinia littoralis broadleaf		VD	
Knightia excelsa rewarewa	720	P	P
Laurelia novae-zelandiae pukatea	460	MD	MR var.
Leptospermum ericoides kanuka		P	MR
Litsea calicaris mangeao	590	ND	
Metrosideros umbellata southern rata		D	
Nothofagus fusca red beech	600	D	MR
menziesii (silver beech)	610	MD	P
Phyllocladus trichomanoides tanekaha	610	MD	MR
Podocarpus ferrugineus (miro)		ND	MR
spicatus (matai)	610	ND	MR
totara	480	VD	MR
Sophora tetraptera kowhai		VD	
Vitex lucens puriri		VD	
Weinmannia racemosa kamahi	600	P	P

12
Tree Selection

The following lists contain the genus names only. For final species selection readers should refer to the text. It is again emphasised that consultation with your local nursery is advisable to ensure that what you buy will match your particular site conditions. This book is only an introduction to farm planting — additional homework is required to ensure success or at least to minimise failure. (Comprehensive lists covering many other species with particular qualities can be found in Stockley's book.)

Deciduous Trees for Autumn Colour

Genus:

Acer	Gleditsia	Nyssa
Ailanthus	Glyptostrobus	Populus
Betula	Juglans	Quercus
Carya	Larix	Sorbus
Diospyros	Liquidambar	Taxodium
Fagus	Liriodendron	Tilia
Fraxinus	Metasequoia	Ulmus
Ginkgo	Nothofagus	Zelkova

Trees for Dry Sites

Genus:

Acacia	Dodonaea ★	Pinus
Acer	Eucalyptus	Pittosporum ★
Ailanthus	Gleditsia	Podocarpus ★
Albizia	Juniperus	Quercus
Brachychiton	Lagunaria	Robinia
Casuarina	Maclura	Schinus
Corynocarpus ★	Metrosideros ★	Tamarix
Cupressus	Olea	

Trees for Damp Sites

Genus:

Acacia	Cydonia	Metasequoia
Acer	Dacrycarpus ★	Nyssa
Alnus	Eucalyptus	Picea
Betula	Fraxinus	Populus
Carya	Glyptostrobus	Pyrus
Casuarina	Hoheria ★	Quercus
Catalpa	Larix	Salix
Chamaecyparis	Laurelia ★	Sequoia
Cordyline ★	Liquidambar	Taxodium
Cupressus	Liriodendron	

★ New Zealand Species

Trees with Fragrant Flowers & Foliage

Flowers	Foliage
Acacia	Calocedrus
Aesculus	Cedrus
Fruit trees	Cinnamomum
Magnolia	Cupressus
Malus	Eucalyptus
Pittosporum	Juglans
Plagianthus	Pinus
Robinia	Populus
Tilia	

Trees for Coastal Planting

This section has been divided into two parts (1) those trees known to withstand constant salt-laden winds in New Zealand and (2) trees recommended by some authorities as being suitable for seaside conditions, but which will not necessarily withstand strong winds. These could be well worth trying if the sites are reasonably sheltered and the climate appropriate.

Trees for Exposed Coastal Sites

Araucaria	Cupressus	Olearia
Coprosma	Griselinia	Pinus
Cordyline	Lagunaria	Pittosporum
Corokia	Metrosideros	Tamarix
Corynocarpus		

Trees for Sheltered Coastal Sites

Acacia	Jacaranda	Quercus
Alnus	Knightia	Salix
Carpinus	Leptospermum	Sequoia
Castanea	Liquidambar	Sophora
Casuarina	Melia	Sorbus
Cinnamomum	Nothofagus	Syncarpia
Cupressocyparis	Paulownia	Thuja
Dodonaea	Phebalium	Ulmus
Eucalyptus	Populus	Vitex
Grevillea	Pseudopanax	Weinmannia
Hoheria	Pseudotsuga	

Appendix 1: NZ Forest Service Policy on Exotic Special Purpose Species (Sept. 1981)

1. Introduction

Although radiata pine is, and will continue to be, the principal exotic forest species planted and managed in New Zealand's State forests, its timber properties are not well suited to some demanding end-uses where high standards in decorative features, dimensional stability and surface hardness are required. With the decline in the supply of indigenous podocarp and hardwood timbers which are suited to these uses, it is essential that exotic special purpose species are established to meet domestic needs and to provide for the possibility of exporting any surplus high value products. Special purpose species are those capable of producing timbers suited to such demanding end-uses as furniture and cabinet work, turnery, handles, ladders, exterior joinery, decorative veneer and plywood, poles, crossarms, strip and parquet flooring, and panelling. In addition the availability of decorative veneers to surface lower grades of radiata pine could enhance the market opportunities for that species.

Only exotic species are considered in this policy as under the terms of the Indigenous Forest Policy the supply of indigenous timbers will fall to the level of sustained yield which is small in relation to national demand for special purpose timbers, although there is scope in the longer term for some indigenous species to meet special purpose timber requirements once management utilisation and environmental requirements have been clearly resolved.

2. Objective

Current estimates of special purpose timbers' supply and demand indicate that a significant deficit in supply is inevitable and will continue into the next century. This shortfall is largely a consequence of the projected decline in the indigenous cut, which will not be offset sufficiently by the production of suitable timber from established exotic resources. A significant change in afforestation and/or reforestation programmes is therefore necessary to meet projected demand levels.

Special purpose timbers have been imported in the past and are likely to continue to be imported in the future. However, on the world scene competition for specialty timbers, especially decorative timbers, is intense and some species are proving to be too expensive for the New Zealand market. Import of timbers from the New Zealand Foreign Aid Projects in the Pacific Islands is expected to increase, but the species concerned are expected to complement rather than compete with New Zealand-grown special purpose species.

There is some risk attached to the establishment of a special purpose species resource because possible non-achievement of planting programmes, uncertainty over silviculture and yields, and losses due to fire and disease may jeopardise the objective of self-sufficiency. In setting establishment targets it is reasonable to establish resources larger than that estimated to meet domestic demand to accommodate forest management risks, and a resource potentially able to supply twice the volume of assessed domestic demand appears appropriate. In the event that this resource proves to be surplus to domestic requirements, exports of the surplus is a possibility.

The objective of establishment of exotic special purpose species will be to meet projected domestic requirements for special purpose timbers currently assessed as approximately $600\,000\,m^3\,(r)$ per annum of sawlogs and to provide at least an equivalent volume as an insurance factor with possible export potential.

3. Potentially Suitable Species

Each special purpose timber use has its own wood quality requirements for optimum performance. Detailed examination of these requirements indicates that the following New Zealand grown species are potentially suitable for selected special purpose uses, and can be grown with reasonable confidence to establish regional resources of special purpose timbers:

Species	Uses
Acacia melanoxylon	Furniture and cabinet work, turnery.
Cupressus macrocarpa	Exterior joinery, boat building.
Eucalyptus botryoides	Furniture and cabinet work.
E. delegatensis	Turnery and veneers.
E. fastigata	Furniture and cabinet work, turnery, handles and veneers.
E. regnans	Furniture and cabinet work.
E. saligna	Furniture and cabinet work, turnery and veneers.
Juglans nigra	Furniture and cabinet work, turnery and veneers.

On the basis of limited studies *Cupressus lusitanica* appears to have similar timber properties to *Cupressus macrocarpa*, but further evaluations are required. *Eucalyptus obliqua* is known to have acceptable timber properties, but exhibits extreme variation in form and vigour; this variation is thought to be provenance-related and could be reduced following adoption of a breeding improvement programme. In the interim widespread planting is not justified.

In establishing special purpose timber resources those eight species listed in the above table will be established on a management scale in state forests and considered for establishment in the private sector under forest encouragement schemes as a means of meeting projected special purpose timber demands, except that certain provenances of *E. obliqua* may be used if recommended by the Forest Research Institute.

Some *Eucalyptus* species are known to produce naturally durable timber, and whilst there is limited demand for such wood on a national scale, there is scope for the development of small resources to meet local farm timber requirements. Accordingly establishment of such species should be encouraged on suitable sites.

Eucalyptus muellerana, *E. globoidea*, and *E. pilularis* will be additional species eligible for consideration for establishment on appropriate sites under forestry encouragement schemes to enable the limited production of naturally durable timbers for farm use.

4. Utilisation Requirements for Special Purpose Species

There is generally in New Zealand little utilisation experience in the processing of the above species from plantation grown specimens which have received optimum silvicultural treatment, although *Cupressus macrocarpa* from woodlots and shelterbelts is known to some sawmillers, and some plywood companies have experience in producing veneers from single tree specimens of a range of special purpose species.

On the basis of current knowledge, there are no special utilisation requirements that require particular silvicultural treatments for *Acacia melanoxylon*, *Cupressus macrocarpa* and *Juglans nigra*; the common utilisation criteria associated with log size, branch defects and taper are appropriate in deriving acceptable silvicultural practices in each region to produce the required end product.

With the eucalypt species, however, it is evident from conversion studies that quarter sawing is preferable, and log size has a pronounced effect on conversion factor and grade recovery. These factors have significant implications in the silviculture of eucalyptus stands.

Further sawing, drying, grading, peeling, veneering and end-use studies will be carried out on the above species as deemed appropriate by the Forest Research Institute and the utilisation development division, as suitable New Zealand-grown material becomes available, to precisely more define silvicultural and utilisation requirements. Management practices adopted in state forests will be based on these requirements. In all cases the production of sawlogs and veneer logs will be the principal objective.

5. Silvicultural Factors

Consideration of silvicultural factors relevant to the establishment of selected exotic special purpose species is necessary, particularly in relation to seed origin, species siting, tending requirements and biological hazards.

Research into silvicultural aspects of the management of special purpose species will be continued by the Forest Research Institute with research results being implemented as promptly as practical. Strict quarantine measures will be continued as essential to the long term successful management of the special purpose species.

6. State/Private Afforestation and the Establishment Programme

The eight principal special purpose species each have particular site requirements and these, together with land tenure, must be taken into account in deriving any establishment programme.

Whilst all species will grow at a faster rate on high fertility soils some species, particularly *Cupressus macrocarpa* and *Juglans nigra* demand high quality soils. With minor exceptions state forests do not have available high quality soils for new planting and accordingly without a change in land tenure, afforestation with *Cupressus macrocarpa* and *Juglans nigra* must be primarily a function of the private sector, augmented by afforestation in state forests to the extent that available sites allow. Private afforestation will be encouraged by the Forest Service through the existing forestry encouragement schemes, with continuing research into silviculture, management and utilisation of the species and by ensuring the availability of adequate quantities of seed and seedlings of desirable provenances. Should a periodic review, undertaken at least every 5 years, indicate that private sector achievement is inadequate to meet the establishment targets set out in this policy, or subsequent targets derived from better information, consideration

will be given to the Forest Service acquiring land of suitable quality for afforestation to ensure that regional new planting targets for special purpose species are achieved.

Other special purpose species, particularly the *Eucalyptus* species and *Acacia melanoxylon*, do not have such critical site fertility requirements and these species will be established on available sites in state forests. In the case of *Eucalyptus* species, which have a critical resource size for processing, at least 100 ha must be established per annum in each region on a continuing basis to ensure long term availability of the resource. Private afforestation with the *Eucalyptus* species and *Acacia melanoxylon* will be eligible for encouragement loans/grants as a further means of achieving sector targets.

The national and regional annual targets for afforestation or reforestation with special purpose species for sawlog production by both the state and private forest encouragement sectors are as follows:

	Cupressus (ha)	Eucalyptus (ha)	Other (*) (ha)	Total (ha)
Auckland	150	290	50	490
Rotorua	150	300	10	460
Wellington	180	280	40	500
Nelson	20	100	10	130
Westland	100	190	10	300
Canterbury	-	-	10	10
Southland	70	130	10	210
	670	1290	140	2100

(*) includes *Acacia melanoxylon* and *Juglans nigra*.

7. To ensure that a plethora of species with widely differing timber properties and with little utilisation potential do not eventuate, production afforestation or reforestation in exotic state forests and under forestry encouragement schemes is to be limited to the species set out in this policy, as well as *Pinus radiata* and *Pseudotsuga menziesii*. Establishment of other species for research purposes will be permitted only when undertaken in accordance with research work-plans endorsed by the Forest Research Institute. When establishment for amenity or landscaping purposes is contemplated, consideration should be given in the first instance to using the species outlined in this policy. Where these species are deemed unsuitable other species may be established provided the principal objective of such establishment is the enhancement of amenity or landscape values, and not the production of wood.

(This policy will be reviewed at five-yearly intervals.)

Appendix 2: Extracts from Forestry Council Bulletin No. 8: "Policy Guidelines for Private Indigenous Forests"

Objectives
It is recognised that New Zealand's lowland indigenous forest area has largely disappeared and that the portion remaining in private ownership needs to be accorded complementary attention to that granted to the State's forests. Such private indigenous forests are generally quite small in area but can contain many of the recreation, protection and scientific features which are applicable to larger indigenous forest tracts although production aspects do not have the same flexibility. In considering the use of private indigenous forests, the objectives must be:
— To maintain the traditional link of the owner with his land.
— To recognise the aspirations and economic situation of the owner.
— To encourage forest species regeneration.
— To provide for recreation and learning.
— To preserve natural landscapes of outstanding scenic quality.
— To preserve areas of outstanding scientific value.
— To protect soil and water values.
— To recognise that timber or other production is a legitimate use of such forests.
It is recognised that the above objectives may be mutually exclusive in some areas. However, all facets of potential management should be carefully considered before giving any one objective undue precedence over the others.

[Authors' note — We think the following objective should have been included: To preserve the habitat of birds and other fauna.]

Policy Guidelines

SUMMARY
The rights and wishes of the private owner are to be respected.
Owners should be encouraged to promote the regeneration of forest species for those forests requiring rehabilitation.
Owners should be encouraged to allow controlled recreation in their forests.
Forest areas of high scientific value should be preserved.
Changes to existing landscape should be one of the factors considered before a decision to log indigenous forest is taken.
Where the logging of indigenous forest is undertaken it should be done in such a manner as to
— be in accordance with the Forest Operations Guidelines published by the National Water and Soil Conservation Organisation
— retain the forest structure
— allow for adequate regeneration.
The decision to clearfell should not be taken lightly.

GENERAL
The history of land use in New Zealand has been such that the indigenous forest element has now largely disappeared from most of the lowland rural areas of New Zealand — with the major exception of the West Coast of the South Island. The main highway traveller from Auckland to Wellington no longer travels through any native forests worthy of the name. Small remnants of indigenous forests in our farmed countryside (as distinct from distant, forested ranges) serve as scenic reminders of what primaeval New Zealand may have looked like.

OWNERSHIP
The owner of private indigenous forest often has a traditional link with the land which may go back several generations. Also, the owner is motivated by his personal interests and aspirations. It is not suggested at all that the private owner should be under State control. Some farmers are prepared to donate or sell forested areas with significant environmental values as public reserves; others who wish to see the forest areas remain, prefer the retention of ownership which gives them a sense of involvement, perhaps also being prepared to adopt a formal means of protection, for which a number of alternative approaches are available.

RESERVES ACT 1977
The Reserves Act 1977 provides for the purchase, leasing, exchange and gifting of land to the Crown for reserve purposes to ensure protection and preservation of forested lands for recreation, scenic, scientific and allied purposes. In addition the Act offers a variety of techniques for protecting indigenous forest on private land without the land owner having to relinquish his title to the land. Details of the provisions are:
Conservation Covenants may be negotiated by the Crown or Local Authority to protect areas of private or Crown lease land to preserve its natural character. The terms and conditions of the covenant are mutually agreed between the Crown or Local Authority and the owner or lessee and may be in perpetuity or for a specific time. However, once registered against the title of the land, the covenant provisions are binding on subsequent owners. In effect this constitutes a joint management agreement which gives the landowner access to expert advice and assistance to manage and protect bush or other natural features etc which justify preservation.

A purchase price may be paid by the Crown or Local Authority to the owner or lessee for the covenant — i.e. a form of compensation — but this is not obligatory. Similarly all or part of any fencing costs may be met.

A Declaration of Protected Private Land is also a mutual agreement but in this case it can only be between the Crown and the landowner or lessee. It is very similar to a conservation covenant except that the land must be sufficiently fenced and it must be of such quality to qualify for nature, scientific, historic or scenic status under the criteria set out in the Reserves Act. In other words the quality of the resource would justify full reserve status if the owner or lessees was willing to sell the land for such purposes.

Again this is in effect a joint management agreement which enables the Crown to provide expert advice and assistance by way of a financial payment and rating relief as well as affording the land protection under the offences provisions of the Reserves Act.

Protection of Land that is not a Reserve under Section 38 of the Reserves Act is a further provision which enables the Crown or the administering body of an adjoining or nearby reserve to enter into a joint management agreement on a similar basis to the Protected Private Land approach. However, in this case there are no criteria specified for the resource and this provision generally enables more flexibility to enable active recreation on the land.

Again a payment may be made for the use of the land and a contribution for any legal costs incurred by the owner for the preparation of the agreement.

Technical Assistance in terms of Section 39 may be provided without charge to the administering body of any reserve or any person, trustee, trust, voluntary organisation etc appointed under the provisions of Section 38. This assistance may take the form of silvicultural advice, planning for resource management or where appropriate for visitor usage. In many cases a landowner is faced with uncontrolled usage or access over his land or the mangement of an area of bush and is in need of expert advice and management assistance. The Reserves Act 1977 provides ample opportunities not only to protect the resource but also to provide the owner with management assistance.

QUEEN ELIZABETH II NATIONAL TRUST ACT
1977 [Refer page 41].

SOIL CONSERVATION AND RIVERS CONTROL ACT 1941
WATER AND SOIL CONSERVATION ACT 1967
These two pieces of legislation are largely non-executory. The operation of the first Act is, by and large, limited to the prevention of erosion, principally by rivers, but does give local Catchment Boards some powers to require an area of forest to be preserved for protection purposes. The second Act is essentially designed around the licensing of the use of natural water but does not operate to facilitate positive steps towards rehabilitation or protection.

OTHER MEANS
The Ministry of Works and Development, the Department of Lands and Survey and the New Zealand Forest Service are all available for information and advice.

TOWN AND COUNTRY PLANNING ACT 1977
As the empowering legislation for regional district planning schemes, this Act is perhaps the most important statutory measure for implementing policy guidelines for private indigenous forest.

There are, however, clear limitations to the powers of the Act so it should be regarded as being only complementary to other measures such as financial incentives. A basic principle in the legislation is that the provisions of planning schemes can only operate to control changes in the use of land, and cannot bring about the termination of established, existing uses. In the case of rural land uses it can be very difficult to determine what contributes a change — for example logging of an area of bush or clearing a bush-covered property could be claimed to have been continuing slowly over a long period. Another principle is that because control of the rights of landowners to use their land is not only a limitation of a basic freedom but also can affect the profitability and value of a property, such control must be clearly justified. Consequently the Act provides broad rights for objection and appeal in respect of proposed control powers and of the application of such powers once a planning scheme is in operation.

The legislation sets out (in section 3) matters of national importance which are to be recognised and provided for in the preparation, implementation and administration of planning schemes. Included in these are the conservation, protection, and enhancement of the physical, cultural, and social environment, and the wise use and management of New Zealand's resources. These are essentially qualitative and subjective expressions, and provide the basis on which judgements can be made, balancing the various considerations about the justification for applying controls in particular circumstances.

Measures to bring about the protection of indigenous forest would come within the matters quoted from section 3, but there are others in the section in respect of which the wording is more prescriptive. However, amendment of the Act would be needed for indigenous forest to be included with these, and interpretation in a particular case would still need to be in terms of the section as a whole.

Notwithstanding the limitations, regional and territorial local authorities can effectively protect forested areas by means of policies and ordinances where the justification for these can be sustained and where destruction or modification of forest would clearly be a change of land use.

Appendix 3: Trees — the No. 1 Power Problem in Rural Areas

Introduction
Most farmers utilise and depend on a reliable electricity supply to a very large extent, for many purposes and on all types of farms whether they be pastoral, agricultural or horticultural.

The Power Board, in supplying the electricity, continuously strives to ensure that the supply is uninterrupted and offers many services to help you enjoy its benefits.

Although there is a continuous programme of line maintenance, storms and accidents can disrupt power without warning at any time of the day or night.

The problem
In rural areas, trees in close proximity to power lines are the major cause of interruptions to supply.

Electric Power Boards are specifically required by the Electric Supply Regulations to take steps to ensure the removal of any tree or part of a tree likely to damage a power line as well as being generally obliged by the regulations to take all reasonable precautions to secure continuity of supply and immunity from danger at all times.

This applies to main distribution lines — whether these are located on road reserves or across country. It also applies to service lines (these are the lines which bring the power from the main lines to the buildings requiring supply).

Stock electrocutions
In some instances stock have been electrocuted when they have contacted live overhead service line wires which have fallen to the ground during windy weather after being damaged by trees which had been allowed to grow up through or near the lines.

Farmers (and horticulturalists) should ensure that trees, including large shrubs and fruit trees, are cut well back from near overhead service lines to avoid accidents such as the above.

The Board's fault staff will deaden service lines, generally without charge (provided reasonable notice is given) to allow tree cutting to proceed.

The value of stock electrocuted can be considerable these days, as can be the loss of production. Further, farmers are faced with the cost of stock replacement which can be quite a burden if not recoverable from insurance.

Danger to human life
Quite apart from the aspect of stock electrocution, there is of course always the danger to human life, especially to young children (and for that matter, property).

Recently a 20 year old man was electrocuted by a wire which had fallen to the ground, following contact with trees. The coroner inferred that the fatality was attributable to the failure of the power board concerned to ensure the removal of the trees. The implications of the above are obvious. Hence, the need for continual vigilance by your power board staff.

However, farmers and others have a responsibility to take prudent action if they see trees or hedges on their property which are interfering, or are likely to interfere with overhead lines. Never hesitate to advise or seek advice from your power board.

Approach by Power Board
If a power board approaches a farmer, then in most cases it is a personal approach, seeking the friendly cooperation of the farmer to have the offending trees removed. Boards prefer an amicable solution to such problems, but sometimes have to resort to certain statutory power available to them, particularly those under the Electricity Act 1968, and the Public Works Act 1981.

It is always the aim of Power Boards to seek the cooperation of farmers to take prudent action to avoid damage to lines by trees in their own interests, rather than to use statutory powers to enforce compliance.

Guidelines
As a general guide, trees should not be allowed to grow within 2.5 m of adjacent electric lines, measured from the nearest part of the tree to the wires (see Fig. 1).

Further, trees and hedges should be kept to such a height that the lines are outside the falling radius of the trees (see Fig. 2).

Service lines should be deadened by Power Board staff before tree cutting is attempted, and in the case of main distribution lines, adequate notice should be given to the Board so that shutdowns of main lines can be advertised if this is necessary, and other arrangements are made to ensure safe working procedures while the trees are being felled or trimmed.

(Contributed by the Electric Power Board Association of NZ)

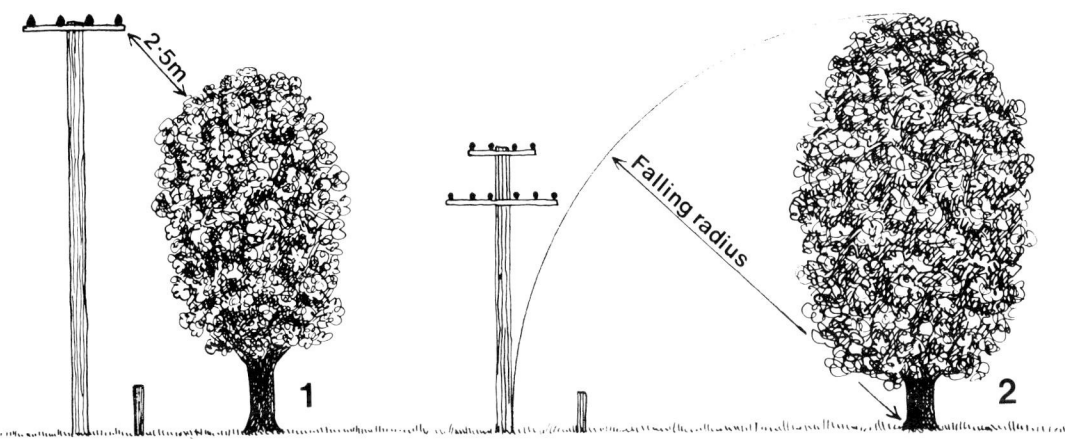

Appendix 4: Reducing Competition to Young Trees Using Herbicide Applied with Knapsack Sprayer

The growth of newly planted trees can be considerably reduced where these trees must compete with other vegetation for nutrients and water. Where the competing vegetation is well established the effect on the trees can be such that mortality results. This is particularly so when long periods of dry weather occur in the summer following planting.

Broadleafed tree species (hardwoods) are much more sensitive to competition than conifers (softwoods) so that the commonly planted radiata pine can survive in situations where eucalypts or for example, walnuts, could not because of the influence of weed growth. However the initial growth of all tree species is enhanced if competing vegetation is controlled during the early stages of growth. This can be achieved in a variety of ways including the physical removal of weeds by cultivation, by smothering weeds as in mulching, or by the use of chemicals to kill established plants and control the germination of weed seeds.

With the planting of trees in established pasture it is essential that grass competition is not allowed to interfere with tree growth. The use of herbicide is an economical way of controlling grass. Although weed growth that develops after planting can be controlled selectively with appropriate chemicals in the case of radiata pine, other tree species are less tolerant and spraying should be carried out before planting unless trials have shown that the species being grown is tolerant of the herbicide being used.

Information on the type and rates of herbicide and the control of particular weeds without harming the planted seedlings can be obtained from representatives of chemical companies, advisory officers of the Ministry of Agriculture and Fisheries, and Forest Advisory officers with the Forest Service.

Where herbicides are to be used as an aid to the establishment of trees one of the most convenient methods of application is the use of a knapsack sprayer.

The only problem associated with the use of this type of spraying equipment is regulating the rate of application. The following account is given as a guide.

To calibrate knapsack spraying equipment
The following directions assume that an area of about 1 metre square is to be sprayed for each tree prior to planting. If a different sized spot is to be used the calculations should be adjusted accordingly.

Mark out with chalk several squares 1 x 1 metre on dry concrete or asphalt. Using the normal spray equipment filled with water only determine the time taken on average to spray each spot. This could be between 3 to 5 seconds. Using a graduated measuring vessel and with the sprayer maintained at normal running pressure collect the volume of water sprayed over a standard time period of say 30 seconds. Repeat this until an average amount can be determined. Divide the standard time by the number of seconds to spray a single spot (1 metre square) to get the number of spots sprayed in that time. Divide the average volume of water delivered in the standard time by the number of spots to obtain the volume of water per spot.

Example: It is found that four second spray is required to cover the spots. At normal working pressure, 200 ml of water are delivered in 30 seconds.

Thus $30 \div 4$ or 7.5 spots require 200 ml of water to cover.

The volume of spray/spot can also be calculated by taking the time to fill a container of known volume. Thus in the above example, it would have taken 90 seconds to fill a 600 ml milk bottle and $600 \div (90 \div 4) = 26.67$ ml/spot.

The volume of water sprayed/spot is then used to determine the amount of herbicide material required for the job. If the recommendation is for 8 kg of active ingredient/hectare for the particular product you are using the amount required for a knapsack is calculated thus.

Example: If product is 50% active ingredient 16 kg of product must be sprayed/hectare (10 000 sq m). Each spot is about 1 sq m in area, so the amount of product/spot is $16/10000 = 0.0016$ kg, or 1.6 grams.

The capacity of the knapsack sprayer is 12 litres or 12 000 ml.

Each spot requires 26.67 m so 12 000/26.67 or 450 spots can be sprayed with one knapsack load.

Therefore the amount of product for one knapsack is:

$450 \times 1.6 = 720$ grams.

(New Zealand Forest Service handout)

Appendix 5: Forestry Encouragement Grants

Introduction
In the 1982 budget Government endeavoured to provide a degree of equity in financial incentives between the various categories of private forest growers. This has been achieved by removing the range of alternative incentives previously available to private forest growers and replacing them with a flat rate grant. As a result of the change the tax deductability of commercial forestry costs by companies has also been revoked. The scheme is administered by the New Zealand Forest Service and commenced on 1 April 1983.

Background
In the 1981 budget the Minister of Finance indicated that following the New Zealand Forestry Conference to be held in that year, the Government would undertake a review of incentives and taxation concessions available to forest industries.

The new grants scheme amalgamates two of the three recommendations of that 1981 Forestry Conference (Recommendations 9 (ii) and 9 (iii)

Scope
Forestry encouragement grants apply to certain qualifying costs incurred in the establishment, tending and maintenance of commercial forest crops. Such costs may be associated with the tending of existing crops or the establishment of new crops and include the restocking of previously logged areas. Forestry encouragement grants may be considered in one of two categories:
- (1) Production grants — those which are established for commercial purposes only, and
- (2) Protection/Production grants — those which, besides being productive, also have a soil protection role.

Eligibility
Grants will be paid to any forest grower who holds a verifiable interest in an existing or proposed forest area. Such growers may include companies, groups of companies, individuals (including trusts and partnerships), societies, boards, local authorities, or corporations. There is no minimum or maximum qualifying area of annual or total planting, but such plantings must be completed with recognised commercial wood-producing species.

Production Grants
Annual grant payments at the rate of 45% of certain qualifying expenditure incurred year by year will be made. There is no upper financial limit applied per hectare for such payments either annually or over the rotation of the crop. However, claimed costs will be subject to audit inspections which may be carried out to confirm the validity of such costs. Audit inspections will normally be restricted to random checks.

Protection/Production Grants
These grants will be subject to the same scrutiny as Production Grants. To qualify for payment, however, the concurrence of a district Catchment Board Officer will be required in writing prior to the first payment being made.

Annual grant payments at the rate of $66^2/3\%$ of certain qualifying expenditure during the preparation and establishment phases will be paid under this category of grant. The establishment phase will cease at the completion of release clearing or in any case not later than year three. Following successful establishment, further work, including tending and maintenance, will receive annual grant payments at the rate of 45% of certain qualifying costs.

Where the planting area has only a limited or doubtful productive potential any incentive scheme should be administered by the appropriate Catchment Board as a wholly protection exercise.

Applications
Although no formal application will be required to participate under the grants scheme, those intending to make annual claims should advise the regional Conservator of Forests of their proposed programme. Such advice should be provided by 30 June in the year prior to a claim being made and should include details of operations, area, species, finance required, and financial balance date. This advice will allow the Forest Service to prepare informed financial estimates in the year before payments are made.

New Zealand Forest Service Extension Officers will be available to assist applicants with operation planning and costing guidelines at the time projects under investigation and advice are being prepared.

District Planning Schemes
Any forest grower considering establishing a forest or woodlot should first check the district planning scheme of the local authority within whose jurisdiction the land concerned is located. This is a means of ensuring that there are no adverse restrictions from which a dispensation would be required.

Production Species
Any species which have proven, within New Zealand, to have a commercial wood production use will be considered eligible under the grant. Plantings for roundwood or firewood production will be considered under the scheme, as will the tending of indigenous regeneration areas. Emphasis should be placed on the NZ Forest Service Policy on Exotic Special Purpose Species.

Size or Area of Plantings
There is no minimum or maximum area of annual or total planting. However, the area must be definable as a productive unit and a reasonable assessment of area able to be established.

Shelter
Trees established solely for agricultural or horticultural shelter purposes will not qualify for the grant.

However, where there is an intention for plantings to be utilised primarily for wood production purposes and secondly to provide shelter such plantings can be considered for the grant. To qualify for the grant such plantings should be not less than three rows in width and of wood production species.

It should be noted that the costs of plantings for agricultural and horticultural purposes are deductible from income under the Income Tax Act 1976.

Qualifying Costs
The following costs will qualify for reimbursement under the grants scheme:
- (1) Expenditure incurred in planting, restocking, tending, or maintaining trees on the land, or in preparing or otherwise developing the land for forestry operations. This includes costs of:
  - Clearing and preparing land for forestry. (Note: preparation for restocking must be clearly segregated

from logging operations.)

— Cost of trees, planting, blanking, and release cutting and spraying.
— Cost of forestry hand tools.
— Pruning and non-commercial thinning.
— Chemicals and fertilisers and their application.
— Access tracks and temporary roads and their associated culverts and bridges. (Note: any road formation of a minimum standard suitable for establishing and tending one tree crop only can be classed as a temporary road.)
— Disease and pest control (insect, fungal, and animal).
— New fencing. (Note: only fencing adequate for the protection of the crop will be considered.)
— Fire protection and suppression. (Does not include capital items, eg lookout towers, fire engines, or rubber dams.)
— Forest huts. (Provided they are temporary huts.)
— Hiring or leasing plant or equipment used wholly or principally in preparing or developing the forest land, or in planting, tending, and maintaining the tree crop.
— Professional forestry service and advice.
— Subscriptions to a Farm Forestry Association and/or a Forest Owners' Association.
— Directors' fees. (Apportioned if necessary between the forestry activities and any other business undertakings.)
— Administration expenses. (Stamps, stationery, and other office expenses, etc.)
— Repairs and maintenance to:
  * access tracks, temporary roads, and their associated culverts and bridges,
  * plant and equipment used wholly or principally in preparing or developing the forestry land, or in planting, tending, and maintaining the tree crop,
  * fences and temporary forest huts.
— The full price of forest management work carried out on contract.

(2) Expenditure incurred by way of rents, rates, land tax, insurance premiums, or other like expenses.
— Rent on land used for forestry.
— Rates.
— Land tax on land used for forestry.
— Insurance premiums.

(3) Expenditure incurred by way of interest on money borrowed and employed as capital for the purpose of forest planting, restocking, tending, or maintaining trees on the land, including the purchase of vehicles, plant, machinery, and land.

(4) Depreciation on plant and machinery acquired or constructed on or after 1/4/83 which is used wholly or principally in preparing or developing forestry land, or in planting, tending, or maintaining the tree crop, not exceeding the rate as determined for tax purposes by the Commissioner of Inland Revenue. Where such items as motor vehicles, plant, and machinery are sold or disposed of for an amount which differs from their "written down value" (ie cost price less grants paid for depreciation) grant adjustments will be made to reflect the actual loss in value over the period of ownership of the asset. Depreciation on motor vehicles, plant, and machinery acquired prior to 1/4/83 by companies will continue to be claimed as a deduction for taxation purposes.

(5) The value of the owner's labour or his/her family at no higher than the rate of payment known in the New Zealand Forest Service as Forest Hand I.

— Up-to-date rates can be obtained from the New Zealand Forest Service.
— The amount reimbursed for such labour is regarded as income for the recipient for the year in which paid and is liable for income tax.

Other Costs

Apart from these qualifying costs there may be additional expenses which will not qualify for reimbursement under the grant scheme and which cannot be capitalised to "cost of bush". Such forestry costs are:

— Cost of land, as well as associated legal, survey, and valuation fees.
— Initial consultancy fees relating to the feasibility of a forestry project.
— Permanent buildings erected or purchased.
— Machinery and equipment not directly associated with the management of the tree crop, eg roading equipment.
— Permanent roads and bridges. (If road formation is on a permanent access route or is to be used during the life of the crop and for successive crops, it is a capital improvement to the land.)

The costs listed below also do not qualify for grants but may be claimed for tax purposes in the manner specified. It would be as well, however, to check with the tax authorities to ascertain the correct method of dealing with them.

— Depreciation of assets not directly associated with management of tree crop, such as administration buildings and workshops. (Carry forward as a loss or deduct from income from any source.)
— Repairs to and maintenance of permanent assets including permanent roads, bridges, fences, and buildings. (Carry forward as a loss or deduct from income from any source.)

Claims

Claims for grant payment on qualifying expenditure must be submitted to the regional Conservator of Forests following the 31 March or such other financial balance date as applies to the grantee.

Claim forms are available from Forest Service offices.

Before submission the claim must be signed by the Company's or Local Authority's Auditors or a chartered or practising accountant, independent of the grantee.

Claims presented must refer to costs incurred in the period between the claimant's last two balance dates.

Completed claims are checked by the Forest Service who will then arrange for an audit to be undertaken where required.

The Forestry Encouragement Grants Regulations require the Forest Service to send a copy of all paid claims to the Inland Revenue Department.

Audits

Audits are undertaken on a random basis with the aim of the audit being to ensure that:

Only qualifying expenditure is claimed, and was genuinely incurred.

Audits may be undertaken over part or all of any total claim.

Every endeavour will be made to ensure that audits are carried out over a range of growers from the smallest to the largest.

Forestry Encouragement Loans

Approved forestry encouragement loans with farmers and local authorities will remain active under the terms and conditions of existing registered agreements. If the maximum finance approved under such loans is exhausted grants money may be claimed in the normal manner for operations not financed by the loan. Repayment of the approved loan will be required under the conditions of the loan agreement.

Advisory Services

Forest Service officers will provide an advisory service, free of charge, to small forest owners. The advisory service staff are trained in such matters as the assessment of the viability of any proposal, species and siting requirements, management regimes, shelter and agricultural planting.

For larger operations it may be desirable to employ the services of a qualified forestry consultant. Forest Service advisory officers can provide enquirers with a list of consultants for various areas.

Further Information

The grants scheme is administered by the New Zealand Forest Service. If you have any queries please write to, telephone, or approach any of the offices listed below:

New Zealand Forest Service Offices

Head Office
Wellington
Private Bag, Wellington Tel: 721-569

Conservancy Offices
Auckland
C.P.O. Box 39, Auckland 1 Tel: 33 269
Rotorua
P.O. Box 1340, Rotorua Tel: 80 089
Wellington
P.O. Box 647, Palmerston North Tel: 89 109
Nelson
P.O. Box 140, Nelson Tel: 81 175
Westland
P.O. Box 138, Hokitika Tel: 1225 or 1226
Canterbury
P.O. Box 25-022, Victoria, Christchurch Tel: 791 040
Southland
Private Bag, Invercargill Tel: 88 075

District Offices
Blenheim
P.O. Box 228, Blenheim 88 099
Dunedin
P.O. Box 495, Dunedin Tel: 779 662
Geraldine
P.O. Box 4, Geraldine Tel: 456
Gisborne
P.O. Box 944, Gisborne Tel: 5078
Harihari
P.O. Box 9, Harihari Tel: 33 021
Kaikohe
P.O. Box 249, Kaikohe Tel: 671 or 109
Kaingaroa Forest
Kaingaroa Forest, via Rotorua Tel: 39 899
Masterton
P.O. Box 191, Masterton Tel: 80 060
Napier
P.O. Box 348 Napier Tel: 53 129
Reefton
P.O. Box 100, Reefton Tel: 853
Tapanui
P.O. Box 7, Tapanui Tel: 48 441 or 48 541
Taupo
P.O. Box 840, Taupo Tel: 89 210
Tauranga
P.O. Box 1026, Tauranga Tel: 87 677
Te Kuiti
P.O. Box 38, Te Kuiti Tel: 144
Thames
P.O. Box 78, Thames Tel: 86 772
Wanganui
P.O. Box 23, Wanganui Tel: 54 593
Waitemata
Riverhead Forest R.D. 2, Kumeu Tel: 4 128 514
Western
P.O. Box 37, Tautapere Tel: 15

(A handbook of the New Zealand Forest Service, Wellington; 2nd edition, 1983.)

Footnote to 1987 reprint:
This grant scheme was abolished in 1984.
The N.Z. Forest Service is being replaced from 1 April 1987 by the Ministry of Forestry. There will inevitably be some rearrangement of the Forestry Offices shown above.

Appendix 6: New Zealand Farm Forestry Assn (Inc).

At various places in this book there has been emphasis on the necessity of becoming familiar with the local scene: looking at what grows well in a district and talking to those who have had experience. The most effective way of doing this is to join the New Zealand Farm Forestry Association which was formed in 1957 and has more than 3000 members in branches throughout the country.

The main objects of the Association as set out in the Constitution are:

(a) To encourage the planting of trees and all other plants and shrubs suitable for farm shelter, farm beautification, and for any other farming purposes and to take all steps necessary to increase knowledge amongst farmers and throughout the community of the characteristics and uses of different species of trees, plants and shrubs, of their care and management, and of the utilisation, treatment and marketing of timber.

(b) To take all reasonable steps to educate the farming community and the public in the proper selection and planting of species of trees, shrubs and other plants for various farming and other purposes.

(c) To take all reasonable steps to educate the farming community and the public regarding the urgency and importance of the promotion and preservation of all forms of farm forestry.

The Association is not a group that is interested only in radiata pine. On some sites, and for many commercial plantings, radiata pine is the best species, but members are also concerned and active in growing other tree species. Many of the quality timber species that increasingly need to be grown do best on farmland sites. These trees include eucalypts, Australian blackwood, black walnut, cypresses and other species. There is interest too in trees that provide fodder for livestock, food for bees and birds, naturally ground-durable wood and edible fruits. Farm foresters are interested in trees in the widest sense, including their effect on the landscape.

Although it is called the Farm Forestry Association, members are not all farmers but most are involved in the use of trees in one way or another. While some members are interested in commercial forestry, others are more interested in trees for shelter, soil and water conservation, and the multiple use of trees, for example shelter and timber production or agroforestry — combining forestry and grazing animals.

Members find that as they become more knowledgeable on the best siting and use of trees, they get the best landscape effects and the most effective returns. Some members are also interested in the better management of existing native stands on their properties. In many situations this means protection and preservation, in others the management to provide a sustained yield of special-purpose timber.

Most activity takes place at branch level where relevant practical local knowledge is available at field days and meetings.

The national conference is held each year in a different part of New Zealand, and is regarded by many as a particularly happy combination of informative discussion and relaxation, incorporating visits to sites of particular relevance. Matters of national interest are raised by branches and debated at the conference.

The Association publishes the *New Zealand Tree Grower* which is distributed to members quarterly.

Anyone wishing to join the Association can find the address of the local branch by inquiring at the nearest office of the New Zealand Forest Service or Ministry of Agriculture and Fisheries.

Bibliography

(Other reference books are listed at the end of chapters)

Allan, H.H. 1961: *Flora of New Zealand* Vol 1, Government Printer, Wellington

Brooker M.I.H., Kleinig D.A: *Field Guide to Eucalypts Vol I South Eastern Australia* 1983 Encounter Press, Melbourne.

Burstall S.W: "Historic and Notable Trees of New Zealand" unpublished report, New Zealand Forest Service.

Chavasse C.G.R. (Editor) 1977: *New Zealand Institute of Foresters (Inc) Forestry Handbook*, NZ Institute Foresters.

Cockayne, L., Phillips Turner, E. 1967: *The Trees of New Zealand*, Government Printer, Wellington.

Collingwood G.H. & Brush W.D. 1974: *Knowing your Trees*, The American Forestry Assn.

Constantine Albert Jnr 1975: *Know Your Woods*, Charles Scribner's Sons.

Eagle A. 1965: *Eagle's Trees and Shrubs of New Zealand in Colour*, Collins, Auckland.

Eagle, A. 1982: *Eagle's Trees and Shrubs of New Zealand Second Series*, Collins, Auckland.

Evans B. 1983: *Revegetation Manual*, Queen Elizabeth II National Trust.

Edlin H.L. & Nimmo M. 1974: *The World of Trees*, Orbis Publishing.

Gorer Richard 1980: *Illustrated Guide to Trees*, Kingfisher Books.

Hall, Johnston & Chippendale 1970: *Forest Trees of Australia, Government Publishment Service.*

Handbook of Hardwoods 1972: Her Majesty's Stationery Office.

Handbook of Softwoods 1977: Her Majesty's Stationery Office, Second Edition.

Harrison Richmond E. 1974: *Handbook of Trees & Shrubs*, A.H. & A.W. Reed, Wellington.

Hillier's Manual of Trees & Shrubs, 1974: David & Charles, Revised Edition.

Kelly, S. 1969 Eucalypts Vols I & II Nelson.

Kirk T. 1889: *The Forest Flora of New Zealand*, Government Printer, Wellington.

Laing, R.M. Blackwell E.W. 1927: *Plants of New Zealand*, Third Edition, Whitcombe & Tombs.

Leathart, Scott 1977: *Trees of the World*, Hamlyn.

McWhannell F.B. 1960: *Eucalypts for New Zealand Farms, Parks & Gardens*, Pauls Book Arcade.

Macoboy, Stirling 1979: *What Tree is That?* Landsdowne Press.

Matthews, B. 1979: *Growing Native Plants*, A.H. & A.W. Reed, Wellington.

Metcalf, L.J. 1972: *The Cultivation of New Zealand Trees & Shrubs*, A.H. & A.W. Reed, Wellington.

Mitchell Alan 1978: *A Field Guide to the Trees of Britain & Northern Europe*, Collins.

Phillips Roger 1978: *Trees of North America and Europe*, Random House.

Poole, A.L. Adams, N.M. 1964: *Trees & Shrubs of New Zealand*, Government Printer, Wellington.

Rendle B.J. 1969: *World Timbers* 3 Vols., Earnest Benn Ltd.

Salmon, J.T. 1980: *The Native Trees Of New Zealand*, A.H. & A.W. Reed, Wellington.

Stockley George 1973: *Trees Farms and the New Zealand Landscape*, Northern Southland Farm Forestry Assn.

Sunset Western Garden Book 1967.

Weston G.C. 1957: "Exotic Forest Trees in New Zealand", Bulletin No. 13, New Zealand Forest Service.

Photo credits:

Gill Brann, p208; Forest Research Institute, pp44, 141 (left); Bruce Gibson, p138 (right); Denis Hocking, p129 (left); Grant Hunter, pp50, 96 (top), 120 (lower), 121 (lower), 125, 164, 210; John Mackay, p63; J.W. Montgomery, p83; New Zealand Forest Service, p197; Karen Nichols, pp132, 142, 163, 179, 186 (lower), 187 (top), 188 (top), 191; Michael Selby, p 66; Dick Thevenard, p152; H. van Puffelen, p79; Waikato Valley Authority, 67. The authors apologise if they have overlooked any acknowledgement.

Index